LAND USE LAW

IN A NUTSHELL®

THIRD EDITION

PATRICIA E. SALKIN
Senior Vice President for Academic Affairs and Provost
Graduate and Professional Divisions
Touro College

JENNIE C. NOLON
Senior Staff Attorney, Land Use Law Center
Adjunct Professor
Elisabeth Haub School of Law
Pace University

WEST ACADEMIC PUBLISHING

444 Cedar Street, Suite 700
St. Paul, MN 55101
1-877-888-1330

Printed in the United States of America

ISBN: 978-1-68467-929-4

To those who preceded us:
Robert R. Wright and Morton Gitelman

Original Land Use Nutshell

John R. Nolon

co-author with Patricia Salkin on the 1st and 2nd editions of this current series

To our families who support us.

To those in whose hands this critical body of law is placed: the students and teachers of Land Use Law.

PREFACE

This summary and exploration of land use law is written with great respect for the relevance, breadth, and complexity of the subject matter. There are nearly a dozen law school casebooks on land use law; they contain over 10,000 pages of cases, commentaries, notes, and problems. Predictably—with such a vast and important subject—the content of these books is intricately varied and diverse. In a nutshell, writing briefly and simply about this mystifying subject is a challenge.

Robert R. Wright wrote the original volume of *Land Use in a Nutshell* and was assisted in its fourth edition by our friend Morton Gitelman. It served students, professors, and interested professionals for over a quarter of a century. In 2006, John R. Nolon and Patricia Salkin considered various approaches to West's invitation to write a new version in response to the rapid changes on the land and in the law. To help navigate this extensive terrain, the authors reviewed every case contained in current casebooks and let that material dictate the content and organization of this book. A Nutshell's principal users are students, and it is anticipated that they will consult the book primarily to find out where each case fits into the grand tapestry of land use law. This caused the authors to abandon the framework of their own casebook, one that was inherited from Professors Wright and Gitelman. This approach continued in the second edition, and now the third edition with a new co-author, Professor Jennie C. Nolon replacing Professor John R. Nolon.

We begin the story with a brief history of the common law origins of land use law, which demonstrates the firm foundation upon which today's public system of land use regulation rests. Many of our contemporary land use laws borrow liberally from the common law and seek to accomplish the same objectives, but in a more complex, challenged, and populated society. The cases teach that the comprehensive, or master, plan is the predicate for zoning and other land use regulations, so that topic comes next. Zoning—America's unique adaptation—follows planning, as it should in practice, but also because it was the principal technique employed to replace common law controls and the first to aspire to the realization of safe and livable communities and landscapes. Chronologically, subdivision and site plan regulations were next on the scene, so they follow zoning in these pages as they did in the relatively rapid development of the modern land use system in the twentieth century.

We struggled with the issue of where to discuss the controversial subject of regulatory takings and its less idiosyncratic constitutional sibling, due process. Because the cases that establish these relevant Fifth Amendment doctrines implicate the full range of land use practice, we decided to place them after discussing the basic land use regulations and then to follow that presentation with other constitutional and statutory limits on land use power. The student's knowledge of the basic land use system and its intricate operations is deepened, we believe, by studying the legal limits placed on land use controls; that study teaches the complete system, what can go wrong in its operations, and how to prevent successful challenges. This prepares them for what comes next.

Land use law continued its evolution in the second half of the twentieth century; its objectives broadened significantly as society demanded that it do more and more. We begin this story with housing and urban redevelopment in the 1950s, follow its evolution in cities and developing suburbs to the present; we then turn to the advent of local environmental law as a complement to local land use law, and continue with the important issues of aesthetic, historic, and cultural interest protection. The Nutshell winds down with a review. By looking at how land use laws can be initiated, amended, or overturned by the people, how stakeholders can aid land use agencies in preventing and mediating land use disputes, and how the courts review and rule on land use decisions, the student is able to revisit the workings of the system in full. The Nutshell ends in the present, with a discussion of a key emerging issue intimately connected to land use law—climate change. To aid the curious in following and understanding this continuing saga, there is an appendix: a guide for further study that discusses and contains a host of internet sites.

Litigation regarding regulatory takings and the deprivation of due process is brisk and controversial. It pits property rights advocates against public regulators and conveys the impression that today's heated battles that shape and define the law of the land are unique to our time. Long ago, however, Blackstone noted that property owners enjoy "despotic dominion" of their land, subject only to the "reasonable laws of the land." This enigmatic utterance properly characterizes our ongoing attempt to resolve the tension between our confidence in private ownership and society's need to control private land use to protect the land and its resources. We hope that our summary and interpretation of land use law will help others understand it and to employ it with care so that this critical balance is maintained.

PATRICIA E. SALKIN

JENNIE C. NOLON

June 2021

OUTLINE

TABLE OF CASES

References are to Pages

LAND USE LAW
IN A NUTSHELL®

THIRD EDITION

CHAPTER 1

INTRODUCTION AND COMMON LAW ORIGINS

§ 1. HISTORY

A. THE ORIGINS OF OUR LAND USE SYSTEM

The United States is not alone in having a governmental system for controlling land use, nor is the notion of regulating land use a new idea. In the early Roman period, around 450 B.C., a commission was formed to draft legislation regulating private behavior and public affairs. The result was the Twelve Tables, which include the following site planning provisions: "Whoever sets a hedge around his land shall not exceed the boundary; in the case of a wall, he shall leave one foot; in the case of a house, two feet. . . . If a well, a path, an olive or fig tree, nine feet." Treasury of Law 71, Nice ed., 1964.

Many of the great Latin American cities founded in the 16th century were developed following distinctly Spanish urban planning concepts. Under the Law of the Indies, decreed in 1572 by King Philip II, cities were laid out according to various guidelines that varied depending on the climate, geography, and characteristics of the place. Viceroys completed surveys akin to today's environmental impact assessments and sent them to Spain, where planners determined which guidelines were to be followed in each location. The Spanish founded new towns—

villas—based on models in Spain, with space for homes, public buildings, and croplands.

The great fire of 1666 in London led to the adoption of municipal building construction laws that required brick exteriors, wider streets, and open space along the Thames River for access to water for firefighting. The use of land was regulated to a minor degree as well, with activities such as breweries and tanneries prohibited in the central city. The law provided for compensation to be paid to any individual lot owner who was prohibited from building. These early land use rules were articulated first in a proclamation by King Charles II, supported by a report from an investigative committee established by the King, and formalized by the Act for the Rebuilding of London adopted by Parliament in 1667. The Act gave the municipality the power to regulate the construction of buildings: their size, height, and placement on the lot, and the materials used.

Sweden enacted an early comprehensive town planning law in 1874, which made provisions for some land use planning in all of its towns and cities. Germany has a strong tradition of comprehensive planning, directed from the top down, with plans at the state, regional, and local level, and with a tradition of self-government where local authorities adopt plans and zoning to control growth around preserved historic centers, with open space retained at the periphery. Early French city planning, which emphasized infrastructure development, particularly transportation planning, was conducted primarily at the national level until 1982, when the French

Parliament adopted a law that transferred significant land use planning and project approval authority to the country's more than 35,000 municipalities.

B. THE AMERICAN APPROACH

(i) The Colonial Era

By the time the American colonies were settled, individuals were thought to hold powerful control over their land—a concept that limited the power of the state to regulate that land. In this early period, land uses were regulated more by the conditions imposed on the land titles conveyed by colonial authorities than by governmental regulation. Colonial settlements evolved into cities, townships, and counties, which eventually achieved governmental status and the power to legislate. These municipalities were regarded not as sovereign entities but as creatures of the state, authorized by state law to exercise a wide variety of powers affecting the health, safety, and welfare of their citizens. Most were deemed to have only those express powers delegated by their state legislatures, and those additional powers fairly implied in that delegation.

(ii) The Federal Republic

The U.S. Constitution was drafted by state-selected delegates and was signed by them in 1787. It created a national government—one of delegated powers, limited to those specifically included in the Constitution. Notably, the full police powers of the states were not delegated to the federal government. The principal power given to the federal government that affects private land use is the authority to regulate interstate commerce, under Article I, § 8 of the U.S. Constitution. Article VI of the Constitution grants the federal government the power to enter into international treaties that legally bind federal, state, and local governments in the United States. Under this authority, the United States has entered into many bilateral, regional, and international agreements that promote resource conservation and prevent environmental pollution.

The Tenth Amendment of the U.S. Constitution reserves to the states all powers not delegated by the Constitution to the federal government; this reservation of power protects states against encroachments by Congress that are not within its delegated authority. The weight of legal and political opinion holds that this allocation of power in the federal republic leaves the states in charge of regulating how private land is used, subject to additional federal regulation protecting interstate commerce or enforcing an international treaty. The concept of dual sovereignty is dynamic and leaves room for flexibility in responding to challenges at the state and federal level, with tensions resolved by the U.S. Supreme Court.

C. THE MODERN ERA OF ZONING

(i) Comprehensive Zoning

The nation's first comprehensive zoning ordinance was adopted by New York City in 1916. As happened in England after the great fire of 1666, the march of unwanted land uses uptown precipitated a crisis leading to the creation of a commission that recommended stricter land use controls to protect the city's economy, private property values, and public health and safety. The resulting zoning law divided the city into multiple land use districts, or zones. These districts allowed private landowners to use their land only for the purposes permitted in the applicable district. This protected Fifth Avenue retailers, for example, from the incursion of garment factories—an industrial use—in that retail zone.

A few years after the adoption of this first comprehensive zoning ordinance, a federal commission formulated a model act—known as the Zoning Enabling Act—to be adopted by state legislatures to make it clear that their localities had the power to zone. In the United States, virtually all 50 states adopted some version of this model act; their legislatures have passed relatively similar zoning enabling laws giving municipalities the authority to regulate private land uses.

(ii) Authority

Local governments are regarded as legal instrumentalities of their states. The legislative authority of municipalities is limited to that delegated by the state and extends only to their geographical boundaries, with modest exceptions. Planning and zoning enabling laws specifically authorize municipal governments to control the use of the land by adopting land use plans and creating zoning districts, within which specified land uses are allowed and various construction standards enforced. In most states, zoning regulations must conform to the locality's land use plan, typically called the comprehensive plan. State enabling laws also authorize localities to create administrative and quasi-judicial agencies to review and adjudicate proposals for land development and to hear petitions for relief from zoning regulations.

Municipalities adopt comprehensive plans that lay the foundation for the adoption of local land use laws. In some states, these local plans must be consistent with regional or statewide land use plans. Municipalities also adopt traditional land use laws such as zoning ordinances and standards that regulate land subdivision and site plan development.

In most states, home rule authority is also delegated to local governments, giving them broad power to adopt laws that affect local property, affairs, and government so long as those laws do not conflict with general or preemptive state laws. States utilize a variety of methods to grant home rule powers to their localities. In most states, home rule authority is contained in the constitution. At a minimum, local home rule power authorizes localities to legislate regarding their own property, affairs, and government, except where general or preemptive state laws operate. In nearly all states, home rule authority is not deemed to prevent the state from legislating regarding legitimate state interests by guiding, directing, or preempting local land use control.

Local governments today are empowered to adopt innovative local land use laws that promote smart growth and that create more balanced land use patterns. More particularly, municipalities in many states have used their land use authority to develop a new body of local regulations designed to protect natural resources and prevent environmental pollution. Environmental objectives can now be found in local comprehensive plans, the boundaries of conservation zoning districts can be drawn to correspond to and protect watershed areas, environmental standards can now be found in subdivision and site plan regulations, and localities can adopt stand-alone environmental laws to protect particular unique and threatened natural resources. The clear purposes of these laws are to control nonpoint source pollution and preserve natural resources from the adverse impacts of land development. Although the majority of U.S. communities have not adopted numerous and sophisticated local environmental laws, the increasing number of these laws, in the aggregate, constitutes a significant body of land use practice.

Some land use projects are subject to permitting standards adopted by one or more agencies and levels of government. According to the U.S. Census Bureau, there are about 39,000 governments that have or can be given authority to regulate private land use. In some areas, land developers must receive a permit to build near wetlands from the U.S. Army Corps of Engineers, the state department of environmental protection, and/or a local wetlands commission and/or planning board. Other examples of overlapping regulations that protect watersheds, habitats, surface waters, and other resources abound. As a result, the contemporary challenge is to integrate some of the various governmental influences on private land use to limit waste and redundancy while preserving the need for flexibility in addressing diverse regional, state, and federal interests. Increasingly, municipalities are found integrating federally-prescribed hazard mitigation plans and state-guided waterfront management plans into their comprehensive plan, which then guides the adoption of zoning with some consistency.

(iii) Zoning Procedure and Judicial Review

Local administrative agencies are established to review and approve individual development proposals. These agencies are required to hold public hearings on most proposals, to provide notice to affected parties of the hearings, to hold meetings open to the public, and to ensure that their voting members have no conflicts of interests that prevent their decisions from being objective. Procedures for adopting land use plans and laws provide for public participation in the process with varying degrees of input and effectiveness.

The two consistent standards that all land use laws must meet are that they accomplish a legitimate public objective and that they allow the landowner some economically viable use of the land. The U.S. Constitution also protects individual freedom of speech, and the right to assemble and worship. Land use regulations that affect these individual freedoms do not enjoy the usual presumption of constitutionality that courts otherwise afford local laws.

The judicial branch of government settles disputes among landowners, affected residents, environmental organizations, and governmental regulators. Courts tend to defer to the judgment of land use regulators and impose a heavy burden on those who challenge land use regulations to prove that such regulations are arbitrary, capricious, not within the scope of local authority, deny owners an economical use of the land, or violate other constitutional protections such as equal protection of the law.

§ 2. THE NATURE OF PROPERTY RIGHTS

A. THE RIGHTS OF LANDOWNERS

The subject of land use law explores the extent of the authority of public entities to regulate private property rights by limiting the use, occupancy, and sale of land and natural resources. This requires that we think a bit about property rights. What rights does a private landowner have and to what extent are they protected from governmental interference? In

Property Law, students study how rights to property arise, what estates and interests can be created, and common law limitations on those rights. They learn that, with the fee simple absolute title to land, comes a number of fundamental rights that are protected by common law doctrines and constraints contained in both state and federal constitutions.

Landowners are said, for example, to own the exclusive right to possess their property; they may exclude others from their domains. The right to exclude others from the land is protected by trespass actions in common law courts. Any intentional incursion onto the land of another, whether actual damage occurred or not, is actionable. Liability for intentional trespass is absolute, regardless of motive or harm effected. Damages are assessed in proportion to actual injury caused to the property. Even when no actual damage resulted from a trespass, courts award nominal damages as a means of settling property disputes. The right to possess or occupy the land is often said to be exclusive in nature, limited to the owner, and that every entry without the owner's permission is a trespass.

This right to exclusive possession is akin to the right that landowners have to use their property as they see fit. Similarly, title to land is tenaciously protected by the law; it may not be taken by the government except in very circumscribed situations. Finally, property owners can alienate their land: sell their complete title, or any lesser estate or interest, to third parties. The right to sell includes the right to create lesser estates and interests such as determinable fees, future interests, leases, easements, and covenants.

B. THE LIMITS OF LAND OWNERSHIP

Although they are described as "fundamental," the rights to possess, use, exclude, and alienate have never been absolute. Property theorists are fond of debating how tenacious private ownership is and to what degree it is limited by collective rights and the public interest. Our legal history is not kind to absolutist interpretations of property rights. At the beginning of our common law era, for example, all property was held either by or "of" the King. Those holding under the King were only possessors—always subject to his vast sovereign prerogatives. Beginning with the Magna Carta, the rights of English lords to control their land and insulate themselves from sovereign interference evolved, but slowly. The Statute of Quia Emptores, adopted in 1290, gave those who held land the power to transfer it to the private ownership of others, subject to the state's right to tax, take, and control the land.

Over the centuries, landowners obtained further rights. It took until 1540 for the owners of real property to secure the right to transfer their property at death by will to individuals of their own choice. The right to exclude had fully matured by 1782 when William Blackstone, a respected commentator on the common law, referred to the right of property as "that sole and despotic dominion which one man claims over the external things of the world, in total exclusion of the right of any other individual in the universe." Although few land use regulations existed by this time, Blackstone noted, even then, that property rights were to be enjoyed "without any control or diminution, save only by the laws of the land."

Blackstone could have added that property rights are limited by common law duties and public law entitlements. Under nuisance law, for example, the right to use land is limited by the private owner's duty not to injure the property of others. Commonwealth v. Tewksbury, 52 Mass. 55 (Mass. 1846). The owner of land crossed by a navigable river may not obstruct the public's right to travel on the river or use it for commercial transportation. Owners of riparian, or littoral, lands adjacent to the sea or other tidal waters cannot exclude those who wish to enter upon their tidal wetlands and even to fish there. In Shelley v. Kraemer, 334 U.S. 1 (1948), the conveyance of a racially restrictive covenant was held to be unenforceable under the Fourteenth Amendment of the U.S. Constitution. The entry of federal employees on a farmer's land to talk with migrant workers about their rights was held not to be a trespass. See also, State v. Shack, 58 N.J. 297, 277 A.2d 369 (N.J. 1971). Limitations on the right to exclude have been created in the event of emergencies, necessities, the wrongful taking of a chattel, and to permit the continuance of minor encroachments.

C. PUBLIC CONTROL OF LAND USE

The seminal land use case is Village of Euclid v. Ambler Realty Co., 272 U.S. 365 (1926), a U.S. Supreme Court case. In *Euclid*, the legal issue before the Supreme Court was whether a zoning ordinance adopted by the village that divided the plaintiff's land into three separate use districts was constitutional. The village adopted its ordinance under the police power delegated to it by the State of Ohio. The state legislature had the power under the state constitution to enact laws to protect the public health, safety, morals, and welfare. In the land use area, it chose to protect the public by delegating the power to adopt zoning ordinances to its municipalities, including the Village of Euclid.

The plaintiff landowner objected. How does it accomplish a legitimate public interest—which a local police power regulation must do—to limit the types of uses to which privately-owned land can be put? The Court instructed that, in deciding this issue, the "law of nuisances may be consulted, not for the purpose of controlling, but for the helpful aid of its analogies in the process of ascertaining the scope of the [police] power. Thus the question whether the power exists to forbid the erection of a building of a particular kind or for a particular use, like the question whether a particular thing is a nuisance, is to be determined, not by an abstract consideration of the building or the thing considered apart, but by considering it in connection with the circumstances and the locality." Because the village had shown that certain dangers to the public lurked in the random mixing of industrial, commercial, and residential land uses, the Court upheld local zoning as a valid exercise of the police power.

§ 3. THE LAW OF NUISANCE

A. BACKGROUND

Euclid, Ohio, is a suburb of Cleveland. At the time Euclid adopted zoning, it was in the path of development moving outward from the metropolitan area. The Supreme Court in *Euclid* understood that there was a certain similarity between judicial policies observable in the common law of nuisance and land use law, or zoning. The context surrounding a particular land use matters in determining whether the use is a nuisance or is reasonably restricted by land use laws. This is a matter of reasonableness. We do not want pigs in parlors, but can abide them on the farm.

In Clark v. Wambold, 165 Wis. 70, 160 N.W. 1039 (Wis. 1917), for example, the plaintiff was unsuccessful in seeking to enjoin a piggery because of its foul odors and disturbing sights and sounds. The state court held that raising pigs on a traditional farm in a rural area is a lawful activity and that the odor that carried across the property line did not constitute an actionable nuisance. Contrast this with the holding of Mitchell v. Hines, 305 Mich. 296, 9 N.W.2d 547 (Mich. 1943), in which the court enjoined a large-scale piggery, where dead animals and municipal refuse were brought to and dumped on the fields to feed the animals. In *Mitchell*, there were several nearby residential owners, the intensity of the noxious uses had increased since they moved in, and the degree of nuisance was great indeed, leading the court to comment on the "revolting odors" emanating from the fields.

Historically, the powerful right of individuals to use their land under the common law was balanced to a degree by the doctrine of nuisance, which established that private landowners may not use their property in a way that is injurious to property held by others. Private nuisance actions originated in the twelfth century, in the assize of nuisance which was replaced in the fifteenth century by an action on the case for nuisance. Nuisance remedies were limited, by and large, to injunctions and damages awarded to owners or occupants of adjacent land who could prove substantial injuries. Offensive intrusions included the effects of smoke, dust, noise, odors, heat, or other discernable effects that interfered with or diminished the normal uses of nearby property. Nuisance rules limiting injurious land uses evolved slowly and only in response to one private party's dispute against another.

B. PUBLIC AND PRIVATE NUISANCE

The difference between a public and private nuisance depends on who is affected. "A public nuisance is one which affects at the same time an entire community or neighborhood, or any considerable number of persons, although the extent of the annoyance or damage inflicted upon individuals may be unequal." Idaho Code Ann. § 5–102 (West).

Land uses that significantly interfere with public health, safety, comfort, or convenience are designated public nuisances because they are unreasonable interferences with a "right common to the general public," according to the Restatement of Torts. Such land uses are deemed "unreasonable" when significant interference is proved by evidence produced by the plaintiffs or when the conduct is proscribed by a duly enacted law, ordinance, or administrative regulation. Zoning laws constitute such ordinances; the violation of land use standards found in zoning laws subjects violators to civil penalties, such as fines, or to criminal penalties, including imprisonment. In most cases involving land use that interferes with the public interest generally, zoning enforcement has replaced the public nuisance suit as the tool of choice.

A private nuisance:

> is a legal cause of an invasion of another's interest in the private use and enjoyment of land, and the invasion is either (a) intentional and unreasonable, or (b) unintentional and otherwise actionable under the rules controlling liability for negligent or reckless conduct, or for abnormally dangerous conditions or activities.

Restatement (Second) of Torts § 822.

The Restatement of Torts defines a private nuisance as a nontrespassory invasion of another's interest in the private use and enjoyment of land.

When one property owner brings a nuisance action against another, she is attempting to control land use through a civil action. Only those significantly affected by the nuisance have standing to bring the action, and the court is interested only in balancing and ordering the equities between the plaintiff and defendant. The Restatement's general rule of nuisance law indicates that a landowner is subject to a nuisance action for a land use—such as operating a pig farm—if that land use is "unreasonable." Whether a use is unreasonable depends upon a number of factors. To help courts determine reasonableness, the Restatement uses a number of tests including the suitability of the activity on the land to the character of the place, the value to society of the alleged nuisance, and the hardship on the defendant of an injunction or damage award. The social value of the plaintiff's use of her land is also considered along with the extent to which that use is harmed. Courts weigh the gravity of harm to the plaintiff against the utility of the defendant's use.

C. ZONING AND THE LAW OF NUISANCE

In *Euclid*, the plaintiff alleged that the village's zoning ordinance would "confiscate and destroy a great part of its value. . . , constitutes a cloud upon the land, [and] reduces and destroys its value. . . ." In Restatement terms, this focuses on the financial hardship of the owner of the land creating the nuisance. The Court, in response, centered its attention on the reasonableness of the zoning ordinance, particularly the creation of separate zoning districts for different land uses. It referenced "comprehensive reports" prepared by "commissions and experts" bearing evidence of "painstaking consideration"—reports that recommended the creation of land use districts that separated residential, business, and industrial buildings. Before police power legislation of this type can be declared unconstitutional, said the Court, it must be found that it is "clearly arbitrary and unreasonable, having no substantial relationship to the public health, safety, morals, or general welfare." In this critical and deferential judicial test for measuring the constitutionality of land use laws, the echoes of nuisance law and the Restatement of Torts reverberate. The question is one of reasonableness.

Comprehensive zoning, of the type adopted by *Euclid*, was new in the early 1920s when it was adopted, but the concept of adopting local laws to proscribe land uses in the U.S. was not. In Hadacheck v. Sebastian, 239 U.S. 394 (1915), for example, the Court upheld a local land use law that prevented the operation of a brick kiln in the City of Los Angeles. Prior to the law's adoption, a brick kiln in that place was perfectly legal. The Court held, however, that since the use was first established, the area had become largely residential. Progress, it noted, could not be slowed for the benefit of private interests. In nuisance law terms, the brick operation was in the path of development. The residential owners now in its vicinity had not moved to the nuisance but rather had been carried along with the organic development of the city into the kiln's neighborhood. The brick operation was now "unsuited to the character of that locality," to use the Restatement's terminology.

Today, a brick factory in a residential neighborhood would be considered a *per se* nuisance. In other words, the nuances of nuisance cases do not pertain, and no balancing of the gravity of the harm to the plaintiff against the utility of the defendant's operation is required. Courts recognize that some uses (junkyards, cemeteries, ammunition factories, and brick manufacturing) are always nuisances in urbanized places, particularly in residential zones. Prior to the advent of extensive land use controls, courts effectively exercised judicial zoning in making such determinations. It was well established in American law that certain land uses should be prohibited in certain districts, or zones. In Powell v. Taylor, 222 Ark. 896, 263 S.W.2d 906 (Ark. 1954), for example, the state found a neighborhood to be so residential in character that the conversion of a home into a funeral parlor would constitute a nuisance.

Notice how judicial land use decisions directly, although imprecisely and unpredictably, affected a form of zoning, prescribing and proscribing land uses in certain "districts." We have seen that in agricultural or rural areas, farm uses are favored and those who move into farming areas are unable to proscribe such uses in most cases—they moved to the nuisance. In areas dedicated to industrial uses, we see the same result. In Bove v. Donner-Hanna Coke Corp., 236 A.D. 37, 258 N.Y.S. 229 (N.Y.A.D. 4th Dept. 1932), the court held that the nuisance doctrine does not apply where plaintiff intentionally locates within a known industrial area, regardless of whether the particular source of the nuisance existed at the time the plaintiff located there. Because courts look to the reasonableness of the land use that is the alleged nuisance, location counts. Different conditions pertain in urban, suburban, fringe, and rural areas and the courts are cognizant of these differences. This results in a fair degree of consistency in judicial decisions with certain uses being zoned out—enjoined—in certain areas because they are not consistent, appropriate, or reasonable there.

D. THE EFFECT OF ZONING ON THE LAW OF NUISANCE

What is left of nuisance law now that land uses are so heavily regulated by local zoning? Does zoning trump nuisance claims? Again, it depends. In Maykut v. Plasko, 170 Conn. 310, 365 A.2d 1114 (Conn. 1976), the plaintiff homeowner brought an action to enjoin their neighbor's use of a noise cannon to frighten birds away from their garden. The defendant had a valid permit for use of the cannon under both a state statute and the local zoning law. In awarding an injunction against further use of the cannon, the state court held that although the action was permitted by zoning law, that fact is no defense to an activity that otherwise interferes with the use and enjoyment of a particular neighbor's property.

Zoning creates standards for land uses that are generally harmonious, in the legislature's opinion, with the character of the zoning district, while private nuisance actions allow individual lot owners to prove to the court that a permitted use affects a nuisance in the particular circumstances of the plaintiff's land. In Prah v. Maretti, 108 Wis. 2d 223, 321 N.W.2d 182 (Wis. 1982), the plaintiff brought an action to enjoin the construction of a home on the neighboring lot alleging that it would interfere with access to sunlight for his solar panels. The state court held that although the defendant was otherwise in compliance with all zoning laws, compliance did not automatically bar a private nuisance claim.

In *Maykut* and *Prah*, the zoning laws applied generally to stipulate what land uses are appropriate in each district. The legislators adopting the zoning did not intend to preempt individual nuisance actions where land uses authorized under the law had such extreme effects. This might not always be the situation, especially where the zoning legislation appears to create an exclusive remedy for the matter regulated, but this is not normally the case. Green v. Castle Concrete Co., 181 Colo. 309, 509 P.2d 588 (Colo. 1973) held that where the zoning laws permit an activity, that activity cannot then be considered a *public* nuisance. A judicial finding that a land use constituted a public nuisance would be tantamount to overruling the clear intentions of the legislature that, as a general matter, the use is in the public interest, not inimical to it.

E. MODERN ZONING AND NUISANCE PRINCIPLES

The influence of nuisance law in land use regulation is ubiquitous. In Lucas v. South Carolina Coastal Council, 505 U.S. 1003 (1992), for example, the U.S. Supreme Court held that a land use regulation that prevents all economically beneficial uses of the land is a *per se* regulatory taking and requires the payment of just compensation by the regulator under the Fifth Amendment takings clause. The Court added, however, that the regulation is not a taking if the land use proscribed by the regulation can be enjoined under nuisance law or other background principles of state law.

Zoning ordinances typically allow land uses that are in place at the time of the law's adoption to continue as legal nonconforming uses. Zoning laws state, however, that some uses, such as junkyards, unsightly billboards, and particularly noxious activities, must be terminated immediately or within a relatively short period. In this, the difference between a nuisance *per se* and nuisance *per accidens* is observable. *Per se* activities are judicially declared to be immoral or extra-hazardous, as are land uses that must be terminated by zoning. Nuisances *per accidens* must be proved by the plaintiff to be nuisances in fact. Such land uses are more likely to be called nonconforming uses under zoning law and allowed to continue, because of the injustice that would be done to the owner who had invested in the building before it was proscribed by the zoning ordinance.

Judicial policies that are evident in decisions regarding nuisances *per accidens*—nuisances in fact—are mirrored in variance provisions of zoning ordinances. Variances may be awarded by local zoning boards of appeals to property owners when they can show that the application of the zoning to their individual lot will create a hardship. A variance might be given, for example, to allow a property owner to build closer to a side yard lot line, in violation of a requirement found in the zoning ordinance, upon a showing that a stream or rock outcropping on the other side of the yard would prevent the owner from building a normal sized home on the property. Under many zoning laws, the zoning board of appeals is required to balance the hardship the zoning creates for the regulated owner against the adverse impact of the proposed building on the neighborhood, mimicking the balancing test in nuisance law used by the judiciary.

F. MODERN NUISANCE CASES

Nuisance law has had to adapt to changing times. Large-scale development and intense industrial uses have caused courts to rethink basic principles. When an entire subdivision was built next to the nuisance (a stockyard), the court adjusted the nuisance doctrine by allowing the subdivision to continue and grow, but granted substantial damages to the stockyard to cover the cost of relocation. See, Spur Industries, Inc. v. Del E. Webb Development Co., 108 Ariz. 178, 494 P.2d 700 (Ariz. 1972). The limitations of private nuisance actions as a solution to societal problems are apparent in *Spur Industries*. A comprehensive land use plan and zoning law for the jurisdiction would have prevented the costs of relocation, loss of business, and inflated subdivision home prices.

These limitations are equally evident in Boomer v. Atlantic Cement Co., Inc., 26 N.Y.2d 219, 309 N.Y.S.2d 312, 257 N.E.2d 870 (N.Y. 1970). In *Boomer*, the New York Court of Appeals refused to enjoin the operations of a large cement plant, because of its social utility and the economic hardship to its investors and employees, awarding damages instead to the individual plaintiffs who were adjacent landowners. Previous case law had held that an injunction was the proper remedy for protecting the adjacent owners. See, Hulbert v. California Portland Cement Co., 161 Cal. 239, 118 P. 928 (Cal. 1911), where local farmers brought a nuisance action against a cement factory and the court awarded an injunction, permanently closing the facility.

The *Boomer* case was a particularly complex matter for the court. The cement company had unilaterally appropriated an affirmative easement on the neighbors' property for the purpose of depositing cement dust. In effect, its operations imposed a "servitude" on the plaintiffs' land. By awarding damages for the imposed servitude, the court was placed in the awkward position of awarding damages for the involuntary taking of a property interest of the plaintiffs for a private purpose. The Fifth Amendment of the U.S. Constitution allows private property interests to be taken, but only for a *public purpose* by a public entity accompanied by an award of just compensation. Despite this awkwardness, the court could find no other way of balancing the equities between the parties in the absence of comprehensive zoning in the jurisdiction or other public regulations. Coincidentally, the Clean Air Act, based on the power of Congress to regulate interstate commerce, was amended to control particulate contamination at the same time that *Boomer* was decided.

§ 4. SERVITUDES: EASEMENTS AND COVENANTS

A. INTRODUCTION

Nuisance law is inherently intertwined with the law of servitudes. In a nuisance case, the aggrieved plaintiff claims that the offending land use imposes a burden on the plaintiff's property, adversely affecting its use and enjoyment. In *Boomer*, the burden was physical: discrete contaminants deposited on the land. In *Clark* and *Mitchell*, the burden was physical, in a sense, since the odors of pig farming physically invaded the property. Under the law of servitudes (easements and covenants), we learn that burdens can be placed on private property but that normally those benefiting from these burdens have to purchase such rights from the burdened owners. O can convey to A an affirmative easement to cross O's land to gain access to a public road. Similarly, O can sell a restrictive covenant to A that limits the use of O's property to single-family housing.

Notice how this happens. A approaches O and asks to purchase an access easement or restrictive covenant from O. Lawyers are consulted. The seller's attorney, acting for O, draws up a deed conveying a property right to A. A's lawyer reviews the document and, if all goes well, a deed conveying the servitude is executed by O and filed in the land records, usually in the county where the land is located. All subsequent purchasers of O's land are then on record notice that O's land is burdened by an obligation to A, who is benefited by the limitation on O's parcel.

If this transaction is done correctly, the burden and benefit of the servitude "run with the land." This means that the agreement is not simply a personal covenant between O and A (which of course it is under contract theory), but also a real covenant affixed to the parcels, the consequences of which "run" to subsequent owners of the benefited and burdened lands.

B. TERMINOLOGY

The terminology used to describe servitudes varies from state to state and can be confusing. The simplest terms to remember are servitudes, easements, and covenants. "Servitudes" is a general term, comprising all types of burdens that may be imposed on the lands of another. They are called "nonpossessory" interests in land, yet they are "property rights" protected by the Constitution. In this field of law, burdened lands are called the "servient estate," or tenement, and benefited parcels are dubbed the "dominant estate," or tenement. If A owns the right to travel across O's suburban lot, A owns the dominant estate and O the servient estate.

"Easements" give third parties the right to physically enter and use land. A *"profit á prendre"* gives a third party the right not only to go on the land, but also to sever valuable resources (timber or minerals) from it. "Covenants" restrict the use of the burdened property or impose some affirmative obligation on its owner. Covenants give a third party the right to enforce a restriction on the use of the land burdened. The remedies for the breach of a covenant, depending on the court and type of covenant involved, are two: an injunction that forces the burdened owner to follow the terms of the covenant, or a damage award that compensates the benefited owner for any breach of those terms.

Because of the way that the law developed, covenants can be referred to as real covenants, restrictive covenants, negative easements, or equitable servitudes. A real covenant is one that strictly conforms to early common law rules: the covenant must "touch and concern the land," the parties must have intended the covenant to run with the land, and there must be privity of estate between the benefited owner seeking to enforce the covenant and the current owner of the burdened parcel. Where privity of estate is missing, but the owner of the burdened property had, or should have had, notice of the burden, the covenant can be enforced in equity and may be called an "equitable servitude."

Easements, too, are described by courts in various ways. They may be affirmative or negative, in gross or appurtenant. An affirmative easement gives the third party the right to enter the burdened parcel. A negative easement restricts the use of the burdened parcel giving the owner of the benefited land the right to ask for an injunction or damages. A negative easement is more properly called a restrictive covenant, since it manifests an agreement, or covenant, to restrict the use of the servient tenement. Easements that are in gross benefit their owner personally, rather than as the owner of a parcel of land. If A buys the right to cross O's land to get to the fishing hole so A can fish, the affirmative easement over O's land is "in gross," not attached to, or appurtenant to, any land that A owns. Easements in gross normally are not assignable: the affirmative easement to get to the fishing hole may not be transferred, for example, from A to B. This is not the case if the easement in gross is a commercial one, such as a railroad or utility easement. Commercial easements in gross can be transferred from one railroad or utility company to another.

It is in sorting out these terms that the complexity of the law of servitudes is encountered. The Restatement of Property, Servitudes, published by the American Law Institute in 2000, greatly simplifies the law in this field. It reduces the types of servitudes to three—profits, easements, and covenants—and integrates them into a modern law of servitudes where many of the common law terms are eliminated and the rules are made more uniform. Unfortunately, the Restatement is not the law in many states and, regarding particular servitudes and the terms used to describe them, complexity still exists. If this occurs in the study of land use law, the student should consult a hornbook on servitudes to clarify the matter at hand.

C. MODERN APPLICATIONS

For the purposes of understanding land use law as it is currently practiced, it is sufficient to understand the concepts and techniques that explain how servitudes gave rise to certain land use regulations and how servitudes function together with public regulations to control land uses in certain places. Land use regulations are public rules that limit private land use for the benefit of the community. Servitudes are private rules that limit the use of privately held land for the benefit of the owners of designated parcels of land, and only those owners. Where land use laws stop, servitudes can pick up to meet the needs of modern landowners, most frequently parcel owners in residential subdivisions.

Does zoning trump servitudes? What happens when a neighbor is carefully protected by restrictive covenants but the neighborhood around it is drastically altered because of zoning changes? Such was the case in West Alameda Heights Homeowners Ass'n v. Bd. of County Commissioners of Jefferson County, 169 Colo. 491, 458 P.2d 253 (Colo. 1969). The developer had retained a few vacant lots on what had become a commercial corridor under the local zoning law and applied for a permit to build in conformance with the zoning standards. The neighbors successfully sought an injunction to enforce the restrictive covenants, prevailing over the developer's claim that the covenants should be terminated because of the change of circumstances in the surrounding area. The court said that the purpose of the covenants was to protect the subdivision from just such occurrences. None of the subdivision owners had violated the covenants, the neighborhood retained its internal integrity, and there was no change of circumstances within the protected area. The court noted that, "The covenants have no meaning if external forces and pressures result in their removal." See also, Rofe v. Robinson, 415 Mich. 345, 329 N.W.2d 704 (Mich. 1982).

D. COMMON INTEREST COMMUNITIES

(i) Introduction

A reference to common interest communities explains how zoning has replaced servitudes and how, at the same time, servitudes supplement land use rules. Common interest communities are extremely popular in today's market and much of the country's new housing falls into this category. The terms for such communities include cooperatives, condominiums, townhouse communities, planned communities, new-towns, traditional neighborhood developments, or homeowner associations.

(ii) Prior to Zoning

Prior to the advent of zoning in the 1920s, servitudes provided developers an effective method for creating high quality residential neighborhoods. The developer would buy a large parcel of land, subdivide it into lots, and sell those lots to individuals for the purpose of building homes. To control the quality of the subdivision, each deed would contain a set of covenants prescribing certain land use practices (each house is to be set back from the street by 20 feet, for example) and proscribing certain land uses (the lot is restricted to the construction of a single-family house and a garage).

(iii) Following the Advent of Zoning

Under zoning, this type of private land use restriction was no longer as necessary. Single-family zoning districts prevent the use of the land for any other purpose and require that houses be set back from the street a certain distance. Notwithstanding these public restrictions, a developer might want to develop a more exclusive community, one with deeper setbacks or larger lots, for example, or one that is governed by design standards to create a certain look or feel that is not achieved by the typical zoning ordinance. These more restrictive standards can be imposed by servitudes: covenants placed in the original deeds restricting homebuilding within 35 feet of the street, mandating larger lots than required by zoning, and requiring the use of a certain style of architecture.

As important, developers may want to build common facilities, such as a clubhouse, swimming pool, and tennis courts, and make them available to all homeowners in the subdivision. This will require revenue for operations and upkeep which can be secured by requiring the purchasers of individual lots to join an association created by the developer and to pay annual dues established by the association's board of directors. Many modern subdivisions are created in which lot owners own a common property interest in such facilities, enjoy easements to access them, and are required to pay dues to sustain them. All of these obligations are secured by covenants and affirmative easements included in their deeds, rather than through zoning or supplemental land use laws.

In common interest communities, the deeds contain or refer to a declaration of covenants and restrictions that burden and benefit each lot or unit owner reciprocally. If A purchases a lot from O, the developer, A's lot or unit is both a servient and dominant parcel, limited and enhanced by the declaration. A parallel expression exists in zoning law; the Supreme Court found zoning constitutional, in part, because it exhibits "reciprocity of advantage." The zoning laws of a community burden and benefit all landowners. Land use restrictions limit what can be done by individual owners so that a secure, attractive, equitable, economically sound, and environmentally livable community can be created.

The early common law of servitudes presented several obstacles to the creation of common interest communities governed by declarations of covenants and restrictions. Often the declaration was not contained in a particular purchaser's deed but recorded in the land records regarding the subdivision or evident by observing a common development scheme as the community was built out. In these cases, are the parcel owners in privity of estate? When lot owners are required to pay a monthly fee to the homeowners association to cover operations and capital costs, how does that burden touch and concern the land? Are affirmative burdens like this—the duty to pay—enforceable at all under the common law?

(iv) Equitable Servitudes

The privity of estate requirement was relieved in an early English case, Tulk v. Moxhay, 2 Phil. 774, 41 Eng.Rep. 1143 (Ch. 1848). The purchaser of a famous London park, which was restricted to recreational use to benefit the immediate neighbors, claimed to be free of the restrictions because they were not actually contained in his deed. He argued, therefore, that he was not in privity of estate with the benefited owner on that covenant or restriction. The plaintiff neighbors appealed to the equity court pointing out that the purchaser had actual notice of the restriction, paid a price that reflected that burden on the park, and would be unjustly enriched if the equity court failed to enforce it. The court agreed, holding that actual or constructive notice of a covenant's existence can replace privity of estate. Where the covenant touches and concerns the land, was intended to run with the land, and the subsequent purchaser of the servient parcel has notice of it, the covenant will be enforced in equity by the issuance of an injunction. The park was saved.

The equitable servitude doctrine of *Tulk* was applied in the United States in the case of Sanborn v. McLean, 233 Mich. 227, 206 N.W. 496 (Mich. 1925). The defendant in *Sanborn* had no covenants in her deed that restricted the use of her land. When she began to construct a gasoline station on her lot, the neighbors brought suit claiming that their exclusive residential subdivision should be protected from this deviant use. They showed that the developer had placed a single-family only, restrictive covenant in many of the original deeds and that the subdivision, which was largely developed, bore the stamp of an observable pattern of development. The court held that the defendant should have noticed the common development scheme and inquired further by checking the land records to see whether the lots in the subdivision were burdened by any restrictions that would explain such an obvious pattern. Since the developer owned all the lots at one time and had conveyed many of them subject to the restriction, the remaining lots were impressed with a reciprocal negative easement. Since the defendant owned one of those parcels, she acquired the land subject to that limitation.

In Neponsit Property Owners' Ass'n v. Emigrant Industrial Sav. Bank, 278 N.Y. 248, 15 N.E.2d 793 (N.Y. 1938), the issue was whether an early homeowners association could enforce the requirement that lot owners pay dues. The plaintiff was the association which itself owned no land benefited by the obligation to support its operations. Was it in privity of estate? Further, the burden imposed was that of paying dues. How did such an affirmative obligation touch and concern the land? The court held that to deny the association the right to enforce mutual covenants would be a triumph of form over substance. After all, it exists solely to represent the homeowners who clearly are in privity of estate on the covenants. Further, since the purpose of collecting dues is to maintain the roads, services, and common facilities, without which the subdivision would fail or lose substantial value, clearly the dues affected the owners as landowners, thereby touching and concerning the land.

This holding has been fortified by the Restatement of Property, Servitudes which says that the touch and concern doctrine has been completely displaced by the rule that a covenant is valid unless it can be shown to be illegal, unconstitutional, or against public policy.

CHAPTER 2

LAND USE PLANS AND THE PLANNING PROCESS

§ 1. INTRODUCTION TO PLANNING, LAND USE LAW, AND DEMOGRAPHY

The United States has a finite amount of real property or land mass. Both the movement of people from one location to another (e.g., from the cities to the suburbs) and the continuing population growth impact the way in which society consumes land resources. The United States' population in 1900 was 76,094 million, and by 2015 the nation's population reached over 320,000 million. By 2016 the largest cities by population were: New York City (over 8.5 million), Los Angeles (almost 4 million), Chicago (2.7 million), and Houston (almost 2.3 million).

Whether attributable to the growth of the cities in the 1920s or the exodus from the cities to the suburbs in the 1960s through the early part of the 21st century, demographic change requires local governments to plan prospectively for, and to respond to, the impacts of human settlement patterns.

The building of roads and highways, the siting of schools, the location of commercial, retail and manufacturing facilities, and ensuring affordable housing are just some examples of what land use planning entails. The impact of these decisions on the natural environment is also an important land use consideration. In addition, balancing the need and desire to preserve open space and to protect agricultural land with the demands of the built environment creates many policy and legal challenges for municipal officials involved in land use decision-making.

Land use planning is a process that allows municipalities to consider the impacts of land use decisions and actions on the immediate and long-range protection, enhancement, growth, and development of the community. In essence, planning results in a blueprint for community development and it becomes an important indicator of quality of life in our cities, towns, and villages. It touches upon virtually everything in our daily routines from the amount of time people may sit in traffic during the business commute to the distance people travel to a grocery store, a gasoline service station, and to school; the location of parks and other recreational facilities; and the types of housing options that are available in neighborhoods and communities. The legal system in nearly every state encourages local governments to consider all of this and to create, in response, a land use plan.

Zoning and other land use controls are the legal tools that implement the land use plan. Zoning addresses, among other things, the dimensional aspects of land use (e.g., height, bulk, and density) and the allowable uses of land in various locations (e.g., residential, industrial, business, and agricultural). A local zoning law may address controversial community development issues, such as the location of adult businesses, telecommunication facilities, and group homes. State statutes usually require that local zoning laws be consistent with the local land use plan. This creates a dynamic synergy between the plan and the law. In addition to zoning laws, other regulatory controls such as subdivision laws and site plan laws address more specific design and infrastructure details for proposed land development projects. These laws, too, should be consistent with the plan. Constitutional and other legal requirements that ensure land use plans and laws will not result in discrimination or violate other important protections including private property rights, free speech, and freedom of religion may, at times, temper these decisions.

With such critical decisions at the core of plan development and the creation of zoning and other land use laws, the active involvement by the public is essential to ensure that these documents best reflect the desired quality of life in each community. Meaningful public participation demands more than mere compliance with statutorily required public hearings. Public information sessions, public workshops, and publications that explain proposals are methods that may be employed to achieve informed and effective public participation. Meeting and workshop locations, time and day(s) of the week for public sessions, as well as, where appropriate, notice in languages other than English are appropriate considerations to meet public participation goals.

§ 2. ECONOMIC ISSUES AND LAND USE

Economic considerations in land use planning and zoning decision-making garner the greatest amount of public attention, particularly for landowners who evaluate government regulation of land based upon individual desires to protect personal investments in real estate. Community [re]development, economic development and housing affordability are major themes in the economic impact of zoning and other land use regulations. Fiscal impacts of land use regulations manifest in a variety of other ways including consequences related to property taxation, the loss of potential revenue resulting from restrictions on expansion or enlargement of nonconforming uses as well as from the amortization of these uses.

Sometimes planning and zoning decisions may have the effect of increasing the value of the land and surrounding properties—this could be characterized as a windfall. Other times, the land use decision by a municipality may have the effect of reducing the market value of property, from a slight reduction to a total deprivation of all economic value amounting to a wipe-out. Issues regarding a municipality's obligation to compensate property owners in these cases are discussed in greater detail in Chapter V. Interest groups are quick to challenge government actions that amount to diminution in property value. There has not been, however, as much attention focused on the issue of whether property owners should have an obligation to share with the government and community any potential windfalls realized as a result of land use regulation.

Debates about the economics of land use regulation focus attention on the relationship of the local property tax with fiscal zoning. For example, the allowable uses of a particular parcel of land will impact the required level of government services for that use. This in turn impacts the property tax required to fund the public services. Land use regulations imposed by the government to protect and preserve natural and historical resources may have the effect of creating certain community benefits at the expense of individual property owners. Likewise, land use regulations adopted by the government to restrict certain property for agricultural use may preserve lands for agricultural production, but may not advance the ability of the farmer to continue using the lands for viable agricultural production due to other government policies regarding various farm-related subsidies.

Governments strive to implement land policies that balance market supply and market demand. This requires governments to monitor land markets to ensure, for example, that housing stock remains affordable. When appropriate, local governments should revisit plans and implement regulations to make certain that the public policies influencing the location, timing, type, and amount of growth within the jurisdiction achieve proper economic goals.

§ 3. HISTORICAL DEVELOPMENT OF LAND USE PLANNING

A. THE STANDARD CITY PLANNING ENABLING ACT

Following the publication of the Standard State Zoning Enabling Act in 1922, in 1928 the U.S. Department of Commerce published the Standard City Planning Enabling Act. Herbert Hoover, who was the Secretary of Commerce, believed that "the lack of adequate open spaces, of playgrounds and parks, the congestion of streets, the misery of tenement life and its repercussions upon each new generation, are an untold charge against our American life. Our cities do not produce their full contribution to the sinews of American life and national character. The moral and social issues can only be solved by a new conception of city building." He appointed an Advisory Committee on City Planning and Zoning which included a number of founding members of the American City Planning Institute. The Committee was charged with the task of producing planning and zoning acts to be considered and adopted by state governments "enabling" their localities to adopt land use plans and to control land uses through zoning.

The Standard City Planning Enabling Act covers the following six areas: 1) the organization and power of the planning commission, which was directed to prepare and adopt a "master local plan"; 2) the content of the master plan for the physical development of the territory; 3) provision for adoption of a master street plan by the governing body; 4) provision for approval of all public improvements by the planning commission; 5) control of private subdivision of land; and 6) provision for the establishment of a regional planning commission and a regional plan. The Act focused on city issues rather than on suburban and rural matters.

The Standard City Planning Enabling Act recommended that plans be adopted by planning boards, while zoning ordinances were to be adopted by the local legislative bodies. This separation of responsibility for the preparation of zoning ordinances and land use plans makes sense since a visionary, long-range plan for the community has long-term impacts on property values and neighborhood character. It is also less likely to arouse impassioned resistance. Planning boards are usually made up of appointed, rather than elected, members, so the pressure of the electorate is felt less in their deliberations. The Act has been criticized because it made planning optional rather than mandatory and because it failed to include a precise definition of a local plan.

In 1935, Alfred Bettman drafted a model municipal planning enabling act that closely tracked the model Standard City Planning Enabling Act. Bettman believed that a staffed professional planning department might serve larger localities better than reliance on volunteer planning board members and local elected officials. He suggested that the local plan include "the general location, character, extent and layout of the replanning of blighted districts and slum areas."

Section 701 of the Housing Act of 1954 was the impetus for the next wave of local land use plans. As a condition of qualifying for federal funding for urban renewal and other programs, local governments were required to prepare plans that included land use and housing elements as well as circulation, public utilities, and community facilities elements. This was the last federal program that provided significant fiscal support for the development and adoption of local plans.

B. THE MODEL LAND DEVELOPMENT CODE

While the early Standard City Planning Enabling Act was clearly influential in the adoption of state planning enabling acts across the country, its shortcomings are apparent in hindsight now that the nation is more fully developed. For example, at the time of the adoption of the enabling Act, there was no interstate highway system, which many have identified as a significant factor in suburban sprawl. Approximately 50 years after the Act was introduced, the American Law Institute published a Model Land Development Code in an effort to modernize the state planning and zoning enabling acts that were based upon the 1920s models. This effort resulted in a multi-volume, 12-section report that failed to garner national interest. In fact, with the exception of the State of Florida, which based its development of regional impacts law on the relevant provisions of this Model Code, no other state used the document in any meaningful way.

C. GROWING SMART LEGISLATIVE GUIDEBOOK

The 2002 preface to the American Planning Association's Growing Smart Legislative Guidebook noted the failure of the Standard City Planning Enabling Act to address twenty-first century challenges. For example, in the 1920s government was simpler and there was less of it. Planning was viewed as a local, as opposed to a regional, state, or federal concern. It was not until the 1950s that significant transportation, housing, and environmental programs were promoted as federal issues. At the beginning of the last century, land was viewed more as a commodity to be bought and sold, while in modern times land is viewed more as a resource, and an ethic of resource sustainability has emerged. Today there is more informed and active public interest and involvement in land use planning decision-making. The legal landscape surrounding the regulation of land use has matured from simple nuisance actions to sophisticated and complex constitutional issues that often stress the critical importance of an open planning process.

The Growing Smart Legislative Guidebook is the result of a seven-year effort to help to modernize state planning and zoning enabling legislation. The two-volume 1,500-page document was issued during a time when there had been unprecedented active efforts to modernize state planning and zoning enabling legislation across the country. The Guidebook is intended to help communities respond effectively to changing conditions, and as such contains model statutes for planning and the management of change along with commentary that highlights critical issues and options. Key, however, is the philosophy that there is no "one-size-fits-all" approach to land use law reform. The Guidebook is organized into 15 chapters covering dozens of topics including: starting a state reform effort, types of state planning agencies, content of state plans, process for developing and adopting plans, siting of state facilities, designation of areas of critical state concern, developments of regional impact, regional planning and intergovernmental issues, local planning, land development regulations, zoning, review of plats and plans, development rights, exactions and impact fees, sequencing of development, development agreements, transfer of development rights, historic and architectural design review, land use incentives, administration and judicial review of land use decisions, enforcement of land development regulations, integrating environmental review, financing of local planning, tax base sharing, redevelopment and tax relief, agricultural districts, and geographic information systems.

Language from the Growing Smart Legislative Guidebook was incorporated into new land use laws in more than a dozen states. While the full extent of the influence of this modern reform effort will not be known for some time, it is clear that its impact will be farther-reaching than prior initiatives such as the

Model Land Development Code. Unlike prior efforts, the Guidebook also contains useful model language for municipalities to incorporate into local zoning and land use laws.

In 2008, a joint task force of the State and Local Government Law Section and the Administrative Law Section of the American Bar Association promulgated a model statute on local land use process to focus on the administrative procedures in the land use decisionmaking process. https://landuse law.wustl.edu/ModelLandUseCode.pdf. Since that time there have been no further efforts to produce model acts or procedures in the land use regulatory arena.

§ 4. PARTICIPANTS IN THE LAND USE PROCESS

Lawyers must be mindful of the various individuals involved in the land use planning and zoning process, including their respective roles and legal authority. Richard F. Babcock, in his book THE ZONING GAME: MUNICIPAL PRACTICES AND POLICIES, identifies the following "players" in the zoning game: local decision-makers (e.g., members of local legislative bodies, planning boards, and zoning boards), professional planners, lawyers and judges, code enforcement officers, engineers, architects, and other related boards (e.g., historic preservation commissions, architectural review boards, and conservation advisory committees) as well as members of the public.

Since local governments are creatures of state governments, local government officials, including members of planning and zoning boards and elected members of local legislative bodies, derive their authority and powers primarily from state constitutional and statutory provisions such as the planning and zoning enabling acts. In many cases, state statutes give local legislative bodies the authority to choose to retain certain planning and zoning powers or to delegate such roles to planning or zoning boards. In addition, local governments may, at their option, establish and empower, by local law, various associated bodies, such as architectural review boards and historic review boards. Therefore, it is critical to consult applicable local zoning codes, in addition to state statutes, to determine exactly which board is responsible for various actions and the relationships among and between the various boards. Similarly, code enforcement officers are vested with certain statutorily derived powers and duties, and they may be expanded as a matter of local discretion.

A. THE ROLE OF PLANNERS

Professional planners guide the development of both short-term and long-term plans that help communities realize growth and revitalization while guiding local officials to make decisions concerning social, economic, and environmental challenges. Planners report on the current use of land in communities, including an examination of public infrastructure (e.g., roads and highways, sewers and water), an inventory of housing stock and commercial and business uses, demographic trends and projections, and employment and economic forecasts. On the basis of this and other related data, planners provide recommendations and input on the design and layout of future land uses, including the suitability of various types of development in different areas of the community.

In addition, planners are involved on a daily basis with both the drafting and the interpretation of various land use regulations. Planners may assume responsibility for drafting of zoning ordinances or subdivision regulations with or without input and review from legal counsel. Planners may also function as advisors, offering opinions to various local boards regarding the application of a state or local land use law to a particular situation. By the very nature of the close intersection of planning and law, planners may be put in the awkward position of being asked for legal advice by their employer. Planners should be careful, however, to remind employers that they are not attorneys and that where legal opinions and reviews are requested, a competent attorney should be consulted.

B. THE LEGAL STATUS OF PLANNERS

Planning as a profession is still relatively new. The American Society of Planning Officials was founded in 1934, but it was not until 1957 that the first planning textbook was published (URBAN LAND USE PLANNING by F. Stuart Chapin, Jr.), and in 1959 the American Collegiate Schools of Planning (ACSP) was founded. In 1971 the American Institute of Planners (AIP) adopted its first Code of Ethics for Planners, and in 1977 the first exam for membership in the AIP was administered. One year later, the AIP and the American Society of Planning Officials merged to form the American Planning Association. In 1989, the Planning Accreditation Board was recognized as the post-secondary accrediting authority for professional planning programs.

Only two states, New Jersey and Michigan, require that planners be licensed. In New Jersey Chapter, American Institute of Planners v. New Jersey State Bd. of Professional Planners, 227 A.2d 313 (N.J. 1967), appeal dismissed, cert. den., 389 U.S. 8 (1967), the New Jersey Supreme Court upheld the constitutionality of a statute requiring that planners meet certain minimum educational and practice requirements in order to be licensed, while licensed professional engineers, land surveyors, and registered architects were able to automatically receive a planning license without a similar showing. The court noted that because of the growing importance of community planning, it was reasonable for the State to regulate the planning profession, and that the national shortage of professional planners was sufficient justification to allow other related professions to automatically receive a planning license. Interestingly, however, there is no national licensure program for professional planners, and the remaining 48 states have opted not to regulate the profession at this time.

C. ETHICAL CONDUCT OF PLAYERS IN THE LAND USE GAME

Planners who are voluntary members of the American Institute of Certified Planners (AICP) are subject to the AICP Code of Ethics (last revised April 1, 2016), see, https://www.planning.org/ethics/ethicscode.htm. AICP annually reports on ethics case activities and reports, see, https://www.planning.org/ethics/report/. A Colorado appeals court has held that a planner's opinion as to the best practices and ethics of a type of service does not establish a legally enforceable duty of care under the AICP Code. Stan Clauson Associates, Inc. v. Coleman Brothers Constr., LLC, 297 P.3d 1042 (Colo. App. 2013). The American Planning Association (APA) has adopted Ethical Principles in Planning (1992), see, https://www.planning.org/ethics/ethicalprinciples.htm as guidance to promote professionalism in planning. In addition, other professionals involved in planning and zoning—including lawyers, engineers, and architects—are governed by various national and state professional codes of conduct. These codes are meant to standardize the practice in various professions and to ensure that the public and clients receive appropriate service by each profession.

Courts are involved, however, in deciding myriad questions concerning conflicts of interest that arise in land use planning and decision-making. These situations often involve members of planning or zoning boards or local legislative bodies. At times they focus on relationships that involve planners, lawyers, engineers, bankers, real estate agents, and others participating in cases before planning and zoning boards and commissions. These questions are not examined as matters of professional conduct, but are analyzed according to various state and local laws and regulations pertaining to government ethics. Many times there is no specific state statute or local law on point. The courts then resort to the common law, or caselaw, to determine whether a particular actor in the land use decision-making process is prohibited from discussing or voting on a matter before the board as a result of a conflict of interest.

Disqualifying conflicts of interest in the land use context may arise where a decision-maker or policy-maker could personally or financially benefit from the outcome of the decision, and where close family members might benefit financially or otherwise. Other types of situations that can pose questions of conflicts of interest come up as a result of alleged *ex parte* conversations between applicants and board members, or where a member of the public or an applicant believes that a decision-maker is biased because of personal associations, affiliations, or residency, or where a decision-maker is alleged to have prejudged an application based upon statements made during a campaign or at other times prior to the final decision being rendered on the evidence.

Unfortunately, issues of corruption in the land use process arise where local officials have been convicted of accepting bribes in the form of money or other services (e.g., home repairs) in exchange for approvals of land use permits. When these situations occur, the U.S. Department of Justice, along with local law enforcement are called upon to prosecute the public officials.

D. ETHICAL CONDUCT OF LAWYERS

Lawyers must be aware of the various ethical issues that may arise when they function both as legal counsel to land use decision-making bodies and when they serve as members of local bodies authorized to make land use decisions. For example, a conflict of interest may arise where a lawyer serves on a planning commission and a potential applicant attempts to retain the lawyer on non-land use matters. The appearance is that the lawyer is being retained to curry favor on future land use matters. In other situations, lawyers in private practice who represent local planning or zoning boards may find themselves with a conflict when they no longer represent the municipality but rather have new clients who desire building permits, site plan review, or other zoning approvals from the locality. Law firms may be ethically prohibited from the subsequent representation. Other recent cases have centered on questions of relationships between board members and law firms representing applicants (e.g., familial relationship and business relationships).

§ 5. LAND USE PLANS

As the land use system evolved, basic concepts were left undefined, including the definition of a comprehensive land use plan. The document itself has been referred to as, among other things, a master plan, a comprehensive plan, a comprehensive master plan, a land use plan, a comprehensive land use plan, a local land development plan, local general plan, and an official master plan. There was no clear agreement as to whether this document should limit itself to physical phenomena, or should include economic, demographic, and social matters. What is meant by comprehensive itself is unclear. Most definitions presuppose a local focus, but some include regional and statewide considerations. The precise relationship of the comprehensive land use plan with the zoning ordinance, the zoning map, and the official map was never entirely agreed upon. The elements of a plan—that is, the subjects to be covered in it—have been described in numerous ways as well.

A. COMPREHENSIVE PLANS OR MASTER PLANS

The comprehensive plan creates a blueprint for the future development and preservation of a community. Often referred to as the "master plan," it is the essential foundation upon which communities are built. A good comprehensive plan guides not only the physical and economic development of the municipality, but also accommodates social, environmental, and regional concerns.

The planning process offers an opportunity to look broadly at local programs such as housing, economic development, provision of public infrastructure and services, and environmental protection, and how they relate to one another by presenting a "big picture" look at the community today and articulating goals for the future. The local comprehensive land use plan resembles a series of goals and policies that are then used to guide future land use regulations and decisions, including zoning and subdivision. In addition to the many benefits for municipalities that engage in the planning process, the private sector benefits as well when plans clearly articulate the desires and aspirations of a community.

According to a 1994 survey conducted by the American Planning Association, approximately 15 states mandate local planning and another 25 states conditionally mandate local planning. Statutes in 10 states provide that local planning is optional, and a few states even require that local plans be "certified" by a state or regional agency.

(i) Development of the Plan

The local comprehensive land use plan is developed pursuant to state statutory authority. The local legislative body typically appoints either the planning board or a special board or committee to develop a proposed plan. Good planning practice incorporates a significant public participation process in the development phase. Public participation is important prior to the adoption of a comprehensive plan, with statutes requiring at least one public hearing prior to adoption. The traditional approach of public hearings to garner input is no longer the accepted norm in practice. Modern planning processes seek to engage public input from the start through, for example, workshops, surveys, and questionnaires. In Creative Displays, Inc. v. City of Florence, 602 S.W.2d 682 (Ky. 1980), the Kentucky Supreme Court held that where a new area-wide plan is developed, it is not sufficient to simply compile the existing individual comprehensive plans for the jurisdictions in the area and merge them into one new area-wide comprehensive plan, as these pre-existing individual plans are not likely to address the proper needs and goals for the new area-wide planning unit. The court noted that by simply merging the existing plans, there is no opportunity for important public input as to the future planning and zoning of the new area.

This discussion presupposes that the comprehensive plan is a written document. However, the New Jersey Supreme Court in Kozesnik v. Township of Montgomery, 131 A.2d 1 (N.J. 1957) found no such requirement in state statutes and held that the plan may simply be the end-product zoning ordinance. This is consistent with the holding of New York's highest court that a comprehensive plan need not be a written document per se, but rather that the test should be one of "comprehensiveness of planning" determined by "examining all relevant evidence," which can include the municipality's previous land use decisions, as well as the zoning ordinance. See, Udell v. Haas, 235 N.E.2d 897 (N.Y. 1968). Based on the information presented, the court will decide whether the challenged action was adopted in conformance with the community's "total planning strategy" or reflects "special interest, irrational ad hocery." Obviously, this approach allows the court great discretion. In the absence of a comprehensive plan, a regulation can appear to be arbitrary or capricious, or simply a response to the complaints or concerns of neighbors. The modern approach, however, is to require that comprehensive planning be done separate from, and prior to, the adoption of zoning.

(ii) Content of the Comprehensive Land Use Plan

State statutes vary widely in terms of directing the content to be covered in local plans. Generally, plans should address, at an appropriate level of specificity, a general statement of goals and objectives, principles and policies, and standards upon which the land use decisions are to be made. The plan should contain an inventory of existing and proposed locations and intensities of various land uses, including public facilities (e.g., sewer and water, roads and other transportation networks, educational facilities, emergency services, parkland and other recreation areas, and utilities), commercial and industrial facilities, and significant natural and environmental resources. Existing housing resources and future housing needs should be discussed in conjunction with a consideration of population, demographic, and socio-economic trends including future projections. The plan should take into account regional needs including the existing plans of neighboring jurisdictions, and the plan should coordinate with other existing municipal plans and programs. It is important to note that each plan is different as it is tailored to the specific culture and need of the locality.

(iii) Plan Consistency

Consistency with the comprehensive land use plan and zoning regulations is generally required. Since the requirement that zoning be "in conformance" with the plan is statutory, the failure of a zoning law to conform to the plan is beyond the authority of the locality to adopt, or *ultra vires*. Therefore, land use regulations are often challenged as "not in accordance with a comprehensive plan." Elysian Heights Residents Association, Inc. v. City of Los Angeles, 227 Cal. Rptr. 226 (Cal. App. 2nd Dist. 1986). When there is a written, up-to-date plan, the court is best able to discern whether the regulation is a permissible exercise of local authority. These plans are given great weight, and courts are hesitant to invalidate a regulation adopted to implement such a plan. There is little doubt that a regulation that accomplishes an express objective of the comprehensive plan "substantially advances a legitimate public objective," the judicial standard by which challenged regulations are measured. However, courts have not held municipalities to a literal interpretation of "in accordance with a comprehensive plan" and for example in Bone v. City of Lewiston, 693 P.2d 1046 (Idaho 1984), the Idaho Supreme Court noted that to do so would elevate the comprehensive plan and land use map to the status of a zoning ordinance and that it would be illogical to conclude that a projected pattern of land use identified in a plan, equates to an entitlement for a property owner with respect to present day zoning. In Haines v. City of Phoenix, 727 P.2d 339 (Ariz. App. 1986), the Arizona court stated that when considering whether a rezoning was consistent with the general plan, it will look for evidence that the legislative body made a proper determination that the rezoning was in "basic harmony" with the plan.

(iv) Adopting and Amending of the Plan

Although in some states a planning board or other special board may be given the task of developing the comprehensive land use plan, the adoption of the plan is a legislative act requiring action by the local legislative body to become effective. Cochran v. Planning Bd. of City of Summit, 210 A.2d 99 (N.J. Super. L. 1965). After a public hearing, the legislative body may accept the plan as recommended and adopt it as is, or it may make changes. Plan amendments are also required to be adopted by the local legislative body in the same manner as the initial plan was adopted. Dalton v. City and County of Honolulu, 462 P.2d 199 (Haw. 1969). In Creative Displays, Inc. v. City of Florence, 602 S.W.2d 682 (Ky. 1980), the court held that failure to follow proper procedure for the adoption of a plan nullified the local comprehensive plan.

There is a difference of opinion as to the legal significance of the comprehensive land use plan once adopted. Some states, such as New Jersey, view the plan as a mere declaration of policy and an indication of intention which does not take effect until implemented through the adoption of land use control ordinances. Cochran v. City of Summit, 210 A.2d 99 (N.J. Super. L. 1965). In Oregon, however, the plan is considered legislative in nature, and where a municipality adopted a comprehensive plan but failed to conform previously adopted zoning regulations to the new plan, the court in Baker v. City of Milwaukee, 533 P.2d 772 (Or. 1975), found that the comprehensive plan would be controlling, not the zoning ordinance. In Fasano v. Board of County Commissioners of Washington County, 507 P.2d 23 (Or. 1973), the Oregon Supreme Court held that the comprehensive plan is a legal governing document, that an action for a rezoning is an exercise of judicial as opposed to legislative action, and that the burden of proof to demonstrate that the rezoning is in accordance with the comprehensive plan rests with the municipality.

(v) Periodic Review

A municipality may engage in comprehensive planning at any time, and it may review and amend the plan whenever necessary. Although many plans contain long-term strategies for community development and conservation, comprehensive plans need to be revisited as change occurs. Planners recommend reviewing the plan every five to 10 years and updating it as necessary. State statutes may require localities to set forth in the comprehensive plan the intervals at which the plan shall be reviewed. The American Planning Association recommends that local governments employ benchmarks as part of the periodic review process to ensure accountability in planning.

B. OTHER PLANS AND PROGRAMS

Municipalities may adopt other special purpose land use plans such as neighborhood plans or "specific plans" covering a discrete area, open space plans, coastal zone management plans, and disaster mitigation plans. These plans may be adopted separate from comprehensive land use plans because they are adopted pursuant to a federal or state requirement or because they are undertaken at a different time. These plans should be considered part of the ongoing comprehensive planning process, and subsequent plans should reference the intent to incorporate the newer plans with the existing comprehensive plans. Capital improvement plans and capital budgets can be effective tools for implementing the local comprehensive land use plan.

Under the national Disaster Mitigation Act, state and local governments are to prepare Hazard Mitigation Plans (HMP). Many such plans call for land use solutions to the risks of hazards such as flooding, sea level rise, storm surges, mudslides, wildfires, high winds, drought, and others. Louisville Metro, a merged city-county government, developed its HMP in conjunction with its comprehensive plan ("Plan 2040"), which allowed Louisville Metro to incorporate the hazard mitigation plan's objectives into the comprehensive plan, with which zoning is to comply. Plan 2040 translated these objectives into specific policies, such as to "encourage design elements that address the urban heat island effect." Such design elements include "the planting and preservation of trees, cool roofs and green infrastructure." Plan 2040 also emphasizes the importance of mitigating flood-related hazards.

To implement these policies, Louisville Metro amended its Land Development Code to require tree planting: certain developers must meet the plan's tree canopy standards. The Code was amended to incentivize developers to use high albedo and vegetated roof surfaces through a point system that determines residential density bonuses. In addition, to locate development away from flood-prone areas, the Code requires buffer areas along protected waterways. These requirements, among others, effectively translate Louisville Metro's hazard mitigation plan into law.

§ 6. STATE PLANNING

Throughout planning history, the subject of state-level land planning has garnered significant interest, but in practice it has been controversial. From 1933 through about 1943, the federal National Planning Board and its successors promoted state-level planning by offering federal financial assistance to states that established state planning boards with professional staff. From the 1940s through the early 1950s, interest in state-level planning waned as this function was largely viewed as local in nature. Beginning with Hawaii in the late 1950s, a number of states have taken a more proactive role in land use planning, requiring state agencies to engage in the development of a statewide land use plan and requiring local governments to submit land use plans to state or regional agencies for review. This effort was supported in part by the availability of federal funds and by the authority of state and regional planning organizations to review and comment on applications for federal funds and their relationship to state and regional plans, goals, and policies. State plans are typically focused on economic development, broad environmental issues, infrastructure, housing, and coordination between the various levels of government to accomplish plan goals.

The growth management movement that started in the 1960s and continued through the 1990s, labeled as "smart growth," has been responsible for a resurgence of interest in state-level planning. States have adopted varying approaches to planning roles. For example, some states, including Oregon, Florida, Rhode Island, and Washington, mandate local planning and require that local plans be consistent with regional and state plans. At the other end of the spectrum are states that do not take an active role in mandating or reviewing plans, but rather provide technical assistance and incentives to encourage local planning. Vermont, Hawaii, Florida, and Oregon offer early examples of the role of state government in planning. The Hawaii statute organizes the state into four major land use districts and establishes a state land use commission. New Jersey adopted a State Plan that includes a system of cross acceptance—or both horizontal and vertical consistency between and among state and local plans. Vermont's Act 250 requires, among other things, that certain projects require mandatory approval from state-created regional environmental review agencies. See, In re Juster Associates, 396 A.2d 1382 (Vt. 1978).

While there is no federal land use plan per se, over time the federal government has assumed an increasing role in the area of land use planning and reform by influencing state and local land use decisions through myriad regulations, funding programs, and other agency-level technical assistance programs. Although the federal government's efforts lack coordination among the various agencies and programs, major programs have been legislated that do require certain land use planning actions by states including the Coastal Zone Management Act and the Disaster Mitigation Act. In addition, as will be discussed in Chapter VI, the federal government has enacted a series of statutes influencing certain local land use decision-making in areas involving fair housing, accommodations for the disabled, religious uses, and telecommunications.

§ 7. REGIONAL PLANNING

There is a growing recognition across the country that the impacts of local land use decisions know no political boundaries. As a result, states have adopted various approaches to addressing significant land use concerns in a more regional context. In some states, such as Maryland, the county has the authority to develop land use plans. In other states, such as New Jersey and New York, sub-county governments, such as cities, towns/townships, boroughs, and villages, are vested with this authority. Statutory schemes often trigger notice and referral requirements to county and regional planning boards for certain local land use actions, but these referrals are usually more for informational purposes and input rather than for permission to proceed.

Political considerations, especially home rule—or local control—concerns, present a challenging environment for regional planning programs. State statutes may either require, or simply authorize at local option, the creation of regional planning boards. Where optional, it typically takes two or more counties to form (and fund) a regional planning agency. While there is little dispute as to the value of looking at planning issues from an interjurisdictional perspective, few local governments are willing to give up coveted land use planning and decision-making authority.

Some states, such as New York, choose to protect significant natural resources through the establishment of special purpose agencies that span multiple jurisdictions. The Adirondack Park Agency, for example, was designed in 1971 to conserve, protect, preserve, and develop approximately six million acres of land in the State-designated Adirondack Park. Although there are 12 counties and 105 towns and villages within the six million acres, the Act specifically vests the regional Agency with authority to develop and implement a region-wide plan, and regulate land uses within the area. These state legislative acts are upheld by the courts since they protect assets of statewide, as opposed to local, significance. See, Wambat Realty Corp. v. State of New York, 362 N.E.2d 581 (N.Y. 1977).

Metropolitan Planning Organizations (MPOs) exist across the country and offer another vehicle for regional planning. MPOs were established primarily for the purpose of transportation planning. Recent federal transportation funding bills have elevated the planning and coordination roles of MPOs as local governments compete for a limited pool of federal fiscal assistance.

§ 8. INTERMUNICIPAL PLANNING

Local governments are authorized in every state, by state constitution or by statute, to voluntarily cooperate to accomplish a number of local municipal responsibilities including planning. In the land use context, this provides an opportunity to plan for and manage greater than local issues. It also presents an opportunity to maximize sometimes scarce fiscal resources. Local governments may opt to develop joint comprehensive land use plans or establish a joint overlay zoning district. Municipalities may cooperate to form joint planning or zoning boards. Smaller, more rural, municipalities may decide to jointly hire a full-time professional planner who can work part-time at each locality.

Compact planning, a method of voluntary areawide planning, has also met with some recent success. Through the compact process, participating local governments agree that they will prospectively adopt local plans and plan amendments consistent with a county or regional plan. Ultimately, the participating municipalities agree on the direction for growth and preservation in the region, and they agree to conform their actions to advance the shared vision and goals. States may specifically allow for compact planning and may provide technical assistance and incentives for voluntary participation.

§ 9. INTERSTATE COMPACTS

Congress may enact interstate compacts to empower two or more states to join planning efforts to protect sensitive natural areas that cross state boundaries. The Lake Tahoe Regional Planning Agency is an example of an effort resulting from an interstate compact between California and Nevada, created to develop and enforce (through the adoption of regulations) a regional plan that covers land use, transportation, conservation, recreation, and public services and facilities. The broad authority granted to the Lake Tahoe Regional Planning Agency as opposed to the power of individual local governments in the area was upheld by the California Supreme Court in People ex rel. Younger v. County of El Dorado, 487 P.2d 1193 (Cal. 1971) on the basis of the significant state interests in protecting and preserving the Lake Tahoe region.

CHAPTER 3

ZONING DISTRICTS AND THE SEPARATION OF LAND USES

§ 1. INTRODUCTION

A. OVERVIEW

At the beginning of the twentieth century, cities needed new techniques to control private development to prevent fires, promote public safety, and protect property values. In New York City, Fifth Avenue merchants were upset with the encroachment of other land uses, such as garment factories and offices, into their high-end retail neighborhood. There was broad sentiment that the city was becoming too densely settled, largely because of the spread of skyscrapers. In 1913, the city appointed a commission to investigate a completely new idea: the division of the city into land use districts.

Based on the commission's recommendations, on July 25, 1916, the City's Board of Estimate and Apportionment, by a 15 to 1 vote, adopted the nation's first comprehensive zoning ordinance. It divided the city into multiple land use districts, or zones. These districts allowed private landowners to use their land only for the purposes permitted in the applicable district. This protected Fifth Avenue retailers, for example, from the incursion of garment factories—an industrial use—in that retail zone.

This concept spread quickly. By the mid-1920s, nearly 400 local governments had adopted comprehensive zoning laws. Initially, municipal authority to control private land use so comprehensively was in doubt. In 1922, the U.S. Department of Commerce issued a model law called the State Zoning Enabling Act. It was intended to be considered and adopted by state legislatures to make it clear that the adoption of zoning laws is within the legal authority of municipal governments. All 50 states adopted some variation of this statute delegating authority to municipalities to regulate private land uses. Over time, these statutes have been changed; today the states vary in how broadly they empower local governments, to what extent they guide them—mandating certain local approaches to land use control—and when they foreclose local action through preemptive, statewide laws.

Despite the common source of local zoning law authority, students and practitioners should be alert to the great differences in terminology and practice encountered from state to state, even from locality to locality, in individual states. The form of municipal government adopted in each state varies depending on the customs of those who settled the territories and the date of their statehood. In some states, counties have been given zoning authority. In other states, counties do not exist. What municipalities are called, whether they have charters, and the contents of the statutes that provide them their basic authorities differ in degree. Boroughs may exist here, villages there; towns in one state may be called townships in others. The power of cities may vary depending on their size and classification.

To make matters more confusing, there has never been a general agreement regarding the denomination of zoning districts or precisely how uses and building are regulated within such districts. The classic suburban zone, which may be designated on the zoning map as "R40," generally means that parcels in that zone are limited to residential, single-family houses on lots of 40,000 square feet in size or larger—the so-called "zoning acre." In the neighboring community, however, that zone may be called "R1" and the lot size may have to be an actual acre: 43,560 square feet. How high the single-family home may be and how far back from the street or side lot lines it must be set will vary too, although only slightly. Finally, differences in the names and functions of local land use boards will be encountered. In nearly all communities, there will be a legislature to adopt land use laws, an administrative board to approve or deny projects, and a quasi-judicial board to which matters of land use law may be appealed.

Regardless of the variations, all zoning laws contain standards that dictate what, where, and how building occurs on the land. The owner of a parcel of land consults the zoning map, which is adopted as part of the zoning ordinance, finds the location of her property, notices that it is in a designated zoning district, such as a single-family residential, one-acre zone, and then consults the texts and tables of the ordinance to find the dimensional requirements that govern construction on her land.

Architects and engineers who work for landowners must follow the prescriptions of zoning. These include the use to which the property can be put (use restrictions), the size of the lot necessary for certain land uses (minimum lot size), how much of the lot can be built on (lot coverage), how far back from streets and property lines buildings can be built (set backs), how tall buildings can be (height restrictions), and important miscellaneous matters such as parking requirements, grades and slopes, driveway construction, and the like. In effect, the law dictates building and site design.

Within each zoning district, each parcel of land is assigned at least one *as-of-right* land use. The *accessory uses* that customarily accompany the principal use allowed on the land are also permitted by most zoning laws, as long as they are incidental to the principal permitted use. A variety of *home occupations,* such as professional offices, may be allowed in residential zones, again if they are incidental to the principal residential use of the property. Some land uses, particularly intense in their impacts on surrounding properties, or unusual in some way, will be designated as special uses and allowed in certain zoning districts, but subject to the imposition of conditions needed to render them harmonious with the location; these are authorized by *special use permits,* known in some jurisdictions as *conditional use permits* or *special exceptions*. Land uses that pre-exist the adoption of a zoning law or amendment usually are allowed to continue as *nonconforming uses*, but are not allowed to be expanded or enlarged. *Variances* of the standards may be awarded when landowners can prove that the zoning standards impose unnecessary hardships.

B. AUTHORITY

Local governments are regarded as legal instrumentalities of their states, their legislative authority is limited to that delegated by the state and extends only within their geographical boundaries. The states have created various types of local governments—cities, towns, townships, villages, boroughs, or counties—and delegated them authority to legislate regarding specific interests.

Local governments are formed as municipal corporations. Just like business corporations they can have charters that enable them to carry out governmental activities and are further limited by state law governing municipal corporations. Lawyers for municipalities that have charters begin their exploration of their clients' legal authority by looking at this foundational document. Many localities do not have charters; they get their authority under various statutes adopted by state legislatures which govern charter municipalities as well. The principal state statute relevant to local land use control is called the zoning enabling act and it is from that law and complementary supplemental laws that localities get their power to control the use of privately owned land within their jurisdiction.

Municipal corporations are governed by local legislatures composed of legislators elected by the people. Local legislatures enact zoning laws and provide for the formation of administrative agencies to administer land use regulations. Residents of the locality are appointed or elected to be members of these administrative agencies. Again, local practice varies. What these boards are called, how many of them there are, how citizens become members of them, and what duties are delegated to each board, differ from place to place.

C. LOCAL ZONING BOARD PROCEDURES

In most municipalities, the most critical land use decisions are made by the legislative body, which adopts and amends the zoning law and other land use regulations and decides which other land use boards and agencies to establish. Occasionally, local legislatures determine that their existing land use controls are incomplete or out-of-date. In some states, they may adopt a moratorium on development until the local legislature adopts regulations to meet new challenges.

Important roles are assigned by local legislatures to the planning board, board of appeals, and the zoning enforcement officer, which are charged with reviewing development proposals and enforcing the zoning law's provisions. Planning boards—or commissions—are established in most communities to review and approve individual development proposals. Zoning boards of appeal—or boards of adjustment—are created to hear applications to reverse adverse determinations of zoning enforcement officials or to provide relief from the strict application of zoning standards that create unnecessary hardships regarding unique parcels of land. Other boards—such as historic district commissions, conservation advisory boards, architectural review boards, or wetlands agencies—may be created if authorized by state law, usually (but not always) at the discretion of the local legislative body.

The local legislature—known as the county legislature, city council, village board of trustees, borough council, town board, etc.—adopts and amends the zoning law: a *legislative* function. It normally then delegates to an administrative agency the authority to review site plan, subdivision, and special use permit applications of private developers: an *administrative* function. When the zoning board of appeals—or board of adjustment—hears appeals from the zoning administrator or grants variances, it is acting in a *quasi-judicial* capacity. These are important distinctions since courts often apply different standards when they review challenges to legislative, administrative, and quasi-judicial actions.

Before beginning any serious construction, the landowner must secure a building permit that certifies that the proposed construction meets the standards of the applicable building, fire, plumbing, and electrical codes. In the typical community, when an application for a building permit is submitted to the local building inspector or zoning enforcement officer, that administrator must ascertain, before issuing the building permit, that the proposed construction is in compliance with the zoning law and other land use regulations.

If the proposed development is not in compliance with the use and dimensional requirements of the zoning law, then the permit must be denied. This denial can be appealed to the board of appeals, which can reverse the officer's interpretation of the zoning provision if it is in error. Alternatively, the landowner may ask the board of appeals or adjustment for a *use* or *area variance* allowing the construction to prevent a hardship caused in the individual circumstance. Variances must be issued in conformance with the local zoning ordinance and the standards of state law. When zoning boards of appeal decide these matters they serve as quasi-judicial bodies and exercise appellate jurisdiction; the determinations of the zoning enforcement officer—or the applicability of the strict letter of the ordinance to the proposed development—are appealed to the board.

When the decisions of a board of appeals are appealed to a court, the court can certify the record of the quasi-judicial body and, in most states, does not conduct a de novo trial on the facts determined by the board. Boards of appeals conduct their proceedings in a formal fashion, allow evidence to be presented and confronted, create a record, and make fact-based decisions that are supported by that record. These decisions must be filed in a timely manner with the municipal clerk or in another designated office, and aggrieved parties are allowed to appeal them to the courts within a prescribed time after the date of the filing. Courts in most states defer to the discretion of boards of appeals and affirm their decisions unless the appellant can prove affirmatively that the decision is arbitrary or unreasonable, not based on facts on the record, or does not conform to applicable standards.

If, on the other hand, the proposed development complies with the zoning provisions, but requires subdivision, site plan, special permit, or other approval, the applicant will be referred to the appropriate administrative agency for its review and determination. Local land use boards receive applications from landowners for approval and neighbors and other affected parties become involved in the local process to protect their interests.

Planning boards or commissions are normally assigned the task of approving landowner applications for subdivision or site plan approval and the issuance of a special permit. In some localities, boards of appeal may be given one or more of these assignments, most likely, if any, the task of issuing special use permits. In hearing and determining applications for these land use approvals, the board serves in an administrative capacity and exercises original jurisdiction. The decision-making process for zoning approvals must follow prescribed time periods, honor requirements to provide public notice of the matter and hold public hearings, maintain a record of the agency's deliberations, and file and circulate a final determination on the matter with the local clerk. Most states have laws requiring that local agency meetings are open to the public and that copies of local records be provided to the public upon request.

State courts normally defer to the determinations of administrative agencies when they make fact-based decisions such as site plan and subdivision approvals or denials or determine whether a special permit should be issued. Their decisions are made, most often, after facts are gathered, a public hearing is held, and deliberations occur at open sessions of the body. These decisions are filed and then may be appealed by aggrieved persons within a period established by state-created statutes of limitations.

Only if the standards of local land use regulations are met and the proposal is approved by the administrative agency can a building permit be issued. In most communities, one may not commence construction without a building permit and may not occupy buildings without a certificate of occupancy. To qualify for a building permit and certificate of occupancy, the property owner must honor any conditions imposed by the approving agency and construction plans for the development must conform to the requirements of the applicable building, fire, plumbing, and electrical codes.

§ 2. THE EARLY CASES

By the end of the nineteenth century in the United States, building construction limits were firmly established and accepted under state and municipal law, but they were relatively simple and focused on prescriptions and prohibitions. In Hadacheck v. Sebastian, 239 U.S. 394 (1915), for example, the U.S. Supreme Court upheld an ordinance which prohibited the operation of a brickyard or brick kiln within certain limits in the City of Los Angeles.

When zoning first became popular at the beginning of the twentieth century, the notion that the right of a private landowner to use her land to meet market needs, when that use was not clearly injurious or dangerous, was a new idea and much more controversial. In the state of Ohio, the constitutional authority of the Village of Euclid to adopt and enforce use limitations was challenged by Ambler Realty Company in the early 1920s. The case, Euclid v. Ambler Realty Co., 272 U.S. 365 (1926), is so important that it is contained in every published casebook on land use law. Ambler claimed that separating uses through zoning districts accomplished no legitimate governmental purpose and, on its face, was unconstitutional. The plaintiff's technical claim was that zoning violated its constitutional right to due process: to be protected from arbitrary or unreasonable laws that did not further a legitimate public purpose.

The U.S. Supreme Court disagreed. In 1926, it handed down its decision in *Euclid* holding that the separation of land uses among zoning districts accomplished a legitimate public purpose, using nuisance limitations on private property use as an analogous doctrine. The Court reasoned that the effect of zoning was to create land use standards that protected neighbors from nuisance-like uses of nearby land. In technical terms, the due process clause of the Fifth Amendment was not violated because use separation was a reasonable method of protecting the public interest. Thereafter, establishing zoning districts that carefully prescribed land uses within each zone became the principal method of controlling private land use in the interest of building safe and economically efficient communities. Following this decision, the adoption of uniform building and use standards within various land use districts became known as "Euclidian Zoning."

A year and a half after *Euclid*, the U.S. Supreme Court, again speaking through Justice Sutherland, declared a zoning ordinance unreasonable and unconstitutional as applied to the plaintiff's particular tract of land. See, Nectow v. City of Cambridge, 277 U.S. 183 (1928). In *Nectow*, the property owner showed that the local zoning law permitted only residential uses and that there was no market for residential use of his land in the neighborhood. The owner's argument was that the zoning law, as applied to the parcel, did not accomplish a public purpose because of market conditions. In essence, the law allowed the owner no economical use of the land. Following *Nectow*, the U.S. Supreme Court handed down no significant decisions implicating local land use matters for the next four decades. Nectow's claim is called an "as applied" challenge to local zoning authority because it challenged the application of the zoning law as it applied to the plaintiff's property, while Ambler Realty's claim is referred to as a "facial" attack, since it challenged the constitutionality of the zoning ordinance as a whole, and not specifically the application of the law to Ambler's property.

It was by no means certain that courts would ratify the bold new concept of comprehensive zoning. Before *Euclid*, there were state court decisions that went the other way. In 1925, for example, Maryland's Court of Appeals, in Goldman v. Crowther, 147 Md. 282, 128 A. 50 (Md. 1925), invalidated Baltimore's zoning ordinance. It was concerned that zoning violated "those guaranties of the State and Federal Constitutions which assure to every citizen the right to hold and enjoy and use his property in any manner he pleases so long as he does not thereby injuriously affect the health, security or welfare of his neighbor or the public, as the words health, security and welfare have hitherto been understood in this State." Noting that the law arrested the organic evolution of a complex city "at a stroke," the court called the Baltimore ordinance "an artificial plan of segregation."

Two years before *Goldman*, the Wisconsin Supreme Court sustained local zoning in State ex rel. Carter v. Harper, 182 Wis. 148, 196 N.W. 451 (Wis. 1923). The plaintiff's application to enlarge his dairy and milk pasteurizing facility was denied pursuant to the city zoning ordinance that prohibited the enlargement of facilities used for nonconforming uses (a use that was legal and in existence prior to the adoption of the zoning ordinance). The dairyman argued that the ordinance was unreasonable and oppressive and deprived him of equal protection of the laws. Plaintiff also claimed that the ordinance was a taking of his property without due process and without just compensation. The Wisconsin Supreme Court held that the ordinance was valid and that it did not deprive the landowner of the use of his property in violation of the Constitution. The landowner was permitted to use the property as it was zoned and could not use the property in a way that harmed the community.

The enabling statutes require that local zoning regulations be made in accordance with a comprehensive plan and accomplish a number of other purposes, including conserving the value of buildings; maintaining the character of zoning districts; facilitating the provision of transportation, water systems, sewage treatment, schools, and parks; lessening traffic congestion; preventing overcrowding; providing adequate light and air; and containing damage from fires, floods, and other dangers. New York's highest court has stated that "the decision as to how a community shall be zoned or rezoned, as to how various properties shall be classified or reclassified, rests with the local legislative body; its judgment and determination will be conclusive, beyond inference from the courts, unless shown to be arbitrary." Rodgers v. Village of Tarrytown, 302 N.Y. 115, 96 N.E.2d 731 (N.Y. 1951).

§ 3. ADMINISTRATION AND FLEXIBILITY

A. VARIANCES

What happens when the strict application of zoning's use and dimensional requirements cause a real hardship to a landowner? From its inception, zoning included a provision that allowed a local board of appeals to adjust standards where they caused serious problems for individual property owners. The local board can grant a use variance if a parcel owner can prove that the use provisions of zoning are unreasonable and do not allow a reasonable return on the property, constituting an unnecessary hardship. The board can vary the area and dimensional standards of zoning that cause owners practical difficulties. The variance device allows the zoning board of appeals to permit owners with such claims to use and develop their properties in ways that are at variance with the strict use and area requirements of the local zoning code. The variance is a safety valve that responds to unique circumstances, avoids "as applied" legal challenges by property owners, and preserves the spirit of the ordinance as drafted by the legislature.

Some states have codified the tests for use and area variances in state statute, and in other states common law tests are applied. Typically it is more difficult to obtain a use variance than to obtain an area variance. Municipalities who find themselves routinely granting variances in the same zoning districts would be well served to review the use and/or dimensional requirements in their zoning ordinances to determine whether a legislative amendment would be appropriate.

(i) Use Variances

Use variances allow property owners to use their buildings and parcels for purposes otherwise prohibited by the zoning law. Since use separation is the fundamental characteristic of zoning, this is precariously close to a legislative determination, and boards of appeal are quite limited in their discretion to award use variances. In some states, use variances may not be given. Where they are, they often are limited to parcels of land that cannot be used profitably under any of the use categories allowed in the relevant zoning district.

In Puritan-Greenfield Improvement Ass'n v. Leo, 7 Mich. App. 659, 153 N.W.2d 162 (Mich. Ct. App. 1967), the grant of a use variance by the zoning board of appeals to allow the owner to establish a medical clinic was overturned by the court because the board failed to find, as it must, that the property could not be reasonably used in a manner consistent with the code. The property had been used as a legal single-family home for years and there was no showing that it could not profitably continue to be used for that purpose. A showing that the property will not yield a reasonable return under any use permitted in the applicable zoning district is required to be made before a use variance can be granted.

The court in Topanga Ass'n for Scenic Community v. County of Los Angeles, 11 Cal. 3d 506, 522 P.2d 12 (Cal. 1974), similarly overturned a use variance to allow a mobile home park. California statutory requirements for a variance demand that the owner show special circumstances such as unique lot size, shape, topography, location, or surroundings, which were absent in this case. The *Topanga* case illustrates the fine line that separates the local legislature's role in zoning from that of the zoning board of appeals. Use provisions established by the legislature in the zoning code cannot be varied unless there are special circumstances affecting a particular parcel that merit taking it out of the general rules created legislatively. If the conditions affecting a single parcel are not unique and a variance is given, the zoning board would be assuming a legislative role: overriding the legislature's determination of the standards that prevail in the district in general.

Zoning boards of appeal must justify their award of use variances with competent, material, and substantial evidence on the record of the proceedings. In Janssen v. Holland Charter Township Zoning Board of Appeals, 252 Mich. App. 197, 651 N.W.2d 464 (Mich. Ct. App. 2002), a challenge to a use variance on a 100-acre parcel allowing residential development in an agricultural zone was defeated by the court because the board had based its determination on the unique circumstances demonstrated by the substantial proof placed on the record by the property owner. See also, Matthew v. Smith, 707 S.W.2d 411 (Mo. 1986), where the grant of a variance was overturned because insufficient evidence of unnecessary hardship was presented to the board by the property owner. The matter was remanded to the board to allow the owners to show that the use provisions of the ordinance deprived them of a reasonable return.

A unique justification for a use variance appears in DeSimone v. Greater Englewood Housing Corp. No. 1, 56 N.J. 428, 267 A.2d 31 (N.J. 1970). The zoning board of appeals awarded a use variance in a single-family district to a housing corporation allowing it to build a multi-family building to serve as a relocation housing resource for tenants to be relocated from a severely blighted area of the city. The applicant for the use variance was the housing corporation that proposed redevelopment in the blighted area and which, under New Jersey law, had an obligation to provide relocation housing affordable to the displaced tenants. The court sustained the use variance in light of public policy and the law of the land constituting a proper "special reason" for which variances can be awarded under the state statutes.

(ii) Area Variances

An area variance may be given when property owners encounter practical difficulties in complying with the dimensional or physical requirements of the applicable zoning regulations, such as height or set-back requirements. Boards of Appeals typically are allowed to issue area variances but are required to impose limiting conditions on variances to protect neighboring properties against the possible adverse effects of the use of the property benefited by the variance. In Kisil v. City of Sandusky, 12 Ohio St. 3d 30, 465 N.E.2d 848 (Ohio 1984), the court reversed the zoning board's denial of an area variance from the minimum lot and set-back requirements. The owner demonstrated that many other properties were on substandard-sized lots and that the variance would not adversely affect the character of the surrounding neighborhood. In this case, the owner proved sufficient practical difficulties caused by the zoning standards. An area variance was properly denied by the court in McMorrow v. Board of Adjustment for City of Town & Country, 765 S.W.2d 700 (Mo. Ct. App. E.D. 1989). The McMorrows applied for an area variance from set-back requirements to allow them to build a swimming pool on an irregularly shaped lot. The variance was denied because the board found no practical difficulties where the family was using the home reasonably for living purposes and because state law disfavors the award of variances.

The Wisconsin Supreme Court created a less stringent standard for area variances in Ziervogel v. Washington County Board of Adjustment, 269 Wis. 2d 549, 676 N.W.2d 401 (Wis. 2004). It explained that the integrity of zoning ordinances is threatened in a qualitatively different manner by the grant of an area variance than it is by a use variance, which can potentially cause great change in neighborhood character. Prior to the *Ziervogel* case, applicants for both use and area variances were required to prove unnecessary hardship. In this case, the court established a more discretionary standard for area variances based on an examination of whether the area and dimensional requirements of zoning are unnecessarily burdensome. New York's statutory balancing test was applied and explained for the first time in Sasso v. Osgood, 86 N.Y.2d 374, 633 N.Y.S.2d

259, 657 N.E.2d 254 (N.Y. 1995). The zoning board of appeals granted the owner of a waterfront parcel of substandard size an area variance. The highest court in the state affirmed the award based on a 1992 amendment to the state law regulating zoning variances. Applying the prescribed five-factor balancing test, the court deferred to the board's finding that it had properly considered each of the factors in balancing the benefit to the applicant against the detriment to the neighbors and the neighborhood.

(iii) Limitations

The limited range of relief allowed by variances is demonstrated in Larsen v. Zoning Board of Adjustment of City of Pittsburgh, 543 Pa. 415, 672 A.2d 286 (Pa. 1996). In *Larsen*, the state court held that the zoning board of appeals had exceeded its authority to grant variances when it allowed homeowners to construct a back porch as a play area for their child. A neighbor appealed the board's variance award to the trial court, which held that the homeowners did not meet the criteria for the grant of a variance; the Supreme Court of Pennsylvania affirmed. The court held that there are four criteria to be met in support of a variance: (1) an unnecessary hardship exists that is caused by unique physical features of the property and was not caused by the landowner, (2) the variance is necessary for the landowner's reasonable use of the property, (3) the variance will not alter the character of the area, impair development of adjacent land, or be detrimental to the public's welfare, and (4) the variance affords the least intrusive solution. In the court's opinion, the landowner failed to meet all four criteria, and the zoning board abused its discretion in granting the variance.

B. SPECIAL OR CONDITIONAL USE PERMITS

While a variance allows a property owner to use her land or buildings in a manner that is prohibited by the ordinance, a special use permit authorizes land uses that are allowed and encouraged by the ordinance and declared to be harmonious with the applicable zoning district. The distinction between variances and special permits is that variances allow the landowner to do something that is prohibited by the zoning law, while a special permit is issued for a use that the zoning law expressly permits, in stipulated circumstances. In most states, there is a brisk pace of litigation that results from the impact of board decisions regarding variances and special use permits on the property values and the daily lives of the affected parties.

In addition to permitting certain land uses *as-of-right* in zoning districts, the zoning law authorizes other uses to be made of the land, but only if landowners desiring to dedicate their land to a stipulated use receive a special—or conditional—use permit issued from a local administrative agency. Typical land uses that are permitted by special or conditional permits include religious institutions, nursing homes, and day care centers. In most states, when such uses are listed as specially permitted uses in the zoning law, they are declared by the local legislature to be uses that are harmonious with *as-of-right* uses, with the recognition that, in a specific location, they can negatively impact adjacent properties and may need to be limited or conditioned to mitigate such impacts. If an applicant for a special use permit can demonstrate conclusively that no such impacts will result, or that the proposal mitigates those impacts effectively, the special use permit will usually be granted. There is a growing trend to categorize fewer uses as permitted as of right, and an increasing number of uses to be permitted subject to special or conditional use permit review.

Where the local zoning ordinance specifies the standards that an applicant must meet to be eligible for a special use permit, the local board cannot deny it on other grounds. In City of Chicago Heights v. Living Word Outreach Full Gospel Church and Ministries, Inc., 196 Ill. 2d 1, 255 Ill. Dec. 434, 749 N.E.2d 916 (Ill. 2001), a church applied for a special use permit to conduct religious services in an area zoned for commercial use. The city zoning board denied issuance of the permit citing that granting a permit for a noncommercial use in a commercial district would be at odds with the comprehensive plan. The zoning ordinance contained six standards that must be met to qualify for a special use permit, and conformance with the comprehensive plan was not one of the criteria. The denial was overturned by the court.

§ 4. AMENDMENTS OR REZONING

Zoning amendments are perfectly proper when they are undertaken at the initiative of the local legislature itself in response to land use changes that have occurred since the ordinance was first adopted. This is particularly the case when studies have been done, the comprehensive land use plan is amended, and the zoning conforms to the new plan. Quite often, however, legislatures are petitioned to amend the zoning ordinance by individual landowners or developers. The power to amend the zoning ordinance and change district lines, or the use designations on the zoning map, provides a degree of flexibility in adjusting land use law to community changes and the need for new or different land uses.

In most cases, the legislature that is petitioned for a zoning amendment may simply refuse to act, since the power to amend local law is usually a discretionary act. If the landowner's petition requests a zoning change because the current provisions cause a hardship, the legislature may properly refer the owner to the zoning board of appeals or adjustment. If the petition suggests that the zone change is beyond the authority of the board of appeals and that public health, safety, or welfare will be advanced by the proposed zoning change, the legislature may consider the matter. In some states, localities are required to show that circumstances have changed which necessitate the amendment. Amendments are tested by essentially the same standards that courts apply to determine the validity of the zoning ordinance itself: whether the new provision bears a reasonable relationship to the public health, safety, welfare, or morals.

The court upheld a legislative zoning change that applied to a single parcel in Bartram v. Zoning Commission of City of Bridgeport, 136 Conn. 89, 68 A.2d 308 (Conn. 1949). The parcel in question was limited to residential use. The owner sought to build a drug store, hardware store, grocery store, bakeshop, and beauty parlor in a neighborhood removed from the nearest shopping district. The amendment was granted, appealed by the neighbors, and invalidated by the trial court. On appeal, the Connecticut Supreme Court held that the rezoning was valid, noting that the means of achieving the purposes of zoning are within the discretion of the zoning authority and not subject to review of the courts unless the authority abused its discretion. "A court is without authority to substitute its own judgment for that vested by the statutes in a zoning authority."

§ 5. SPOT ZONING

Challenges by neighbors to the rezoning of individual parcels often claim that such changes are "spot zoning" and illegal because they single out small parcels for different treatment from other land in the applicable zoning district. The allegation is that small parcel rezoning is not uniform, as zoning is supposed to be, or that the differential treatment of the rezoned parcel is arbitrary and capricious, effected just to benefit the landowner, not the public. The rezoning can be invalidated where the amendment singles out a parcel of land for special treatment or privileges not in harmony with the other use classifications in the area and without any apparent circumstances which call for different treatment.

In many jurisdictions, spot zoning is a shorthand description of the legal flaw that exists when a zoning amendment does not conform to the comprehensive plan. In a broad sense, spot zoning is any change that departs from the comprehensive plan. More specifically, it is the singling out by a zoning amendment of a small parcel of land that permits the owner to use it in a manner inconsistent with the permissible uses in the area. Some courts, in discussing such changes, apply the terms "arbitrary," "capricious," "unreasonable," and similar adjectives. See, e.g., Cassel v. Mayor and City Council of Baltimore, 195 Md. 348, 73 A.2d 486 (Md. 1950); and Pierce v. King County, 62 Wash. 2d 324, 382 P.2d 628 (Wash. 1963). In the oft-cited *Cassel* case, the court stated:

> Spot zoning, the arbitrary and unreasonable devotion of a small area within a zoning district to a use which is inconsistent with the use to which the rest of the district is restricted, has appeared in many cities in America as a result of pressure put upon councilmen to pass amendments to zoning ordinances solely for the benefit of private interest. * * * It is, therefore, universally held that a 'spot zoning' ordinance, which singles out a parcel of land within the limits of a use district and marks it off with a

> separate district for the benefit of the owner, thereby permitting a use of that parcel inconsistent with the use permitted in the rest of the district, is invalid if not in accordance with the comprehensive plan and is merely for private gain. (195 Md. at 355, 73 A.2d at 488–489.)

See also, Griswold v. City of Homer, 925 P.2d 1015 (Alaska 1996), where the court said, "The classic definition of spot zoning is the process of singling out a small parcel of land for a use classification totally different from that of the surrounding area, for the benefit of the owner of such property and to the detriment of other owners. Spot zoning is the very antithesis of planned zoning." When considering whether a zoning amendment constitutes spot zoning, the court considers: (1) whether the zoning is consistent with the comprehensive plan, (2) the benefits and detriments of the amendment to the owners, adjacent landowners, and the community, and (3) the size of the area rezoned.

§ 6. CONTRACT OR CONDITIONAL ZONING

The traditional idea of zoning is that the provisions of the ordinance alone burden and limit land uses. When a project is approved but conditioned by the administrative body on meeting standards or restrictions contained in the zoning law itself, no problem is raised. In some circumstances, however, land use boards will approve projects that meet the zoning standards, but subject them to restrictions not expressly found in the zoning ordinance. Some state courts call this practice contract zoning and others refer to it as conditional zoning.

The basis of the invalidity of contract rezoning is that a city cannot bargain away its police power. A process of negotiation between the municipal government and a private person leading to zoning reclassification of land in order to accommodate private interests is not in furtherance of legitimate public purposes and invalid. It is often referred to as spot zoning, which is discussed above. Conditional zoning can be invalidated where the court finds that the administrative body acted beyond its authority in imposing conditions not found in the zoning ordinance or other applicable land use laws.

The majority view regarding contract zoning is expressed in Church v. Town of Islip, 8 N.Y.2d 254, 203 N.Y.S.2d 866, 168 N.E.2d 680 (N.Y. 1960). In *Church*, the state high court upheld the rezoning of a property subject to reasonable conditions. The court found that conditions to restrict the maximum size of the building and to erect fences and shrubbery of a specific size and type did not rise to "contract zoning" but were in response to the community's need to respond to increasing population and commercial needs. Where the zoning designation of a parcel of land is changed by the local legislature, it can impose stricter conditions on that parcel than contained in the district's rules under the zoning. The court stated that the power to rezone includes within it the power to add new restrictions where the particular circumstances require.

§ 7. NONCONFORMING USES

A nonconforming use is created when zoning changes prohibit existing land uses that were valid when they were established. Pre-existing land uses that do not conform to zoning are allowed to continue, but they are not favored. The ultimate goal of the zoning law is to achieve uniformity of property uses within each zoning district, which can only be accomplished by the elimination of uses that do not conform to the specifications of district regulations.

Nonconforming land uses are expressly defined in most local zoning laws. A typical provision defines a nonconforming use as "any use, whether of a building or tract of land or both, existing on the effective date of this chapter, which does not conform to the use regulations of the district in which it is located." Nonconforming use issues arise when the zoning law is first adopted or when amendments to the zoning ordinance are later adopted. When a district is zoned residential, for example, all existing nonresidential uses in that district are rendered nonconforming.

The policy of allowing nonconforming uses to continue originated due to concerns that the application of zoning regulations to uses existing prior to the regulations' enactment might be construed as confiscatory and unconstitutional. It was assumed that by limiting the enlargement and reconstruction of nonconforming uses, they would disappear over time which, for a variety of reasons, they tend not to do. The allowance of nonconforming uses has been characterized by the courts as a "grudging tolerance" of them. The right of municipalities to adopt reasonable measures to eliminate them has been recognized.

When property owners propose a change to their nonconforming property use, they must be certain to comply with local regulations governing those matters. Normally, these regulations are found in a discrete article of the local zoning law, entitled "Nonconforming Uses." That article will prohibit or limit changes in buildings and lot uses that are nonconforming and will provide for the termination of nonconforming uses in a variety of ways, such as (1) simply terminating them after the passage of a stipulated amount of time, (2) limiting their expansion or enlargement, (3) disallowing the reestablishment of nonconforming uses after they have been discontinued for a time, or (4) prohibiting the reconstruction of damaged structures.

A. AMORTIZATION

Some local ordinances require certain nonconforming uses to be amortized over a specified period at the end of which they must be terminated. The term "amortization" is used to describe these provisions because they allow the owner some time during which to recoup his investment in the nonconforming use. In general, courts look to see whether the benefits to the public of eliminating the preexisting use are sufficiently great to balance the detriment to the property owner. This is a case-specific investigation.

Contexts in which amortization provisions are likely to be upheld are:

- When the common law of nuisance would allow neighboring property owners to enjoin the continuation of a nonconforming use. For example, a gravel pit, auto wrecking operation, or junkyard, harmful to children in a developing residential area, might be enjoined under a private nuisance action. Likewise, a zoning law can legally require such a nonconforming use to be terminated in an appropriate case. Any grace period allowed by the ordinance is gratuitous if, in fact, the owner's use may be enjoined as a nuisance.

- When the nonconforming use is not a nuisance under the common law but is somewhat noxious and the owner has little investment in it. For example, a provision requiring the owner to cease raising pigeons on the roof or to remove an old outdoor sign might withstand challenge because of the minimal nature of the owner's investment and the significant harm done to the zoning scheme if the owner's activity is allowed to continue. Harder cases are presented when the owner has a demonstrable investment in the use and the public interest in removing it is clear, but the threat to public health and safety is not imminent.

In City of Los Angeles v. Gage, 127 Cal. App. 2d 442, 274 P.2d 34 (Cal. App. 2 Dist. 1954), the court held that a zoning ordinance that required the discontinuance of a nonconforming use over the five-year period was a valid exercise of the state's police power and not unconstitutional. Defendant was required to discontinue operation of his plumbing business over the period of five years following the rezoning of the area for exclusively residential uses. The evidence showed that the costs of relocation were not great, that there were areas zoned nearby for the plumbing business to move, and that the new land uses allowed the businessman on the site were profitable.

B. EXPANSION OR EXTENSION

Local zoning laws often prohibit the enlargement, alteration, or extension of a nonconforming use. To allow the expansion of nonconforming uses would defeat the zoning law's underlying policy of eliminating them over time. Typically, the law allows the owners of nonconforming land uses to conduct normal maintenance and complete internal alterations that do not increase the degree of, or create any new, noncompliance with the locality's zoning regulations.

Courts have upheld prohibitions on the construction of an awning over a courtyard outside a restaurant, on the theory that it would create additional space for patrons to congregate and, in this sense, increase the degree of the nonconforming use. Prohibiting the conversion of seasonal bungalows to year-round residences has also been upheld as an acceptable method of preventing the enlargement of a nonconforming use.

In State v. Perry, 149 Conn. 232, 178 A.2d 279 (Conn. 1962), the court prohibited the addition of a trailer equipped with freezer storage to the facility's existing buildings. The ordinance prohibited the extension or expansion of a nonconforming use, and the defendant owner was prosecuted for violating the zoning ordinance by the municipality. The court held that where the defendant would be directly prohibited from building an extension, he could not achieve that same effect indirectly by attaching a trailer. In Conforti v. City of Manchester, 141 N.H. 78, 677 A.2d 147 (N.H. 1996), where rezoning rendered a movie theater as a nonconforming use, the use of the facility for live performances was an impermissible expansion or extension of the nonconforming use. The New Hampshire Supreme Court held that live performances were "substantially different" from showing movies.

Nonconforming use provisions in zoning laws vary considerably from one locality to another. A municipality particularly intent on eliminating nonconforming uses may prohibit any physical expansion of a building; another may favor property use by allowing, for example, the construction of an additional story because it does not increase the footprint, or lot coverage, of the structure.

C. DISCONTINUANCE OR ABANDONMENT

A property owner's right to continue a nonconforming use may be lost by abandonment. In some states, this may require a voluntary, completed act of abandonment by the owner—the concurrence of an intention to abandon and some act, or failure to act, that implies a lack of interest on the part of the owner to retain the use. In other states, courts uphold zoning provisions that define abandonment as any discontinuance of the nonconforming use for a specified period, such as six months or a year. Courts hold that such provisions are sufficient to establish the owner's intent to abandon the nonconforming use as a matter of law. Where the established period is reasonable, discontinuance of the use for that time amounts to an abandonment of the use.

D. DESTRUCTION

The local zoning ordinance may prohibit the restoration of a nonconforming structure that suffers significant physical damage and may require that any such reconstruction be for a use that conforms to the zoning law. Significant physical damage is usually defined as damage that exceeds a certain percentage of the structure's value. Typical standards range from 25% to 50%. These provisions are premised on the theory that owners do not have a right to reconstruct a nonconforming building after damage by fire, weather, natural disaster, or otherwise. In such a case, their property rights were destroyed by the disaster, rather than by the law. The owner is in a situation similar to the owner of a vacant lot, who must comply with the applicable zoning restrictions.

In Moffat v. Forrest City, 234 Ark. 12, 350 S.W.2d 327 (Ark. 1961), the plaintiffs purchased a home in a residential district and began operating a meat market on the premises. The area was later zoned as exclusively residential and the meat market became a nonconforming use. When a fire caused significant damage to the premises, the city sought to enjoin the plaintiffs from rebuilding pursuant to the zoning regulations that prohibited restoration of a property that was more than 60% destroyed. Although the court noted that the zoning ordinances should be strictly construed in favor of the property owner, it was bound to follow the ordinance and refuse restoration if destruction was greater than 60%.

§ 8. ACCESSORY USES

Generally, zoning laws state that lot owners may use their land for a permitted principal use and for activities that are accessory to that use. Accessory uses are uses of land that are found on the same lot as the principal use and that are subordinate, incidental to, and customarily found in connection with the principal use. For example, a garage may be accessory to the residential use of a property because it is customarily found in connection with, and is incidental and subordinate to, the principal residential use.

To be *incidental*, an accessory use must be reasonably related to the principal use. For instance, a garage or recreational use is reasonably related to the principal residential use and thus is deemed incidental. To be *subordinate*, the accessory use must be proportionately smaller than the principal use. The garage is generally smaller than the house, for instance. A use is *customary* if it commonly, habitually, and by long practice has been reasonably associated with a principal use. A most common example of this is vehicle parking for a residence or business. But a municipality need not be limited to specific uses that are customary, so long as the type of use is customary. For instance, a court upheld a zoning board of appeals determination that the construction of a skateboard ramp, when skateboarding was a new recreational activity, was customary because recreational uses of property that serve the needs of the occupants are customary in a residential district. The test is whether the recreational use is incidental to the residential use, not whether landowners in the town are engaged in similar types of recreational activities. Collins v. Lonergan, 603 N.Y.S.2d 330, 198 A.D.2d 349 (N.Y.A.D. 2nd Dept. 1993).

Accessory use provisions in zoning laws allow a range of incidental uses of property that owners expect to engage in when they purchase their property for its principal use. By permitting uses customarily incidental and subordinate to the principal activity, zoning ordinances allow property owners additional beneficial use of their property. Regulations that limit the accessory uses allowed in a district also recognize that some neighborhoods should be protected from accessory uses that are not consistent with the expectations of the property owners.

§ 9. HOME OCCUPATIONS

Historically, single-family homes have been used by their occupants for a variety of occupational uses such as beauty parlors, dressmaking, laundries, and day care. Zoning limits single-family homes to residential uses and to those uses that are customarily associated with residential use and are incidental and subordinate to that residential use—accessory uses. Does this mean that a single-family homeowner can conduct a particular business in a particular neighborhood as an accessory use, or is the occupational use prohibited?

In some communities, this question is answered on a case-by-case basis without benefit of any special regulations. The zoning authorities examine the proposed occupational use and determine whether it is customary, incidental, and subordinate to the residential use. Other municipalities define "home occupations" or "home-based businesses" more specifically in their zoning laws, requiring homeowners to conform their occupational uses to those definitions. Some adopt a list of permitted occupational uses of homes, while others prohibit a specific list of occupations.

A typical definition of "home occupation" reads as follows: "An occupation, profession, activity or use that is clearly a customary, incidental and secondary use of a residential dwelling unit and which does not alter the exterior of the property or affect the residential character of the neighborhood."

Permitting occupations to be conducted in single-family zoned neighborhoods honors expectations of homeowners that such uses have been permitted historically and are within the bundle of rights purchased with the single-family home. Zoning restrictions limiting the occupational use of homes recognize that residential districts must be protected from home occupations that are out of character with the neighborhood and are not uses that homeowners expect to be affected by when they purchase a home in a single-family area. One of the original purposes of zoning is to separate uses that are inconsistent with one another into distinct zoning districts. Traffic, noise, signs, and parking issues are just some of the common complaints neighbors raise about some home occupations.

§ 10. LOCALLY UNWANTED LAND USES

Two types of "locally unwanted land uses," short-term rentals and the production, processing, and sale of medical or recreational marijuana, are relatively recent land use activities, not previously regulated by local law; they raise serious concerns that municipalities are challenged to control. Emerging regulations of these newer land uses raise many legal questions that regulators, property owners, and the judiciary must confront.

Short-term rentals or transient rentals involve the rental of properties zoned for residential occupancy to individuals and groups usually not known to the property owner. Companies like Airbnb provide an internet platform to connect homeowners, or hosts, with potential guests. The use of residentially zoned properties in this way does not neatly fit into the zoning definitions of local codes. Some local constituents object to such occupancies and the more intense activity they cause and some support the extra revenue they can generate, including licensing fees when such homes are regulated by local laws.

Similarly, the legalization by some states of marijuana raises serious concerns for local governments. Is the production of marijuana plants allowed under local zoning? What about facilities that purchase and process marijuana products? Can local retail establishments advertise and sell such products under current zoning definitions and restrictions?

A. SHORT-TERM RENTALS

The Virginia appellate court found that the circuit court did not err in dismissing challenges to certain amendments to a local zoning ordinance and the imposition of a transient rental occupancy tax. Norton v. Board of Supervisors of Fairfax County, 858 S.E.2d 170 (2021). The court found that the county legislature correctly interpreted the original definition of "dwelling" in the applicable zoning ordinance. Further, it held that its amendments to that ordinance were not unreasonable, arbitrary, or capricious. While the plaintiffs' properties are clearly distinguishable from hotels, motels, boarding houses, and travel campgrounds, those distinctions are irrelevant in determining whether the law allows a locality to levy a transient occupancy tax on short-term rental properties. The legislative body was not required to present evidence because the inherent presumption of validity of local law, and the lower court did not err in dismissing claims challenging the short-term occupancy amendments. Since the original definition did not permit as-of-right, short-term lodging, there is no basis for the argument that the amended definition permits anything more than short-term lodging subject to permitting and other restrictions. Accordingly, the trial court did not err in dismissing the claims related to the short-term lodging amendments.

In Calvey v. Town Board of North Elba, 2021 WL 1146283 (2021), plaintiff absentee property owners claimed that requiring the licensing of certain homes before they can be rented through short-term rental media were illegal in several respects. The court held that, on the particular facts of the case, the plaintiffs constituted a class of one sufficient to raise an equal protection question. It also held that the plaintiff's claim that the law involved an unreasonable search and seizure provision was viable, that they had raised a viable regulatory takings claim, but that their due process rights were not violated by the local regulation.

A federal district court in California validated a city ordinance that banned home-sharing services from collecting fees from hosts whose short-term rentals were not registered with the city. Airbnb, Inc. v. City & Cty. of S.F., 217 F.Supp.3d 1066 (2016), found that the regulation was not preempted by the Communications Decency Act 47 U.S.C. § 230(c) and was not a violation of the First Amendment. The ordinance did not force the media platform service to perform content management similar to a publisher or an editor and therefore did not violate the Communications Decency Act. Further, the local law did not violate the First Amendment finding that the ordinance targeted non-expressive commercial conduct, which is not protected by that amendment.

The Court of Appeals of Texas found that an ordinance that regulated the operation of short-term rentals was unconstitutional. Zaatari v. City of Austin, 615 S.W.3d 172 (Tex. App. 2019). In this case, the regulation created three types of rental houses: single-family owner occupied; single-family, non-owner occupied; and multi-family. The local law banned certain activities in single-family, non-owner occupied homes other than sleeping and limited their use to ten or fewer adults. It gave city officials authority to enter, examine, and survey the short-term rental properties to ensure compliance with the law. The court found these regulations were unconstitutionally retroactive because the ordinance significantly affected well-recognized property rights while serving a minimal, if any, public interest. The court also found that the ordinance's provision restricting assembly violated the Texas constitution's guarantee to due process of law because it infringed on the fundamental right of assembly and was not narrowly tailored to serve a compelling governmental interest.

B. PRODUCTION, PROCESSING, AND SALE OF MARIJUANA

The Court of Appeals of New Mexico held that growing medical cannabis was the cultivation of plants or crops and, as an agricultural use, was permitted as-of-right in a conservation zoning district. In Filippi v. Board of County Commissioners of Torrance County, 424 P.3d 658 (N.M. Ct. App. 2018) the Court of Appeals upheld the local zoning board's determination that the production of plants and crops offsite is an as-of-right use under zoning and that the petitioner did not have to apply for a conditional use permit.

A local law prohibiting retailers from selling, furnishing, or distributing cigarettes, electronic cigarettes, tobacco products, or liquid nicotine to any person under 21 years old is a constitutional exercise of Topeka's home rule power. Dwagfys Mfg. Co. v. City of Topeka, 443 P.3d 1052 (2019). The court found that Kansas Cigarette and Tobacco Products Act did not preempt cities from regulating tobacco products and that the local law did not conflict with the Act by imposing greater restrictions.

In RPF Oil Co. v. Genesee County, 950 N.W.2d 440 (Mich. Ct. App. 2019) the Michigan Court of Appeals held that a local law that prohibits the sale of tobacco products to those under the age of 21 was preempted by the state's Age of Minority Act of 1971. That statute entitles individuals 18 and over to all rights, privileges, and responsibilities not otherwise limited by the state constitution or other state statutes. Since the local law imposed restrictions not found in the

Act, it was in conflict with, and therefore preempted by the state statute.

§ 11. ENFORCEMENT

Local governments provide for the enforcement of their land use regulations in a variety of ways. Most building construction, building uses, and changes in land use must comply with the local zoning law and applicable land use and building regulations. Technically, building codes (fire, construction, plumbing, and electrical) are enforced by specialized building inspectors, while zoning provisions are enforced by zoning enforcement officers. Depending on the size of the municipality and its fiscal resources, there may be large departments with various personnel assigned these tasks or a single ministerial official who serves as both the building and zoning officer. Practice with regard to zoning enforcement and the terms used vary, of course, from place to place. The description here is representative of how enforcement is carried out in general.

Building permits certify that construction plans, submitted by a homeowner or developer, comply with the standards of various building codes. A building permit may not be issued until the responsible local official certifies that the construction complies with all the standards contained in the zoning ordinance and that the developer has obtained all required land use approvals. Local review bodies, such as the planning board, are authorized to impose conditions on subdivision, site plan, and other required approvals in order to enforce the standards contained in the land use regulations.

The zoning enforcement officer is charged with the duty of inspecting construction sites while construction of approved development is proceeding. Municipal law must specifically empower the officer to enter onto private property. In most localities, a landowner's application for zoning approval conveys implicit permission to inspect the premises during and after construction.

The most effective enforcement mechanism when violations are encountered during construction that is proceeding under a land use approval is a cease and desist order, which causes construction to stop until compliance is affected. Another effective technique is to revoke the building permit, which may be done when the construction fails to comply with standards in the building or zoning codes. Such orders are ignored at the developer's risk; they may be successfully appealed if arbitrary or unfounded. Development that does not comply with code standards can be ordered removed by local enforcement officers and will be sustained by courts. In Kosciusko County Bd. of Zoning Appeals v. Wygant, 644 N.E.2d 112 (Ind. 1994), a building permit was awarded for a remodeling project and then revoked when the owners later decided to raze the house and construct a new one without a proper building permit. The refusal of the lower courts to award an injunction and require compliance with the code was deemed to be an abuse of judicial discretion.

If construction has been completed, the structure is occupied, and violations are later discovered, the officer may refuse to issue new permits with respect to that property until all zoning problems have been corrected. Some communities follow the practice of revoking the building's certificate of occupancy until violations are cured. Alternatively, the municipality may issue a cease and desist order to compel a property owner to correct an existing violation. Such violations also subject the landowners to civil and criminal penalties. The extent of the affirmative duty of the zoning enforcement officer to discover and remedy zoning violations was discussed in People v. T.S. Klein Corp., 381 N.Y.S.2d 787 (N.Y. City Ct. 1976). The city's zoning officer frankly admitted that the municipal policy was to enforce zoning standards only when complaints were lodged. The court held that where violations are open and discoverable, the local enforcement officials have a duty to establish an adequate method of providing equal protection of the laws in bringing enforcement actions. Responding to complaints, as the sole method of choosing which offending property owners to prosecute, did not meet equal protection standards.

Adjacent owners in some states are authorized to ask courts to enjoin illegal construction or to seek monetary damages. In Frankland v. City of Lake Oswego, 267 Or. 452, 517 P.2d 1042 (Or. 1973), the Oregon court applied a balancing test to determine whether neighbors who complained of the defendant's construction, which failed to comply with the zoning ordinance's standards, should be enjoined or whether damages should be awarded. The factors to be balanced in such cases are the extent of the depreciation of the neighbors' property and the hardship and cost to the defendant of remedying the violation.

When a property owner refuses to comply with violation notices, the zoning enforcement officer refers the matter to the municipal attorney who may ask a court to issue an injunction requiring compliance or to impose a fine or period of imprisonment as a penalty for the violation. Civil proceedings are the most common method of enforcing zoning and land use regulations. That criminal sanctions are available for zoning violations is evident in People v. Multari, 517 N.Y.S.2d 374 (Albany County Ct. 1987), where three college students were sentenced to prison and fined for violating city zoning requirements permitting traditional family housing rather than student living quarters. Punishment included a prison sentence of 45 days and a fine of $2,750. In any court proceeding on a land use matter, the zoning enforcement officer's records and testimony are critical proofs that must be submitted by the municipal attorney to secure a judicial remedy.

After construction and after a complete inspection of the premises, a certificate of occupancy is issued that certifies that the construction, as completed, meets the specifications of all applicable codes. Until there is a validly issued certificate of occupancy, the building may not be lawfully occupied.

to be balanced in each case are the extent of the [illegible] and [illegible] or [illegible] vation.

When a property owner believes [illegible] complies with [illegible] [illegible]

[illegible]

[illegible] of all applicable codes. [illegible] there is a valid [illegible] certificate of occupancy, the building may not be lawfully occupied.

CHAPTER 4

SUBDIVISION CONTROLS AND DEVELOPMENT BY AGREEMENT

§ 1. HISTORY AND AUTHORITY

Closely related to zoning, subdivision regulations are a form of land use control governing the division of land into two or more lots, parcels or sites for sale or development. Whereas zoning regulates the use, density, and dimensional requirements of land, subdivision regulates the development of the land by focusing on the creation of building lots and the provision of public infrastructure to service those lots. Where a zoning law exists, the lots that are proposed as part of a subdivision must comply with the applicable zoning regulations. Typically, planned suburban neighborhoods are developed based upon a subdivision review process.

Like zoning, the authority that local legislatures have to enact local subdivision regulations is derived from the police power and is specifically found in state statutes (modeled on the Standard City Planning Enabling Act, sections 13 and 14). In most states, the local legislature also creates an administrative agency to review applications from landowners and developers that propose the subdivision of land. Subdivision regulations enable municipalities to guide the appearance and character of a neighborhood and developing community by providing criteria for design review of a proposed development. The regulations also make it possible for municipalities to articulate the standards by which public improvements in the area are to be made by examining the need for, and provision of, adequate public infrastructure, ensuring that street patterns are consistent, and making certain that community services are available to meet community needs. Over the years, subdivision regulation has evolved from an early method of facilitating orderly land sales to a critical land use planning and control technique to address issues resulting from suburban sprawl, including the need to protect and preserve open space and critical environmental areas.

Modern issues in subdivision control focus on the conditions that governments might attach to a proposed subdivision. These requirements, discussed below, may require developers to install certain public amenities on or adjacent to their proposed subdivision, to set aside certain land within the subdivision for public purposes, and to pay a fee to the municipality. Other legal issues in subdivision review today focus on the ability of government to require certain designs such as cluster development and conservation subdivisions for the purpose of preserving open space or protecting significant natural features within the proposed subdivision.

Another issue that continues to garner attention is that of antiquated subdivisions, or subdivisions that were prematurely platted and are presently either not developed or only partially developed, and where their initial platting no longer meets current zoning and subdivision standards. Antiquated subdivisions, which may have been approved forty or fifty years ago, raise serious questions about the proper control and timing of future development. Some techniques that have been used to address these challenges include adequate public facilities ordinances, impact fees, and transfer of development rights.

The authority of local governments to regulate a subdivision is well established as a valid exercise of the police power. However, in cases like Ayres v. City Council of City of Los Angeles, 34 Cal. 2d 31, 207 P.2d 1 (Cal. 1949), the courts focus on the extent to which government may have exceeded this authority under state or local law, or under the police power more generally. In Ridgefield Land Co. v. Detroit, 241 Mich. 468 (Mich. 1928), the Michigan Supreme Court upheld a road dedication as a reasonable condition on a subdivision approval. The condition required the developer to provide streets of a certain width consistent with the city's master street plan. Early key considerations were the reasonableness and necessity of the conditions imposed.

The dedication of streets and highways as a condition of subdivision approval was controversial, with many applicants unsuccessfully arguing that the conditions amounted to an uncompensated taking of their property. The courts were quick to uphold the subdivision review process, and the resulting conditions imposed, by focusing on the fact that these requirements were voluntary for the purpose of obtaining the privilege of having the subdivision plat recorded.

In City of Corpus Christi v. Unitarian Church of Corpus Christi, 436 S.W.2d 923 (Tex. Civ. App. 1968), a Texas church requested a building permit to improve its property for church purposes. The municipality required the church, as a condition of permit approval, to dedicate a strip of land on the plat so that an existing street could be extended. In determining that the city had no authority to require the dedication, the court found that the city ordinance applied only to the subdivision of land, and in this case the church did not request permission to divide its land into two or more building lots, only to make certain improvements on its piece of property.

§ 2. SUBDIVISION APPROVAL PROCESS

Subdivision review is an interactive process between the municipality and the applicant. The application to subdivide land is in effect a request for administrative action ultimately resulting in an approval for proposed development of a tract of land that will yield some number of smaller lots or parcels. While typically subdivision proposals conjure images of residential development, the laws are generally not written to be so restrictive, and they may accommodate the use of property for business, commercial or industrial uses.

Informally, an applicant may begin the subdivision process by simply meeting with the planning staff or other local officials to better understand the local subdivision law and to enable the local government to understand the initial scope of the project. This step is typically not required, but, in practice, it often occurs. The applicant formally begins the process by submitting a preliminary plan or plat. This document shows the layout of the proposed subdivision, including, among other things, road and lot layout and approximate dimensions (e.g., lot sizes and road widths), topography and drainage of the site (this includes identification of significant natural features such as streams and ponds, flood prone areas, large trees and vegetation), and public facilities (e.g., water, storm and sanitary sewers, gas, electric, cable, and fire hydrants). Local regulations seek to assure that the provision of services will be adequate to meet the needs of the new development (e.g., the capacity), that the quality of the materials used is appropriate, and that the design and materials used are compatible with the existing municipal infrastructure system (e.g., uniformity). As a result of the need for coordination and uniformity, subdivision regulations typically require that developers dedicate the roads, water, sewer and other on-site infrastructure to the municipality for future care and maintenance as part of the municipal infrastructure. Legal issues that arise with both on-site and off-site improvements are discussed in Section 4. Lastly, the subdivision review process enables the municipality to examine planning concerns by reviewing, among other things, street layout and connectivity.

In setting forth the purpose of subdivision review and the authority for plat review, statutes vest the municipal planning commission with the responsibility for ensuring that the subject parcel can be developed in a safe manner without peril from fire, flood, drainage or other threats to the public health, safety, and welfare. The subdivision review process is most commonly considered to be a ministerial action by the planning commission. The following list of requirements from the subdivision review statute in New York, N.Y. Town Law § 277, is a good example of common matters that are subject to review: streets and highways of sufficient width and suitable grade; location of streets and highways to accommodate anticipated traffic; adequate light and air; ability for fire protection and other emergency vehicles to service the development (e.g., are the roads wide enough for a fire truck to turn around); conformity and consistency with the comprehensive plan and the official map; the location of suitable monuments at block corners and other necessary locations; appropriate grading and paving of streets and public places; street signs; sidewalks; street lighting, where applicable; curbs; gutters; trees; water mains; sanitary sewers and storm drains; and, where appropriate, fire alarm devices.

In reviewing the preliminary plat, the planning board makes certain that all information required pursuant to the local subdivision regulations is provided to the municipality, and that the requisite design criteria and infrastructure standards are met. The planning commission may request that the applicant make adjustments or modifications to the preliminary plat, or it may approve the proposal as submitted. State statutes provide a time frame within which the planning commission must act on the application. A typical time frame is 60 days, but it varies from state to state.

Following the preliminary review, the applicant must then submit a final plat. Statutes or local laws will also set forth a time frame within which this submission must be made. Usually, so long as the applicant has followed the required conditions from the planning board, the final plat submission is approved. This could be problematic, however, where local zoning laws have changed between the time of initial review and final submission. This is covered below in the discussion of vested rights in Section 6. States may give municipalities the ability to grant a conditional approval of a final plat, which sets forth additional conditions that must be satisfied prior to the signing of the plat by the authorized local official for filing and prior to the granting of any building permits. Where a conditional approval is granted, statutes also provide the time frame within which the applicant must bring his plat into compliance or lose the conditional approval. In addition, municipalities may be authorized to approve a proposed plat in sections. This would allow for the phasing of the project and enable the planning commission to ensure the orderly development of the plat before the next section is approved for construction.

While state statutes set forth applicable time frames within which any required public hearings and decision-making must occur, these dates may often be extended upon mutual consent of the parties. Although developers typically desire to have their projects approved quickly, they may be reluctant to refuse a request for an extension by the planning commission for fear that the project may not be approved without the additional time to present information and make necessary adjustments. However, where the municipality fails to make a decision within the statutorily prescribed time frames, in some states, it can amount to a default approval in favor of the applicant.

Where subdivision regulations exist, landowners are prohibited from filing or recording a plat (development plan/map) until it has been approved and certified by the designated local board. Statutes may also require that a designated local official, such as the chair of the planning commission, sign the plat prior to it being accepted for filing in the office of the applicable municipal clerk. Furthermore, many states require certain additional procedural steps to ensure inter-jurisdictional coordination, such as referrals of the proposed plat to the county or regional planning agencies for their review and recommendation.

Municipalities require applicants to invest a significant amount of money into the installation of adequate public infrastructure to service the development. Developers often do not install all of the infrastructure at once because of the high cost, choosing instead to phase the installation over the duration of the project. Municipalities may require applicants to post a performance bond or other security, such as a letter of credit or deposit of funds into an escrow account, to ensure that all of the agreed to infrastructure will be provided. This arrangement protects both the municipality and the individual purchasers from developer bankruptcies or failures to install certain public amenities.

Some state and local governments apply different levels of review for "major" and "minor" subdivisions. These terms are defined in the local subdivision law. For example, the division of land into six or more building lots may trigger a "major" subdivision review. The minor subdivision review offers an abbreviated process for developments of less significant impact. States may also require subdivision review to be coordinated with the applicable environmental review process.

§ 3. CLUSTER DEVELOPMENT AND CONSERVATION SUBDIVISIONS

As a means of promoting flexible design and development that preserves the natural and scenic qualities of open space, statutes may authorize local governments to either request or require an applicant to submit a "traditional" subdivision plat as well as a "cluster" plat. A cluster plat modifies the existing dimensional requirements set forth in the zoning law and proposes lots that are smaller and closer together to obtain the otherwise allowable density, such as the number of housing units, while conserving areas of open space within the subdivision. Clustering of residential units may encourage interaction in the community by designing the units closer to the street, providing for public gathering places, and encouraging use of parks and community facilities as focal points in the neighborhood.

Some state statutes allow localities to provide applicants with an incentive for the submission of a cluster plat by increasing the otherwise allowable density in exchange for the provision of open space. So, if the developer would normally have been permitted to site 40 lots on a traditional plat, the applicant with a cluster plat may be able to site 44 lots. In other states, however, local governments are vested with the authority to require the cluster plat, and an increased density incentive is prohibited. The planning commission may establish conditions as to use, maintenance, and ownership of the open lands shown on the cluster plat.

Closely related to traditional cluster subdivision, conservation subdivisions also permit flexibility of design in order to promote environmentally sensitive and efficient uses of land. They tend to focus on preservation of unique or sensitive natural resources such as groundwater, floodplains, wetlands, streams, steep slopes, woodlands, and wildlife habitats, as well as the preservation of important historic and archaeological sites. They may permit clustering of houses and structures on less environmentally sensitive soils, which will reduce the amount of infrastructure (including paved surfaces and utility easements) necessary for residential development, and reduce erosion and sedimentation by minimizing land disturbance and removal of vegetation. In addition, conservation design may provide needed space for walking trails and bike paths, both for within the subdivision and connected to neighboring communities, businesses, and facilities, reducing reliance on automobiles. Conservation of scenic views and protection of prime agricultural land, along with the preservation of farming as an economic activity, are also goals of this type of development. Developers tend to favor cluster and conservation subdivisions because by placing the buildings closer together there is a cost savings on pavement for roadways, sidewalks, sewer extensions, and other on-site infrastructure.

In Chrinko v. South Brunswick Twp. Planning Bd., 77 N.J. Super. 594 (N.J. Super. L. 1963), the court noted that preservation of land in its natural state is a widely recognized public purpose, and that even absent specific state statutory authority, a cluster subdivision local law reasonably advances this legitimate purpose. Related in concept is the flexibility offered through a planned unit development, or PUD. A PUD permits mixed use development, typically designing plats where residential development is compatible with other uses such as small neighborhood businesses. Orinda Homeowners Committee v. Board of Supervisors, 11 Cal. App. 3d 768, 90 Cal. Rptr. 88 (Cal. App. 1 Dist. 1970) explains the distinction between cluster development and PUDs—describing clustering as a device for increasing dwelling unit density on some portion of the development area for the purpose of leaving open space in other areas. *Orinda* and other cases also reinforce that the cluster design technique does not violate the uniformity requirement for zoning districts, as it is uniformity of regulations and not uniformity of the layout of dwelling units that is controlled by zoning.

§ 4. PLANNED UNIT DEVELOPMENTS

Another tool that has gained popularity is the planned unit development (PUD) as it allows for greater flexibility of design by enabling mixed uses to exist within a single development plat. The enabling statute in New York provides in part, "Planned unit development district regulations are intended to provide for residential, commercial, industrial or other land uses, or a mix thereof, in which economies of scale, creative architectural or planning concepts and open space preservation may be achieved by a developer in furtherance of the town comprehensive plan and zoning local law or ordinance." N.Y. Town L. 261–c. Planned Unit Development has its roots in cluster zoning, and it borrows from the floating zone, subdivision control techniques, and special permit procedures.

§ 5. EXACTIONS

The most litigated aspects of subdivision review are the monetary fees or land set asides that municipalities may impose upon applicants. Exactions may consist of land, infrastructure, a fee, or any combination thereof that a municipality requires from a developer in return for subdivision or development approval. Exactions may also include a requirement that the developer connect water and sewer lines to the municipal system. Municipalities rely on exactions as a method of ensuring that new development "pays its own way" for certain infrastructure necessitated as a direct result of the development. Developers often view exactions as a public or taxpayer responsibility that is being shifted onto the private sector.

As discussed below, the U.S. Supreme Court has helped to articulate standards by which exactions must be measured to ensure that they are closely related to the needs generated by the development. In addition to these considerations, the imposition of exactions on land use approvals can violate the Takings Clause discussed in Chapter 5. When the condition, for example, requires the conveyance or dedication of land for public use, just compensation may be required. This occurs when the condition is not a proportional response to the adverse impact that the project will have on the community. In other words, the government might be able to acquire land for the intended purpose, but may not require it as a condition of development without a showing that it is necessary to mitigate impacts of the proposed project.

A. TRADITIONAL EXACTIONS

Traditional subdivision exactions involve the requirement that applicants set aside land for parks or other recreational uses, or pay a fee in lieu thereof. Other commonly accepted exactions include requirements for surfacing, curbing, and guttering streets to prescribed standards, and installing and connecting water and sewer facilities. In Petterson v. City of Naperville, 9 Ill. 2d 233 (Ill. 1956), the Illinois court upheld the requirement that the developer provide curbs and gutters as well as water drainage facilities as reasonable exactions, stating, "The imposition of reasonable regulations as a condition precedent to the subdivision of lands and the recording of plats thereof is not a violation of the constitutional requirements of uniformity of taxation or tantamount to the taking of private property for public use without just compensation." These types of exactions are seldom challenged today as it is well settled that, so long as the requirements are not ultra vires with respect to the applicable state enabling act and so long as they are reasonable, they will be upheld as a condition to the subdivision approval.

In 181 Inc. v. Salem County Planning Bd., 133 N.J. Super. 350 (N.J. Super. L. 1975), mod. on appeal, 140 N.J. Super. 247 (1975), the New Jersey Superior Court found a problem with the county's exaction scheme in that it set up an automatic blanket policy of requiring developers to dedicate frontage of land along every county road as a condition of development approval, whether or not there was a present need for such dedication. The court noted that there must be some rational nexus between the requirement and the municipality's proposed use.

B. NON-TRADITIONAL EXACTIONS

The exactions discussed above tend to relate to land and infrastructure located within the proposed subdivision area. Non-traditional exactions refer to exactions, typically consisting of fees, for public infrastructure that is or will be located outside of the property on which the subdivision occurs, but the need for which is necessitated by the new development. To withstand challenge, these exactions must serve the occupants of the subdivision and they must be reasonable.

In Pioneer Trust and Savings Bank v. Village of Mount Prospect, 22 Ill. 2d 375 (Ill. 1961), where the village required the developer to dedicate land for a school and a playground outside of the subdivision, the court in Illinois applied a "specifically and uniquely attributable" test and determined that although the activity of the developer would aggravate the existing need for more school rooms, the record did not demonstrate that the need was specifically and uniquely attributable to this situation. In sharp contrast to the conservative view of the Illinois Supreme Court, in Jordan v. Village of Menomonee Falls, 28 Wis. 2d 608 (Wis. 1965), appeal dismissed 385 U.S. 4 (1966), the Wisconsin Supreme Court upheld an ordinance that required the dedication of land for schools, parks, and recreational facilities, or a fee in lieu thereof.

C. IMPACT FEES

Increased costs of growth, significant decreases in federal and state dollars to local governments, and increased costly mandates on local governments forced municipalities and municipal planners to become more creative in the generation of new revenue to meet local infrastructure and public facility demands. Impact fees are assessed upon developers by municipalities for off-site improvements necessitated as a direct result of the proposed development. They became popular in the late 1980s and early 1990s as a means of generating revenue to pay for a host of community amenities including schools, libraries, fire stations, and ambulance services.

Differences between impact fees and traditional land exactions include: 1) traditional exactions are paid at the time of subdivision plat approval, whereas impact fees are customarily paid at the time of issuance of a building permit or certificate of occupancy; 2) traditional exactions are assessed primarily on subdivisions whereas impact fees are generally assessed on all new development, which enables the collection of fees for a variety of non-subdivision projects, such as condominiums, apartments and commercial developments; 3) traditional exactions are based upon a percentage of the total acreage of the proposed development. Impact fees, in contrast, are based generally upon the individual characteristics of each parcel such as square footage, the number of bedrooms, or the number of living units, and they therefore provide a closer correlation between impacts and assessments; and 4) impact fees are used to fund a greater variety of services and facilities than traditional exactions, which are limited to open space, parks, and infrastructure within the development.

More than half of the states now authorize the assessment of impact fees subject to various regulations. Where there is a lack of specific state statutory authorization, cases have focused on the issue of whether the impact fee is a permitted regulatory fee (the authority for which is derived from the police power), or whether it constitutes an unauthorized tax (unauthorized because local governments can only impose local taxes where they have specific constitutional or statutory authorization to do so). A "fee" is a mechanism used to regulate land use, whereas a "tax" is imposed to raise general revenues. The distinction between the two can be vague, and courts will look beyond the label in order to make their own determination with respect to classification.

§ 6. THE OFFICIAL MAP

The official map was in many respects the precursor to modern subdivision regulation. These maps were developed and adopted by municipalities for the purpose of designating streets and roads so that as development occurred over time, developers and owners would be required to dedicate and improve the mapped streets within the subdivision. Municipalities are authorized by state statute to adopt an official map that is much more detailed than the master plan. The official map sets forth both existing and planned streets, sewer and water lines, parkland and other public facilities, and it may establish set-back lines for future roads and for the widening of future streets. Just over half of the states have enabling statutes authorizing the adoption of an official map.

Edward M. Bassett and Frank B. Williams, the authors of the 1926 New York Official Map Act and a 1935 model official map act, distinguished the official map from the master plan by explaining that, "A master plan embraces many features not included in an official map. The master plan, therefore, does not usually show precise data founded in careful surveys, while the official map, upon which the details of both public and private works must be based, should be capable of accurate interpretation. The master plan, therefore, may be characterized as plastic, the official map as rigid." In some states, the official map is binding upon landowners whereas the master plan is not. This is the case particularly where the master plan is adopted by a planning commission rather than by the local legislative body. In Nigro v. Planning Board of the Borough of Saddle River, 237 N.J. Super. 305, 567 A.2d 1010 (N.J. Super. 1989), the court explained that the official map is binding and that a municipal body may not approve a development application that conflicts with the map. In other cases, the official map has been used to strengthen the master plan where both documents were found to be complementary and not contradictory. See, Lake City Corporation v. City of Mequon, 207 Wis. 2d 155, 558 N.W.2d 100 (Wis. 1997).

State enabling statutes authorize, but may not require, local governments to adopt an official map. Upheld as a valid exercise of the police power, Headley v. City of Rochester, 272 N.Y. 197, 5 N.E.2d 198 (N.Y. 1936) is the leading case upholding an official map act and stating that the adoption of the map and the identification of future streets does not constitute an unconstitutional taking of property because it does not automatically divest the title of the landowner or require the municipality to institute condemnation proceedings to acquire title to such land. This is because although future streets are set forth on the official map, they may never be realized, as only time will prove whether the municipality correctly predicted the future growth and development. Therefore, the municipality is under no obligation to open a designated future mapped street until the legislative body determines it is needed. One likely exception would be if all of the owner's land were to be reserved or where such reservation created an incumbrance on the title. Forster v. Scott, 136 N.Y. 577 (N.Y. 1893).

In Palm Beach County v. Wright, 641 So.2d 50 (Fla. 1994), a landowner with a portion of his property located within the Future Thoroughfare Map in the county's comprehensive plan alleged that the map was an unconstitutional taking of private property. The court disagreed, holding that the map served a legitimate governmental purpose and was a valid exercise of county planning authority. In addition, the court held that just having private property located within a thoroughfare map did not represent a per se taking. Whether a taking had occurred should be determined on a case-by-case basis only after the property owner had filed for a development permit.

To ensure best that an official map reservation can withstand a constitutional challenge, the laws should contain savings provisions that protect individual landowners from hardships that may result from the reservation of their property on the map. Such a provision, similar to the relief that variances offer, may allow for a locality to issue a building permit for an area designated as reserved on the official map where it can be shown that failure to do so would result in an unnecessary hardship. See, State ex rel. Miller v. Manders, 2 Wis. 2d 365, 86 N.W.2d 469 (Wis. 1957).

§ 7. DEVELOPER RIGHTS

Developers invest significant fiscal resources into the subdivision review process. Costs may include the professional services of engineers, surveyors, planners, lawyers, and architects, as well as services for the testing of soils and examination of other environmental and geological aspects of the proposed development. Even when the government grants subdivision approvals and the owner of record files the approved plat, subsequent changes in either the local subdivision law or the zoning law may supercede the prior approval. Absent a state statute on developer agreements, developers and landowners are subject to the "vested rights" common law in their jurisdiction. Each of these concepts is discussed more fully below.

A. VESTED RIGHTS

Some states have chosen to adopt vested rights statutes which set forth criteria for determining when a landowner has acquired a right to develop her property in accordance with an approved plan regardless of whether the regulations subsequently change. The purpose of vested rights is to ensure a balance—the municipality's police power to protect the health, safety, and welfare versus the landowner's right to finish development of his or her land once begun. The majority of states follow common law precedent with respect to vested rights. A landowner typically receives "vested rights" to develop after the government has made a decision to permit the development and where the landowner has then acted in good faith upon such approval by making some improvement to the land or by making a financial investment in reliance on the approval. Many states, either by common law or legislation, are relaxing the requirements of the landowner and letting rights vest earlier in the development process. Just what constitutes "substantial" work or expenditures is the focus of much of the vested right litigation. In New York, for example, a landowner acquires vested rights after a permit is approved and the landowner puts a "shovel in the ground" to begin work in reliance on the approval.

The majority rule requires issuance of a building permit by the municipality, plus substantial construction and/or substantial expenditures before rights vest. However, states interpret the general rule differently. In Dawe v. City of Scottsdale, 119 Ariz. 486, 581 P.2d 1136 (Ariz. 1978), the owner of a parcel recorded an approved subdivision plat prior to the application of a new zoning law, which had the effect of making the lots substandard. The Arizona Supreme Court rejected the owner's assertion that he held a vested right to develop the substandard lots where there was no attempt to improve the property and it had remained vacant from the date of the filing of the subdivision plat through the implementation of the new zoning law. Similarly, in Avco Community

Developers, Inc. v. South Coast Regional Commission, 17 Cal. 3d 785, 132 Cal. Rptr. 386, 553 P.2d 546 (Cal. 1976), the developer had spent more than $3 million to improve the property based upon a final approval of a map and initial approval of a development permit for 7,500 acres of land. The state later changed the regulations and required the landowner to comply with the new law. The California Supreme Court found that the landowner had not acquired vested rights, even though a significant amount of money had been expended, because the landowner never received a final building permit from the agency. The court reasoned that to do otherwise would take away the discretion of the government to control land development policy. A number of states are, however, moving toward earlier vesting due to increasing subdivision activity.

Generally, vested rights are not transferable to subsequent owners who purchase the land before the project is completed. However, some states are changing that by statute. For example, in Colorado vested rights attach to the property and run with the land to subsequent owners so long as the project does not offend the public health, safety and welfare. Colo. Rev. Stat. sec. 24–68–103 (2007). The Tex. Local Gov't Code sec. 245.002(a) similarly provides that, "A regulatory agency shall consider an application for a permit under the regulations in effect at time the original application is filed for review, or a plan for development or plat application is filed with a regulatory agency."

In 2002 the American Planning Association published a Growing Smart Legislative Guidebook that includes two model laws for vested rights—one a "bright-line" vesting rule and one for vesting of rights upon significant and ascertainable development. The Guidebook can be accessed at: https://www.huduser.gov/Publications/pdf/growingsmart_guide.pdf.

B. DEVELOPER AGREEMENTS

A minority of states have dealt with the lack of certainty in the process through the adoption of statutes authorizing developer agreements. The developer agreement is in essence a bilateral contract between the developer and the municipality whereby the municipality agrees to guarantee to the developer the right to develop the project for a defined number of years regardless of future changes to the zoning law or subdivision regulations in exchange for certain negotiated public amenities, or a fee in lieu thereof, that the municipality might not otherwise legally be able to require the developer to contribute. The appeal of the developer agreement is that both sides benefit from the bargain.

Developer agreements remain controversial in many states. It is uncertain whether a municipality illegally bargains away its police power by, in essence, promising not to change its zoning or land use regulations as applied to a particular parcel of land. Local governments are prohibited from contracting away their police powers because to do so would empower one legislative body to bind future legislative bodies. In Giger v. City of Omaha, 232 Neb. 676, 442 N.W.2d 182 (Neb. 1989), in characterizing a developer agreement as a form of conditional zoning, the agreement was upheld where the court determined that the city did not bargain away its police power and that the agreement enhanced the city's regulatory control over the development rather than limiting it.

Municipalities are not without recourse when developers fail to perform pursuant to the terms of the developer agreement. In Bollech v. Charles County, Maryland, 69 Fed. Appx. 178 (4th Cir. 2003), a development agreement required the property owners to install certain public infrastructure in exchange for the right to build a certain number of residential units, all staged over time with specific time frames detailed in the development agreement. The county subsequently changed its zoning, and when the property owners failed to install the infrastructure they had agreed to within the agreed upon time frame, the county was able to void the development agreement. The Fourth Circuit Court of Appeals noted that the failure to perform on the part of the property owner released the county from its obligations under the contract. Similarly, developers are not without recourse when a municipality fails to uphold its part of the agreement. In Mammoth Lakes Land Acquisition, LLC v. Town of Mammoth Lakes, 191 Cal. App. 4th 435 (3rd Dist. 2010) where a town repudiated a development agreement, a jury awarded over $32 million in damages.

C. COMMUNITY BENEFITS AGREEMENTS

A community benefits agreement (CBA) is a private contract negotiated between a prospective developer and community representatives. In essence, a CBA specifies the benefits that the developer will provide to the community in exchange for the community's support of, or quiet acquiescence in, its proposed development.

The CBA is a relative newcomer to the toolbox of strategies that communities may utilize to ensure that development occurs consistently with the sometimes more narrow goals and desires of neighborhood residents, as opposed to the sometimes broader goals and desires of municipal and regional governing bodies. CBAs also provide a mechanism for community groups to organize and work collaboratively to communicate and negotiate with developers to address community impacts and opportunities that the host municipality may not have legal authority, and/or the political will, to discuss. These agreements may require a developer to mitigate potential impacts of the development, but often they also go farther, asking the developer to work with the community to improve housing, employment options, and recreational and cultural facilities. The legal relationship between CBAs and planning is still unclear. Social justice principles, including an emphasis on public participation, are key to the CBA movement.

Enforceability is still a largely untested area of the law with respect to CBAs in two respects: since these are private contractual agreements the local government is not obligated to approve a proposed project just because there is a CBA, nor is the government responsible for the enforcement of the private agreement. The powers and resources that community groups may or may not have to enforce the private agreement also may be uncertain.

CHAPTER 5

FIFTH AMENDMENT LIMITS ON LAND USE REGULATIONS

§ 1. CONSTITUTIONALLY PROTECTED PROPERTY RIGHTS

All land use regulations must conform to the Fifth Amendment of the U.S. Constitution. They are not valid if they deprive any person of property without due process of law and they cannot constitute takings of real property unless just compensation is paid. The structure of the relevant provision of the Fifth Amendment is interesting to study. It reads as follows:

> *No person shall be . . . deprived of life, liberty, or property, without due process of law; nor shall private property be taken for a public use, without just compensation.*

Notice that there is a strategically placed semicolon in this critical constitutional provision. It separates the "due process clause" from the "takings" clause. The first prohibits the federal Congress from passing any laws that do not substantially advance legitimate state interests. This means that a land use regulation is invalid if it does not in fact further a legitimate public purpose. The second requires that, if private land is taken or conscripted for a public use, just compensation must be paid. These clauses are the principal source of the property rights that courts protect from undue interference by legislatures and land use regulators.

The Fourteenth Amendment passes these proscriptions on to the states and the local governments to which state legislatures have delegated the authority to adopt and enforce land use regulations. It specifies that:

> *No State shall make or enforce any law which shall abridge the privileges or immunities of citizens of the United States; nor shall any State deprive any person of life, liberty, or property, without due process of law; nor deny to any person within its jurisdiction the equal protection of the laws.*

In a 1897 case, Chicago, B. & Q. R. Co. v. Chicago, 166 U.S. 226 (1897), the Supreme Court held that the Fourteenth Amendment incorporates the Fifth Amendment protections of property and applies them as limitations on state law as well as local governmental regulations, since local governments are considered legal instrumentalities of the states. All local zoning, subdivision, site plan, and other land use regulations, under this analysis, are subject to and limited by the due process and takings clauses. This chapter explores the extent to which these critical clauses limit the authority of government to adopt and enforce land use regulations.

§ 2. THE DUE PROCESS CLAUSE

In Chapter III, we explored how the due process clause is used to challenge land use regulations, particularly zoning. In Euclid v. Ambler Realty Co., 272 U.S. 365 (1926), the plaintiff claimed that zoning, on its face, did not accomplish a legitimate governmental purpose. This amounted to a claim that the plaintiff's due process rights had been violated by a regulation that was unreasonable and unrelated to the public well being. Some state courts at the time agreed with the plaintiff's position. In Goldman v. Crowther, 147 Md. 282 (Md. 1925), for example, the Maryland court held that zoning constituted an artificial plan of segregation of land uses, had nothing to do with advancing the public safety, health, or welfare, and violated the rights of citizens to hold and enjoy property as they wish so long as they do not injure their neighbors or the public.

Unfortunately for Ambler Realty, the U.S. Supreme Court disagreed with the *Goldman* court. It seriously considered Ambler's position that the separation of land uses among various zoning districts accomplished nothing approximating the public interest. This issue had never been taken up by the Court and was a matter of great importance. The Court referred to reports of planning and land use professionals at the time that supported the segregation of residential, business, and industrial businesses. These reports found that use separation into zoning districts made it easier to fight fires, increased the security of home life, prevented street accidents, decreased noise, and preserved a more favorable environment. The Court found these reasons sufficient to preclude it from finding that zoning, on its face, has no relationship at all to the public health, safety, morals, or general welfare. In other words, Ambler Realty Company's due process rights were not violated; the law properly advanced a public purpose. It did not, therefore, violate the plaintiff's constitutional rights under the due process clause.

Less than two years later, the Court found that a zoning ordinance did, in fact, violate a property owner's due process rights, not on its face as in *Euclid,* but as applied to the plaintiff's particular piece of property. In Nectow v. City of Cambridge, 277 U.S. 183 (1928), the owner claimed that the residential zoning of its property was unconstitutional because it failed to accomplish its objective, which was to further residential development in the particular zoning district. To the Court's satisfaction, the plaintiff proved that because of industrial and other incompatible and noxious land uses in the area, there was no market for housing—the only land use allowed under the applicable zoning regulations. This meant that, as applied to the plaintiff's parcel, the law did not accomplish a legitimate public purpose. Although the objective of providing for exclusive residential development in a neighborhood is a valid and laudable public purpose, since there was no market for such development, the law, as applied to this parcel, was ineffective to achieve that objective. The Court found, therefore, that the zoning violated the plaintiff's due process rights and was constitutionally invalid because it did not substantially advance a legitimate public purpose.

In Lingle v. Chevron U.S.A. Inc., 544 U.S. 528 (2005), the Court returned to the due process question. In examining the proscriptions of the Fifth

Amendment, it explained that due process claims are subject to a test it called the "substantially advances" formula. This suggests that the due process clause involves a means-ends test. It asks, in essence, whether a regulation of private property is effective in achieving some legitimate public purpose. "[A] regulation that fails to serve any legitimate governmental objective may be so arbitrary or irrational that it runs afoul of the Due Process clause." The Court cited County of Sacramento v. Lewis, 523 U.S. 833, 846 (1998), which stated that the Due Process Clause is intended to protect citizens against "the exercise of power without any reasonable justification in the service of a legitimate governmental objective." Combining all this into a single formulation, a land use regulation violates the Due Process Clause if it pursues an objective that is simply not public in nature or if it is not effective in achieving a valid public objective.

§ 3. REGULATORY TAKINGS DISTINGUISHED

The *Lingle* case eliminated much of the confusion that lingered since the U.S. Supreme Court's decision in Agins v. City of Tiburon, 447 U.S. 255 (1980) regarding land use regulations and whether they constitute a regulatory taking in violation of the Fifth Amendment's taking clause. As early as 1922, in the case of Pennsylvania Coal Co. v. Mahon, 260 U.S. 393 (1922), the U.S. Supreme Court held "that while property may be regulated to a certain extent, if regulation goes too far it will be recognized as a taking." As a result, a land use regulation can be invalidated as a "regulatory taking" and compensation can be awarded to the regulated property owner for the damages caused. In *Agins,* the Court stated that a government regulation could be a taking if it does not substantially advance legitimate state interests or denies an owner economically viable use of his land. This is a disjunctive test: if either prong is violated, the *Agins* Court said, a taking occurs and compensation is the proper remedy.

In a unanimous decision, the *Lingle* Court held that the *Agins* "substantially advances" formula is not an appropriate test for determining whether a regulation constitutes a taking under the Fifth Amendment. The "formula prescribes an inquiry in the nature of a due process, not a takings, test, and . . . it has no proper place in . . . takings jurisprudence." The effect of the Court's holding and its explanatory dicta is to clarify the field of regulatory takings law as applied to land use regulations and agency determinations.

In *Lingle*, Chevron challenged a Hawaii statute that placed a cap on the amount of rent an oil company may charge a lessee-dealer. Hawaii enacted Act 257 in June of 1997 in order to protect gasoline prices from inflation due to the effects of market concentration. Chevron filed suit in the United States District Court for the District of Hawaii claiming the Act affected a taking of its property; the company sought a declaratory judgment and an injunction against the application of the rent cap to its stations.

The parties stipulated that Chevron, under Act 257, was earning a return on its investment on its lessee-dealer stations in Hawaii that satisfies any constitutional standard. Patently, Act 257 did not effect a taking because it deprived Chevron of an economically viable use of its property. In *Lingle*, the lower courts held that Act 257 is a taking because it fails to meet the *Agins* "substantially advances" test. These courts held that the Act did not substantially advance the legitimate state interest of controlling gasoline prices. In arriving at its conclusion, the district court weighed the reasonableness of two opposing economists who testified on behalf of the litigants; it found one expert's views more persuasive than those of the other and concluded that Act 257 would not achieve the objective of controlling gasoline prices.

In the Supreme Court's words, using the *Agins* test in this way "would require courts to scrutinize the efficacy of a vast array of state and federal regulations—a task for which courts are not well suited. Moreover, it would empower—and often require—the courts to substitute their predictive judgments for those of elected legislatures and expert agencies." According to the Court, the *Agins* test is "regrettably imprecise" and "such a test is not a valid method of discerning whether private property has been 'taken' for purposes of the Fifth Amendment." "There is no question that the 'substantially advances' formula was derived from due process, not takings, precedents." "[T]he 'substantially advances' inquiry reveals nothing about the magnitude or character of the burden a particular regulation imposes upon private property rights. Nor does it provide any information about how any regulatory burden is distributed among property owners." "The notion that . . . a regulation . . . 'takes' private property for public use merely by virtue of its ineffectiveness or foolishness is untenable." The "Takings Clause presupposes that the government has acted in pursuit of a valid public purpose."

The Takings Clause of the Fifth Amendment provides that property shall not be taken for public use without just compensation. It is designed not to limit governmental interferences with property rights as such, but to secure compensation when a proper interference occurs. In the Court's words, "[t]he paradigmatic taking requiring just compensation is a direct government appropriation of title or physical invasion of private property." "Beginning with *Mahon*, however, the Court recognized that government regulation of private property may, in some instances, be so onerous that its effect is tantamount to a direct appropriation or ouster—and that such 'regulatory takings' may be compensable under the Fifth Amendment." In determining whether a regulation is a taking, the Court states that "we must remain cognizant that 'government regulation—by definition—involves the adjustment of rights for the public good,' and that 'Government hardly could go on if to some extent values incident to property could not be diminished without paying for every such change in the general law.' "

§ 4. FOUR CATEGORIES OF REGULATORY TAKINGS CASES

The Court in *Lingle* identified four categories of regulatory takings cases. The tests created by the Court in each category aim, according to the Court, to "identify regulatory actions that are functionally equivalent to the classic taking in which government directly appropriates private property or ousts the owner from his domain. Accordingly, each of these tests focuses directly upon the severity of the burden that government imposes upon private property rights." The first two categories are per se takings: void on their face once certain facts are proved by the aggrieved property owners.

A. PERMANENT PHYSICAL INVASIONS

Landowners who do not apply for governmental permits are particularly protected from the imposition of conditions that require them to allow others to come on their land. The right to the exclusive possession of one's property is one of the most fundamental property rights recognized in law. The government, of course, can exercise its power of eminent domain and "take" an easement for the installation of a utility line, for example. In such case, it must pay the landowner the value of the property right taken. The Court in *Lingle* stated that in cases of this type "where government requires an owner to suffer a permanent physical invasion of her property—however minor—it must provide just compensation." This is defined as a per se taking.

B. TOTAL TAKINGS

The right to own one's property carries with it the right to use it in a profitable fashion. Regulations that are so severe that they prevent the owner from using her property for any economically beneficial purpose are the equivalent of a direct appropriation, achieved through eminent domain. Some courts and scholars refer to this type of taking as "inverse condemnation." The effect of the government's action is to produce the financial equivalent of the direct condemnation of the land, a so-called total taking. According to the *Lingle* Court, "A second categorical rule applies to regulations that completely deprive an owner of 'all economically beneficial use' of her property." Where the regulated landowner can prove that a total taking has occurred, the Court treats the matter as a taking per se and requires the payment of just compensation, subject to very limited exceptions.

C. FORCED ENTRY EXACTIONS

The third category, land use exactions, involves the imposition by a land use approval board of a condition requiring a landowner to dedicate an easement allowing public access to her property or to convey title to a portion of the subject property to the locality. The effect of these land use conditions, or exactions, is to oust the landowner from a portion of her domain: the physical equivalent of a direct condemnation. Here, although the property owner is allowed to use the parcel as approved, subject to the condition, the Court senses a violation of the fundamental right to exclude others and it looks at the regulation with heightened suspicion.

D. ALL OTHER ALLEGED REGULATORY TAKINGS

When the facts of an alleged regulatory takings case fall outside one of these three "relatively narrow categories," regulatory takings challenges are governed by the standards set forth in Penn Central Transp. Co. v. New York City, 438 U.S. 104 (1978). All other types of land use regulations are subject to ad hoc factual inquires conducted by the Court under a variety of factors articulated in the *Penn Central* case. In this broad category, the Court presumes the constitutionality of the regulation, defers to the regulator, and requires the challenger to carry a heavy burden of proof that the regulation runs afoul of the standards used to measure the validity of the regulations.

§ 5. JUDICIAL TESTS FOR DETERMINING REGULATORY TAKINGS

A. PER SE CASES

Permanent physical invasions and total takings are classified by the *Lingle* Court as per se regulatory takings and, in these categories, much less proof is required of the challenging property owner. The first of these is illustrated by a regulation—imposed outside the context of an application for land use approval—that invades the owner's exclusive right of possession. The seminal Supreme Court case in this category is Loretto v. Teleprompter Manhattan CATV Corp., 458 U.S. 419 (1982). Ms. Loretto challenged a New York City law that required that she, as an owner of an apartment building, permit a cable television company to install its equipment on her property. She had not applied to the city for any land use permit. She simply was required by the law to allow the cable company access to her site and to allow equipment that occupied one-eighth of a cubic foot of space to be permanently attached to her building.

The court noted that, in this context, "[past] cases uniformly have found a taking to the extent of the [physical] occupation, without regard to whether the action achieves an important public benefit or has only minimal economic impact on the owner." In other words, outside the context of application for land use approvals, once the landowner proves that the government requires that another party, even a licensed utility provider, enter the property without consent, the owner has carried its required burden of proof. This, and no more, demonstrates a regulatory taking and requires just compensation to be paid.

The second per se category involves regulations that deny property owners all economically beneficial use of their property. The applicable test here is contained in Lucas v. South Carolina Coastal Council, 505 U.S. 1003 (1992). The trial court had found that the state's Beachfront Management Act rendered the landowner's two beachfront lots valueless. Regulations under the act prohibited development within a set-back line established to prevent erosion along the beach. The regulations did not permit landowners any variance for hardship caused by the prohibition. The Court recognized that "government hardly could go on if to some extent values incident to property could not be diminished without paying for every such change in the general law." It stated, however, that "regulations that leave the owner of land without economically beneficial or productive options for its use—typically, as here, by requiring land to be left substantially in its natural state—carry with them a heightened risk that private property is being pressed into some form of public service under the guise of mitigating serious public harm."

Relying on the trial court's fact-based determination, the Supreme Court found that all economically beneficial or productive use of the plaintiff's land had been taken. It went on to hold that the state must compensate the plaintiff for this value unless, upon remand, it can identify background principles of nuisance or property law that impose the same burden as the regulation. In other words, if the restriction imposed on the land by the regulation is "inherent in the title to the land," it is valid, even where all economically beneficial use is taken. Upon remand, no such principles were found, and the state was required to pay the plaintiff full value for his land.

In total takings cases, the burden of proof is on the challenging property owner to show that the land use regulation permits no economically beneficial use of the land. Once that burden is carried, if the regulator cannot show that nuisance doctrine in the state, or other background principles of law, impose the same burden on the land as the regulation, a regulatory taking has occurred and just compensation must be paid.

Lucas was decided in1992, the same year that the world's nations gathered at the Earth Summit in Rio de Janeiro. There, they adopted three critical agreements and formally declared their concerns with climate change and the inevitability of sea level rise, among many other consequences of global warming. Scalia, in writing for the majority in *Lucas*, said this: "The fact that a particular use has long been engaged in by similarly situated owners ordinarily imports a lack of any common law prohibition (though changed circumstances or new knowledge may make what was previously permissible no longer so). In the subsequent three decades, much has changed and much has been learned about the precarious development of coastal properties that may change judicial attitudes about land use regulations of development in increasingly vulnerable locations.

B. EXACTION CASES

Where land use agencies, when presented with an application to develop property, impose conditions that require owners to allow the public on their land or the government to take title to a portion of the land, courts must determine whether there is an essential nexus and rough proportionality between the condition imposed and the impact of the proposed development on the public. Cases clarifying the rules within this category are Nollan v. California Coastal Comm'n, 483 U.S. 825 (1987) and Dolan v. City of Tigard, 512 U.S. 374 (1994). The *Lingle* Court explains that *Nollan* and *Dolan* "involve a special application of the 'doctrine of unconstitutional conditions,' which provides that 'the government may not require a person to give up a constitutional right—here the right to receive just compensation when property is taken for a public use—in exchange for a discretionary benefit conferred by the government where the benefit has little or no relationship to the property.' "

An exaction is a condition imposed on the issuance of a development approval that requires the developer to dedicate land to the public, to allow the public access to his private land, or to pay a fee in lieu of such requirements. In City of Monterey v. Del Monte Dunes, 526 U.S. 687 (1999), the Court was asked to determine whether such fees are exactions. In *Monterey*, the Court declined to extend the *Nollan* and *Dolan* tests to cases in which the plaintiff challenges a denial of a development permit. In dicta, the Court stated that land use decisions conditioned approval of development on the dedication of property to public use and, by extension, fees in lieu of such dedication, were exactions.

Relatively few land use laws or decisions force the owner to convey an easement or portion of the title to the public to allow public access. Where they do, under *Nollan*, the regulator must show that there is an essential nexus between the condition imposed and the public purpose that is to be achieved by the condition. In addition, under *Dolan*, the Court requires the regulator to conduct individualized impact studies showing that the public benefits obtained by the condition imposed on the property are "roughly proportional" to the adverse impacts of the development on the community.

Applicability of this heightened degree of judicial scrutiny is limited to these conveyance cases—where the owner, in essence, is required to convey an easement or partial title to the government. In *Dolan*, the City of Tigard required a site plan developer to dedicate to the public a portion of her property lying within a 100-year floodplain for the improvement of a storm drainage system along a nearby creek and an additional 15-foot strip of land adjacent to the floodplain as a pedestrian and bicycle pathway. The conditions required the owner to convey an easement to the city allowing it and the public access to her land. The landowner objected, claiming that these requirements were not calculated to mitigate the impact of the proposed development and, therefore, constituted an uncompensated taking.

Citing *Nollan*, the Court stated that when dedication conditions are imposed on a land use permit, they must bear an "essential nexus" to a legitimate public objective. In view of clear findings regarding the seriousness of the flooding and traffic problems in the city and along the creek, such a nexus was found. The Court went on to establish, for the first time, a test that is to be used to determine "the required degree of connection between the [dedication conditions] and the projected impact of the proposed development." For this purpose, the Court wrote, "we think a term such as 'rough proportionality' best encapsulates what we hold to be the requirement of the Fifth Amendment. No precise mathematical calculation is required, but the city must make some sort of individualized determination that the required dedication is related both in nature and extent to the impact of the proposed development."

In *Dolan*, the Court found that the city had not shown why a dedicated public greenway, rather than a private one, was required in the interest of flood control. In regard to the pedestrian/bicycle path dedication, the Court held that the city's finding that the path "could offset some of the traffic demand" was too general. The city did not "meet its burden of demonstrating that the additional number of vehicle and bicycle trips generated by the petitioner's development reasonably relate to the city's requirement for a dedication of the pedestrian/bicycle pathway easement." The Court required the city to "make some effort to quantify its findings in support of the dedication . . . beyond the conclusory statement that it could offset some of the traffic demand generated." The imposition of the burden of proof on the regulator, the stricter scrutiny used, and the failure to presume the validity of the city's determinations are uniquely applicable to cases where land use exactions of this type are challenged.

In 2013, the Court decided Koontz v. St. John's River Water Management District, 570 U.S. 595 (2013), holding that *Nollan* and *Dolan* should not be limited to only those cases involved dedicatory exactions, but rather should be extended to permit denials and monetary exactions as well. The decision has called into question concerns about liability over engaging in the typical land use approval negotiation process, and the decision has left many open questions including: whether unconstitutional conditions challenges are regulatory takings claims or due process claims; and whether it applies only to individualized permit decisions or whether it also applies to legislative exactions that impose conditions on all developers pursuant to uniform formulas, such as wetland banking, solid waste impact fees, and mandatory affordable housing requirements.

In California Building Industry Association v. City of San Jose, 577 U.S. 1179 (2016), the U.S. Supreme Court denied certiorari, declining to review a California Supreme Court decision that upheld the city's imposition of affordable housing requirements on residential developments of 20 or more dwelling units. The California case, 61 Cal. 4th 435, noted that "like many other land use regulations, this condition simply places a restriction on the way the developer may use its property by limiting the price for which the developer may offer some of its units for sale." It stated that "we are aware of [no authority] suggesting that such use restrictions would constitute a taking of property outside the permit process or that a permit condition that imposes such use restrictions on a proposed development would constitute an exaction under the takings clause that would be subject to the *Nollan/Dolan* test. . . ."

C. ALL OTHER CASES: THE BALANCING TEST

According to the *Lingle* decision, when the facts involved in a regulatory takings case fall outside one of these "relatively narrow categories," the matter is governed by the standards set forth in Penn Central Transp. Co. v. New York City, 438 U.S. 104 (1978). In *Penn Central*, the Court adopted a multifactor balancing approach to review New York City's landmarks preservation law and found it constitutional. The landmarks preservation law identified 31 districts containing over 400 landmark buildings that were subject to special regulations. These buildings represented less than one-tenth of one percent of the buildings in the city. The owners of designated properties were required to apply for and obtain a certificate of appropriateness before altering the exteriors of their buildings. Penn Central, which owned Grand Central Terminal, applied for a certificate to allow it to build a modernistic 50-story tower over the station, to greatly alter the historic façade, and to demolish the grand interior lobby. When permission was denied by the Landmarks Commission, Penn Central claimed that the application of the law constituted a regulatory taking.

The Court characterized the type of regulatory takings analysis it uses regarding land use regulations as "essentially ad hoc factual inquiries."

It referred to several factors that previous Court decisions had relied on and balanced to arrive at its decision as to whether a regulatory taking had occurred. They included "the economic impact of the regulation on the claimant," "the extent to which the regulation has interfered with distinct investment-backed expectations," and "the character of the governmental action." In the Court's words, "A 'taking' may more readily be found when the interference with the property can be characterized as a physical invasion by Government. . . , than when interference arises from some public program adjusting the benefits and burdens of economic life to promote the public good." The Court saw a clear analogy between landmarks preservation laws of the type involved in the case and generally applicable zoning laws, "which have been viewed as permissible governmental action even when prohibiting the most beneficial use of the property." This and the fact that the subject property was "capable of earning a reasonable return" were instrumental in the Court's decision that no regulatory taking had been proven by Penn Central.

In Penn Central, the Court rejected the petitioners' argument that the regulation constituted a taking of the air rights above the terminal. The Court stated that the takings analysis "focuses . . . both on the character of the action and on the nature and extent of the interference with rights in the *parcel as a whole* . . . ." It was not until its holding in Murr v. Wisconsin, 137 S.Ct. 1933 (2017), that the Court provided specific guidance on how to identify the relevant "parcel as a whole." In Murr, the Court held that the Wisconsin Court of Appeals was correct to analyze the petitioners' two merged lots as a single parcel in assessing the effect of the challenged county "lot merger" ordinance and that enforcement of the merger provision did not result in a compensable taking.

In affirming the Wisconsin state court's decision, the Court established a three-factor test for determining what constitutes the relevant "parcel as a whole" in a regulatory takings analysis under the Fifth Amendment. The factors are

(1) "the treatment of the land under state and local law"; (2) "the physical characteristics of the land"; and (3) "the prospective value of the regulated land." Under this analysis, courts "should determine whether reasonable expectations about property ownership would lead a landowner to anticipate that his holdings would be treated as one parcel, or, instead, as separate tracts."

In Lake Oswego Preservation Society v. City of Lake Oswego, 360 Or. 115 (Or. 2016), the state legislature adopted a historic designation statute that allowed landowners to refuse the designation or to demand its removal later in their discretion. These refusal and removal provisions were designed to prevent regulated owners from suffering a regulatory taking. The issue in *Lake Oswego* was whether the removal powers could be exercised by subsequent landowners. The court concluded that they could not. It reasoned that purpose of the law was to allow for historic preservation while respecting the investment back expectations of affected landowners.

Subsequent landowners, who bought the property with knowledge of the historic designation, the court held, do not have reasonable expectations to use the property free from the limitations of historic designation.

§ 6. OTHER TAKINGS CONCERNS

A. PRE-EXISTING REGULATIONS

In Palazzolo v. Rhode Island, 533 U.S. 606 (2001), the Supreme Court held that a blanket rule that purchasers who take title with notice of an adopted land use regulation have no right to compensation "is too blunt an instrument to accord with the duty to compensate for what is taken." The Court held that a pre-existing regulation affecting a parcel is not necessarily inherent in the title taken by a purchaser or heir and cannot be used as a *per se* device to deny the right to compensation. In *Palazzolo*, the Court reversed a determination by the Rhode Island Supreme Court that a landowner had no right to challenge a regulation as a regulatory taking when the regulation was in place when title to the land was acquired.

Palazzolo owned a 20-acre parcel, most of which was salt marsh subject to tidal flooding. Development would have required significant fill, up to six feet in some places, to support any development. Under the Rhode Island coastal wetland regulations, development on the tidal wetlands portion of this site was prohibited unless the owner secured a special exception permit for an activity that serves a compelling public purpose that benefits the public as a whole. Since the responsible state agency, in denying Palazzolo's application to fill 11 of 18 tidal wetland acres for a private beach club, made a determination that this type of private development of tidal lands was not eligible for a special use permit, the Court held that the matter was ripe for review. In this unusual context, no further applications by Palazzolo were necessary to determine how the land could be developed under the regulations. An application for a permit to fill fewer acres would not change the determination that the requisite "public interest" was not being served. This constituted a final determination that there can be no filling of this class of wetlands for any ordinary land use and, therefore, the case was ripe for judicial review.

B. RIPENESS

In Williamson County Regional Planning Comm'n v. Hamilton Bank of Johnson City, 473 U.S. 172 (1985), the Court ruled that a landowner must wait until the governmental agency responsible for implementing land use regulations has reached a final decision regarding the application of the regulations to the affected property. This has created some confusion as to how many applications a landowner must submit, and for what intensity of use must be proposed, before it can be determined by the courts whether the regulation has gone far enough to constitute a taking. The *Palazzolo* decision leaves undisturbed the understanding that the landowner must submit applications for development activity sufficient to discover the permissible uses with a reasonable degree of certainty. It is not sufficient to submit, for example, a grandiose development proposal, obtain a denial, and then challenge the regulations as a regulatory taking. In the ordinary context, land use agencies have a high degree of discretion to soften the strictures of the regulations they administer. It remains the law that the landowner must submit applications that give the agency the opportunity to decide and explain the reach of a challenged regulation and a court to determine whether a taking has occurred. Blanket prohibitions of private development activity of the type involved in the Rhode Island coastal wetlands regulations are not found in most land use regimes.

The ripeness issue itself, however, was revisited and revised by the U.S. Supreme Court in Knick v. Township of Scott Pennsylvania, 139 S.Ct. 2162 (2019). The case involved a municipal ordinance requiring that "[a]ll cemeteries . . . be kept open and accessible to the general public during daylight hours." The Township claimed that the ordinance was a codification of common law. The Plaintiff countered that, in federal court, the ordinance constituted a taking of her property. The Third Circuit had held that the federal claim was not "ripe" under *Williamson County* because no state court had denied compensation under state inverse condemnation law. The majority claimed that precluding takings claims under *Williamson County* would, as a practical matter, prevent takings claims from being brought in federal courts. The Court held that *Williamson County* "was not just wrong" but that its "reasoning was exceptionally ill founded and conflicted with much of our takings jurisprudence." Further, "a property owner has a claim for a violation of the Takings Clause as soon as a government takes his property for public use without paying for it" so that the claim may be litigated at once in federal court under the Civil Rights Act, 42 U.S.C. § 1983 regardless of state "post-taking remedies that may be available" to the plaintiff because the right to just compensation rests on the Constitution and not any statute.

The ripeness issue bears on the U.S. Supreme Court's holding in *Palazzolo* regarding the effect of a preexisting regulation on the existence of a takings claim. The Court stated that it would be illogical and unfair to bar a regulatory takings claim because of the transfer of land after a regulation was adopted where the steps necessary to make the claim ripe were not taken by the previous owner. Here, Palazzolo's claim ripened after applications were submitted and denied, became ripe at that moment, and accrued to his benefit as owner.

A New York rule affected by the *Palazzolo* decision was articulated in four cases decided by the Court of Appeals on the same day in 1997. In Gazza v. DEC, 89 N.Y.2d 603, 679 N.E.2d 1035, 657 N.Y.S.2d 555 (N.Y. 1997), the landowner challenged the denial of a variance from a set-back requirement, which prevented any economical use on the affected parcel, a one-acre lot. The landowner purchased the parcel for $100,000 knowing it was subject to wetland regulations from which a variance from the State Department of Environmental Conservation (DEC) would have to be obtained to allow its development as a single-family parcel. The landowner estimated that, if the variances were granted, the land would be worth $396,000. Because the owner could not demonstrate that development under the variances would have no adverse impact on the tidal wetlands contained on the property, the request was denied.

The effect of the denial was to limit the use of the site to a catwalk, dock, and parking lot, activities which would have required variances from the village's zoning board. Rather than pursue these local variances, the landowner challenged the denials as a regulatory taking. The court noted that "[o]ur courts have long recognized that a property interest must exist before it may be taken." A taking claim may not "be based upon property rights that have already been taken away from a landowner in favor of the public." "[R]egulatory limitations that inhere in the title itself will bind a purchaser (citing Lucas v. South Carolina Coastal Council, 505 U.S. 1003 (1992)." See also, Anello v. ZBA, 89 N.Y.2d 535 (N.Y. 1997), Kim v. City of New York, 90 N.Y.2d 1 (N.Y. 1997), and Basile v. Town of Southampton, 89 N.Y.2d 974 (N.Y. 1997).

In Murr v. Wisconsin, 137 S.Ct. 1933 (2017), the U.S. Supreme Court made it clear that regulations in place at the time of purchase are relevant to the landowner's reasonable investment-backed expectations in a takings claim based on that regulation. Although the Court in *Palazzolo* held that an owner who acquired property before the adoption of a regulation is not necessarily barred from challenging it as a taking, Justice O'Conner's concurring opinion asserted that pre-existing regulations should be a relevant consideration. Since four dissenters joined this viewpoint, lower courts have generally accepted it, but the Court has never addressed this issue as a majority until *Murr*. In *Murr*, the majority stated: "[a] reasonable restriction that predates a landowner's acquisition, however, can be one of the objective factors that most landowners would reasonably consider in forming fair expectations about their property."

C. INVESTMENT-BACKED EXPECTATIONS

A majority of the U.S. Supreme Court in *Palazzolo,* while holding that the existence of a pre-existing regulation was not an absolute bar to a takings challenge, could not agree on whether it was relevant in determining whether the purchaser had reasonable investment-backed expectations, one of several factors used to determine if a taking has occurred under *Penn Central*. The Supreme Court remanded the case to the Rhode Island courts for a determination as to whether a taking had in fact occurred. In making its determination, the state court had to consider the debate of two concurring justices in the *Palazzolo* decision.

In her concurring opinion, Justice O'Connor noted that "Today's holding does not mean that the timing of the regulation's enactment relative to the acquisition of title is immaterial. . . ." She cited *Penn Central* for the proposition that several factors are considered in determining whether a regulation constitutes a taking, including whether it interferes with the landowner's legitimate investment-backed expectations. She noted that "the regulatory regime in place at the time the claimant acquires the property at issue helps to shape the reasonableness of those expectations."

Justice Scalia disagreed in a separate concurring opinion. In his view, "the fact that a restriction existed at the time the purchaser took title . . . should have no bearing upon the determination of whether the restriction is so substantial as to constitute a taking." He added that the investment-backed expectations "do not include the assumed validity of a restriction that in fact deprives property of so much of its value as to be unconstitutional."

D. TOTAL TAKING

The issue of most importance to regulators and landowners, of course, is the Court's position on the substantive matter of what constitutes a regulatory taking. On this point, the *Palazzolo* case made little progress. Palazzolo's property contained two upland acres and it was agreed that a substantial residence could be built on that land. The Supreme Court upheld the Rhode Island Supreme Court's determination that the coastal regulations did not constitute a total taking under Lucas v. South Carolina Coastal Council, 505 U.S. 1003 (1992).

Palazzolo submitted evidence that the land was appraised at $3,150,000 under a 74-lot subdivision proposal he had submitted for approval before his private beach club application. The parties agreed that the upland acres had a value of $200,000 for residential development. The Court noted that the development rights on the upland area did not constitute a token interest and that, therefore, the regulations did not leave the land economically idle as must be the case for the *Lucas* total taking rule to apply.

E. TOTAL TAKINGS AND THE PUBLIC TRUST DOCTRINE

That the tidal wetlands regulations of the state in the *Palazzolo* case do not constitute a total taking was affirmed, using additional rationale, in the decision of the Rhode Island Superior Court on remand. Palazzolo v. State, 2005 WL 1645974 (R.I. Super. 2005). The court held that the state's public trust doctrine was part of the background principles of common law in the state. Under that doctrine, Palazzolo had no right to develop the coastal marshlands in the first place. Further, the court found, any development on them would have been so costly that Palazzolo would have lost money attempting to fill, reinforce, and build on the tidal wetland basin, which constituted most of his acreage. Under *Penn Central*, his investment-backed expectations were not frustrated. Under *Lucas*, the regulations were not a total taking.

F. THE TOTAL PARCEL RULE

The Court also refused to consider Palazzolo's claim that the relevant parcel to use in a takings case is the land affected by the regulation, in this case the

18 wetland acres. The majority decision recognized that what parcel of land should be considered when a takings claim is raised is the "persisting question of what is the proper denominator in the takings fraction." Since this issue was not presented in the petition for certiorari to the Court, the majority refused to consider it.

This issue surfaced in Tahoe-Sierra Preservation Council, Inc. v. Tahoe Regional Planning Agency, 535 U.S. 302 (2002). The Court considered whether a moratorium on development constitutes a temporal taking (a total taking for a limited period). It held that a moratorium on all development was not, by itself, a taking. At issue in the *Tahoe* case was the validity of a moratorium on development adopted by the Tahoe Regional Planning Agency to protect the unique environment and tourist-based economy of the Lake Tahoe region. The agency was created by a compact between the legislatures of California and Nevada. The compact gave land use authority over development in the region to the Lake Tahoe Regional Planning Agency. The objective of the regional agency was to coordinate and regulate development in the Lake Tahoe Basin and to conserve its natural resources. The agency was directed by the two states to develop environmental threshold carrying capacities including standards for air quality, water quality, soil conservation, vegetation preservation, and noise. This new legislation halted temporarily all development in critical environmental areas in the region, giving the agency the time it required to consider, draft, adopt, and implement needed regulations.

The legal challenge to the 32-month moratorium was launched by a non-profit corporation representing 400 owners of land in the critical environmental areas of the Basin who had purchased their parcels prior to the changes in the compact legislation. They claimed that the moratorium on the development of their properties was a regulatory taking. Their essential argument was that, even though the regulation does not take the future right to develop, the temporary taking of all development rights, for the 32-month period, itself violates the constitution.

The owners' argument raised the issue of whether property rights in a single parcel of land are severable for the purpose of takings law. If property rights are defined in segments and one of those segments, such as the present right to develop, is totally prohibited by a regulation, does that regulation constitute a total taking under *Lucas*? Broadly stated, the question was whether a regulation that totally limits the use of a portion of the land, whether limited by time, use, or space, deprives its owner of all economically beneficial use under the constitution. Specifically, the legal question addressed by the *Tahoe* case was whether a moratorium on development of land constituted a regulatory taking, *per se*.

The U.S. Supreme Court refused to declare that a moratorium is a categorical taking, regardless of the circumstances. In arriving at this conclusion, the Court also rejected the argument that property interests should be segmented, in time, use, or function, for the purpose of determining whether the interests have been taken.

The *Tahoe* court held that a moratorium, like most other land use regulations, is subject to an ad hoc inquiry that considers the circumstances of the case such as the character of the regulation, the public interest to be achieved, the extent to which it interferes with the owner's investment-backed expectations, and how severely they are affected by the regulation. In other words, a moratorium may be a taking, under the circumstances of a particular case, but is not categorically so. In the *Tahoe* case, the Court noted that the lower federal courts had concluded that the 32-month period was not unreasonable and that the Agency had acted in good faith during that time to do what needed to be done before the moratorium could be lifted. It further recognized that the consensus of land use planners is that moratoria are an essential tool of successful development.

Moratoria prevent landowners from rushing to develop, causing inefficient and ill-conceived growth before a comprehensive plan can be adopted. They prevent regulators from making hasty decisions that would disadvantage landowners as well as the public. The Court recognized that land values can actually increase during a moratorium and that the public and all landowners are reciprocally benefited by moratoria because they protect everyone's interest against immediate construction that might be inconsistent with the provisions of the plan that is ultimately adopted. Of course, moratoria can be enacted that are not reasonable in these ways and they are vulnerable, under *Tahoe*, to challenge.

Note that in Arkansas Game & Fish Comm'n v. United States, 568 U.S. 23 (2012), the Court held that government-induced flooding that is temporary may be a taking, depending on circumstances. Factors pertinent to whether temporary flooding effects a taking include severity, duration, character of parcel, and owner's expectations regarding parcel's use.

G. JUDICIAL TAKINGS

In Stop the Beach Renourishment, Inc. v. Florida Dep't of Environmental Protection, 560 U.S. 702 (2010), the Court unanimously upheld the Florida Supreme Court's decision that the state does not, through beach restoration projects, effect a facial taking of beachfront property owners' littoral rights of accretion and direct contact with water. Nonetheless, the case is significant because four Justices suggested that a "judicial taking" could occur; in other words, the Takings Clause applies to the judicial branch just as to other branches. Four Justices expressed skepticism about takings applying to judge-made law and one Justice did not participate.

§ 7. REMEDIES

In First English Evangelical Lutheran Church v. County of Los Angeles, 482 U.S. 304 (1987), where the government adopted an interim ordinance prohibiting the construction of structures in a flood zone, the plaintiffs challenged the ordinance as a temporary taking. The Supreme Court held that if a regulation is determined to have taken property, the Takings Clause would require that compensation be paid during the time the regulation was in effect. Simply repealing the law would not be enough.

In *First English*, a Los Angeles County interim flood control law was challenged as a regulatory taking. For the purpose of the appeal, the court assumed as true the landowner's allegation that the law affected a total taking of its property value and was therefore invalid as a regulatory taking. This allowed it to consider the question of whether a landowner is entitled to damages for a temporary taking. Such a holding would allow an owner compensation for the period running from the enactment of a regulation that constitutes a taking to the time it is invalidated by the courts. Previously, the rule had been that compensation must be paid for the period beginning with the date a regulation is declared invalid as a taking and only if the government insists on enforcing it. This prior rule allowed the government to amend the offensive regulation and avoid compensating the landowner for the taking even when the regulation had been in effect for many years, as it had been in this case.

The court held "that where the government's activities have already worked a taking of all use of property, no subsequent action by the government can relieve it of the duty to provide compensation for the period during which the taking was effective." It went on to say that this holding does "not deal with the quite different questions that would arise in the case of normal delays in obtaining building permits, changes in zoning laws, variances, and the like which are not before us." On remand, the California courts determined that the flood control law in this case did not constitute a taking. The "temporary takings rule" of the *First English* case, however, endures.

In Wheeler v. City of Pleasant Grove (Wheeler III), 833 F.2d 267 (11th Cir. 1987), the court of appeals expanded on *First English,* by examining how damages for temporary takings should be determined in inverse condemnation proceedings. In this case, a landowner sold a piece of property in the City of Pleasant Grove to a developer who planned to build a 120-unit apartment building on the site. After finding that the proposed land use complied with applicable zoning ordinances, the Pleasant Grove Planning Commission issued a building permit, and the plaintiffs began work in preparation for construction. Following strong public opposition to the project, and a referendum that confirmed that a majority of the city's residents were against it, the city council passed an ordinance that outlawed the construction of apartment complexes in the city limits and stopped plaintiffs' construction. In a prior decision, the court found that the ban on apartment development and the stop work order under these circumstances constituted a regulatory taking. In this case, it turned to the determination of the appropriate measure of damages owed to the plaintiffs.

It began its damage analysis by pointing out that "the owner's loss is measured by the extent to which governmental action has deprived him of an interest in property," and that "the value of that interest, in turn, is determined by isolating it as a component of the overall fair market value of the affected property." When, as here, a temporary taking is at issue, the court looked at whether there was an effect on the property's potential for producing income or on an expected profit. The court remanded the case with instructions that the appropriate measure of damages should be the loss in income-producing potential suffered over the 16 months that the ordinance was in effect.

Upon remand, the district court ruled that the plaintiffs were not entitled to a damage award because their injury did not arise from the unconstitutional enactment of the ordinance, but rather from the prior withdrawal of the building permit under the city's misinterpretation of the ordinance, and the case was again appealed to the circuit court. In Wheeler v. City of Pleasant Grove (Wheeler IV), 896 F.2d 1347 (11th Cir. 1990), the court overturned the district court, affirming that the plaintiff's injury was caused by the unconstitutional ordinance. It then again set out to determine the appropriate level of damages. Using the formula articulated by the court in *Wheeler III*, it awarded damages based on the "market rate of return computed over the period of the temporary taking on the difference between the property's fair market value without the regulatory restriction and its fair market value with the restriction."

CHAPTER 6

OTHER CONSTITUTIONAL AND STATUTORY LIMITS ON LAND USE REGULATION

§ 1. INTRODUCTION

In addition to federal and state constitutional constraints on local control of land use, a number of federal and state statutes have been enacted since the 1980s that either limit or preempt local control in the areas of religious land uses, housing, and telecommunications. This chapter begins with a discussion of issues that arise when land use decision-making intersects with the First Amendment in the regulation of adult business uses and signs and billboards. This is followed by a discussion of federal statutes including: the Religious Land Use and Institutionalized Persons Act, which limits governments' ability to restrict religious uses; the Americans with Disabilities Act and its applicability to local land use decision-making; the Federal Fair Housing Act Amendments of 1988, which impact how local governments can regulate in the area of group homes and certain other housing related issues; and the Telecommunications Act of 1996, which narrows local governments' ability to fully control the regulation of the siting of cellular and wireless facilities. Following a discussion of the Civil Rights Act, the chapter focuses on a host of state laws designed to regulate local control of certain land uses.

There are a number of reasons why the federal and state governments have inserted themselves into what has traditionally been a local land use process. Among these are the inability of many local officials to respond effectively to the concerns of the community that amount to NIMBY (Not In My Back Yard) for uses often believed to be LULUs (Locally Unwanted Land Uses) and the attitudes of those in the community who take a BANANA (Build Absolutely Nothing Anywhere Near Anyone) perspective on future development around them. Perhaps it is because too many local officials adopted a NIMTOO (Not In My Term of Office) approach to land use planning and zoning decisions that advocacy organizations and business organizations were successful in convincing Congress to enact strong federal legislation designed to limit local control over the siting of certain types of land uses.

§ 2. THE FIRST AMENDMENT

The First Amendment guarantees of freedom of expression have produced a body of caselaw that includes significant opinions impacting the ability of local governments to regulate land uses that are subject to First Amendment protections. This section focuses on sexually-oriented businesses. Another important area is sign regulation and this is covered in Chapter 10.

A. REGULATING ADULT BUSINESS

A variety of ordinary commercial uses may be excluded from communities as municipalities exercise their zoning power to safeguard the public health and welfare. The desire of local officials to exclude adult business uses, however, has proved more difficult since the regulation of sexually-oriented businesses is subject to First Amendment considerations. In one of the leading cases on issue, Young v. American Mini Theatres, Inc., 427 U.S. 50 (1976), the Supreme Court upheld a zoning ordinance that prohibited any "adult" movie theater, book store, and similar establishments within 1,000 feet of any other such establishment, or within 500 feet of a residential area, after finding that the regulation did not violate the First Amendment. In reaching this conclusion, the court stressed that, although the First Amendment protects sexually explicit forms of communication from total suppression, municipalities have the power to place reasonable restrictions on the time, place, and manner in which these materials are showcased or sold, if the regulations are necessary to further some significant governmental interest. In *Young*, the Supreme Court upheld the exclusionary ordinance finding that the regulation was needed to develop an overall plan for the community and to regulate the use of commercial property within its borders.

In accordance with this approach, some courts have been more willing to invalidate ordinances on First Amendment grounds where the record is void of any evidence showing the regulation furthers a significant governmental interest. For example, in Secret Desires Lingerie, Inc. v. City of Atlanta, 266 Ga. 760 (Ga. 1996), the Supreme Court of Georgia struck down an ordinance that was enacted to regulate lingerie modeling studios in the City of Atlanta after finding that the ordinance violated the owners' constitutional right to free speech. Although the city argued that the ordinance was needed to curb the undesirable, secondary effects that had become associated with the studios, specifically prostitution, the court found that the city had not presented specific evidence to support its contention. Based on the lack of specific evidence linking the lingerie modeling studios to the undesirable secondary effects the ordinance was enacted to combat, the court concluded that the ordinance violated the property owner's constitutional right to free speech.

Secondary effects studies have become an essential condition precedent to the enactment of local adult use ordinances to support the legitimate governmental interest in regulating these uses. City of Renton v. Playtime Theatres, Inc., 475 U.S. 41 (1986), as well as City of Erie v. Pap's A.M., 529 U.S. 277 (2000), make it clear that municipalities may rely on similar studies in other jurisdictions to support their regulations. Justice O'Connor, however, warned in City of Los Angeles v. Alameda Books, Inc., 535 U.S. 425 (2002), that municipalities cannot get away with shoddy data or reasoning and that "the municipality's evidence must fairly support the municipality's rationale for its ordinance."

The Supreme Court has been willing to uphold local ordinances restricting adult uses when the municipality can show that the regulation is necessary to further a significant governmental interest and the manner chosen is the least restrictive means. In *City of Renton*, for example, the plaintiffs brought suit challenging the constitutionality of a zoning ordinance that prohibited adult motion picture theaters from locating within 1,000 feet of any residential zone, single or multiple-family dwelling, church, park, or school. The Supreme Court held that the ordinance was a valid governmental response to the serious problems created by adult theaters that satisfied the dictates of the First Amendment. Specifically, after finding that the ordinance was "a valid governmental response to the serious problems created by adult theaters," the Court held that it was within the city's power to regulate adult theaters by dispersing them throughout the city, or by effectively concentrating them in one geographic area, so long as they are not prohibited from operating within the city altogether. Similarly, in *City of Los Angeles v. Alameda Books, Inc.*, the Supreme Court, in a plurality opinion, upheld an ordinance that prohibited operation of multiple adult businesses in a single building after finding that the city reasonably relied on police department studies, which correlated crime patterns with concentrations of adult business, when it enacted the ordinance. Based on this evidence, the Court rejected the plaintiff's constitutional arguments, and concluded that the regulation was a valid exercise of the police power aimed at furthering the city's significant interest in reducing crime.

Although courts are willing to uphold exclusionary zoning ordinances that seek to regulate the location and operation of adult business, they have struck down municipal ordinances that seek to ban sexually-oriented businesses altogether. In Schad v. Borough of Mount Ephraim, 452 U.S. 61 (1981), the Supreme Court held that a municipal ordinance, which prohibited the operators of an adult bookstore from introducing a coin-operated machine in their store that would permit customers to watch a live nude dancer behind a glass panel, violated the store owners' First Amendment rights to free speech. In reaching this conclusion, the Court rejected the municipality's argument that the regulation was a reasonable time, place, and manner restriction on the operators' First Amendment right to free speech, and that it was needed to further the borough's plan to create a commercial area that caters to the immediate needs of the surrounding residents. The Court asserted that live nude dancing was a form of expression protected by the First Amendment, and thus, an ordinance that excluded live entertainment completely, while allowing a variety of other compatible commercial uses in the same area, could not be considered a reasonable restriction.

Regulation of uses physically located in one space, but delivered to the public via cyberspace, is a new frontier in the land use regulation arena. For example, the Court in Voyeur Dorm, L.C. v. City of Tampa, 265 F.3d 1232 (11th Cir. 2001) was called upon to interpret the regulation of adult entertainment establishments in Tampa. Specifically, the city's ordinance defined these establishments as premises "on which is offered to a member of the public or any person for consideration, entertainment. . . ." Voyeur Dorm is a multi-million dollar "virtual" business, operating a website that provides 24-hour a day internet transmissions portraying the lives of unrelated residents of a dwelling in Tampa, Florida. The city attempted to shut down Voyeur Dorm as a prohibited use in the district. The Court determined that the business was not regulated by the zoning ordinance since members of the public could not physically attend the premise to patronize the entertainment, and that the zoning ordinance could not reach into "virtual space" on the Internet.

Flava Works, Inc. v. City of Miami, 609 F.3d 1233 (11th Cir. 2010), involved an adult use similar to the one in Voyeur Dorm. The court distinguished the cases, however, explaining that while Voyeur Dorm was not an adult use *establishment* prohibited in Tampa's residential zones, Flava Works' use was an adult *business*, which was prohibited under Miami's residential zoning. These cases raise the importance of clarity in the drafting of zoning ordinances, particularly when it comes to regulating adult uses. It is not uncommon for adult use restrictions to be voided for vagueness.

Local governments may, in addition to regulating the location of sexually-oriented business, regulate the operation of the businesses through certain licensing requirements. Examples of licensing approaches include regulating structural issues, minimum levels of lighting in the establishments, the availability of alcohol on the premises, and hours of operation. These regulations must also undergo First Amendment analysis to ensure that they do not unconstitutionally impinge on free speech.

The law surrounding the regulation of adult business uses through zoning is contentious and remains somewhat unsettled. The case of Schad v. Borough of Mount Ephraim, 452 U.S. 61 (1981) held that adult business owners were entitled to challenge a zoning ordinance that banned all live entertainment as facially overbroad. While the Court found that the borough failed to justify its ordinance offering no evidence that live entertainment was incompatible with commercial business activities, this case is illustrative of how unsettled the law is, as it contains five separate opinions with a plurality opinion of three Justices and three concurring opinions representing the views of four Justices which all differ from each other, as well as one dissenting opinion representing the views of two Justices. More than twenty years later, in *City of Los Angeles v. Alameda Books*, the Supreme Court is still issuing plurality opinions. Recent changes on the Court may bring more clarity to this area when the Court has an opportunity to revisit these issues.

§ 3. FEDERAL CONTROL

In general, our federal system permits individual communities to define their own specific community development goals, and to employ various land use planning and land use control tools allowing them to achieve their individual notions of the "public good." As a result, when Congress restricts the ability of local governments to make certain land use decisions, the federal influence on state and local land use planning and zoning authority becomes most apparent.

There are a growing number of subjects over which the federal government exercises some level of control over local land use regulation. These include: satellite earth stations; receiving dishes and antenna; airports; hazardous waste facilities; wireless communications; gaming facilities; and discrimination within housing including, but not limited to, manufactured housing and group homes. The following examples are illustrative of this phenomenon.

A. AMERICANS WITH DISABILITIES ACT

The Americans with Disabilities Act of 1994 (ADA), codified at 42 U.S.C. § 12000, prohibits public entities from discriminating against individuals on the basis of their disability. The Act states in part that, "no qualified individual with a disability shall, by reason of such disability, be excluded from participation in, or be denied the benefits of the services, programs, or activities of a public entity, or be subject to discrimination by any such entity." In addition, public entities are required under the Act to make "reasonable accommodations" for individuals with disabilities. Although it was largely undisputed that the ADA prevented municipalities from discriminating against individuals on the basis of their disability when hiring employees for government positions, many municipalities challenged the Act's application to zoning ordinances, arguing that zoning does not constitute a "service, program, or activity." While the statute did not contain a specific reference to zoning or land use controls, a technical assistance manual published by the Department of Justice did refer to zoning as an example of a public entity's obligation to modify its policies, practices and procedures to avoid discrimination.

The Second Circuit, in Innovative Health Systems v. City of White Plains, 117 F.3d 37 (2d Cir. 1997), examined the anti-discrimination provisions of the ADA in order to determine what effect, if any, these provisions had on the local zoning power. In reaching the conclusion that the ADA prohibits municipalities from discriminating against individuals on the basis of their disability when enacting and implementing zoning ordinances, the court asserted that making zoning decisions is part of the "normal function of a governmental entity" and therefore can be considered an "activity" or "program" under the Act. This interpretation accords with previous Supreme Court jurisprudence previously prohibiting discriminatory zoning practices.

The Supreme Court held in City of Cleburne v. Cleburne Living Center, 473 U.S. 432 (1985), that municipalities could not require a special operating permit for a proposed group home that would house mentally disabled individuals. The court struck down the city ordinance after finding that the city had no legitimate interest in requiring a special use permit for such facilities, while other care and multi-dwelling facilities, such as an apartment house, sorority, hospital or nursing home, were freely permitted. Based on this evidence, the Court concluded that the city's failure to present evidence to show that it had a rational basis for requiring additional operating permits for group homes housing mentally disabled persons, violated the Due Process Clause, making the ordinance invalid and void.

Examples of "reasonable accommodations" in zoning under the ADA include waiver or modification of rules prohibiting elevators in buildings where this would prohibit certain people from residing in the buildings (see Oconomowoc Regional Economic Community Action Program, Inc. v. City of Middletown, 294 F.3d 35 (2d Cir. 2002)); and a variance from the distance restrictions for the operation of group homes (see Residential Programs v. City of Milwaukee, 300 F.3d 775 (7th Cir. 2002)). Often, ADA claims are coupled with alleged violations of the federal Rehabilitation Act, 29 U.S.C. § 794, which also prevents discrimination based upon disability.

B. FEDERAL FAIR HOUSING ACT (FHA) AND THE FAIR HOUSING ACT AMENDMENTS OF 1988 (FHAA)

Like the ADA, the language of FHA does not refer specifically to land use planning or zoning. However, courts have interpreted the language to encompass land use regulation. The FHAA makes it unlawful to refuse to sell or rent, or otherwise make unavailable or deny, a dwelling to any person because of race, color, religion, sex, familial status, disability or national origin. 42 U.S.C. § 3604. Specifically, the phrase "or otherwise make unavailable or deny" has been interpreted to prohibit discriminatory zoning practices and land use regulations. Much of the litigation under the FHA involves municipal defendants and challenges to land use policies on the ground of their discriminatory intent or discriminatory effect.

(i) Discriminatory Intent

Prior to the 1988 Amendments, courts around the country were struggling to decide whether a showing of discriminatory intent was required by the Fair Housing Act. In Village of Arlington Heights v. Metropolitan Housing Development Corp., 429 U.S. 252 (1977), the Supreme Court held that evidence showing a "discriminatory effect" was insufficient to invalidate a zoning regulation under the Fourteenth Amendment, and that under normal circumstances, a "discriminatory purpose" or intent would be required. As far as due process and equal protection were concerned, the Court held that, although suburban communities are generally permitted to enact exclusionary zoning ordinances, the requirements of the Fair Housing Act might necessitate a different standard as to public housing. To answer this question, the Supreme Court remanded the case back to the Seventh Circuit. Metropolitan Housing Development Corp. v. Village of Arlington Heights, 558 F.2d 1283 (7th Cir. 1977). The Seventh Circuit first addressed the critical factors to be considered and stated, in essence, that: 1) "discriminatory effect" is relevant when it has a greater adverse impact on one racial group, or when it serves to perpetuate racial segregation in a community; 2) the question of discriminatory intent is relevant so long as there is sufficient evidence presented, even where the evidence is inconclusive; 3) the interest of the defendant in taking such action is pertinent if it is a governmental body acting within the scope of legitimate authority; and 4) courts should be more reluctant to grant relief when affirmative action to compel action is requested than when a plaintiff simply seeks relief from a defendant's refusal or prohibition. The Seventh Circuit held that the Village of Arlington Heights had a statutory obligation under the Fair Housing Act to refrain from zoning policies which effectively foreclosed construction of publicly financed housing for low-income families in its borders.

(ii) Disparate Impact

Courts have continued to rely on the Supreme Court's holding in *Village of Arlington Heights,* following the adoption of the 1988 Amendments to the Fair Housing Act. For example, in Huntington Branch, NAACP v. Town of Huntington, 844 F.2d 926 (2d Cir. 1988), the Second Circuit applied the disparate impact test of Title VII employment discrimination cases to strike down a refusal to rezone for multi-family housing. Pursuant to this test, discriminatory effect, not intent, is the appropriate standard. Thus, if the plaintiff can establish that a particular land use regulation has a discriminatory effect, the burden shifts to the municipality to "prove that its actions furthered, in theory and in practice, a legitimate, *bona fide* governmental interest and that no alternative would serve that interest with less discriminatory effect."

Applying this test, the Second Circuit concluded that the refusal to rezone, in order to enable a multi-family, subsidized housing development to be located outside the urban renewal area to which such projects were restricted by the local zoning ordinance, created "a strong prima facie showing of discriminatory effect." The court was particularly concerned with the disproportionate impact the ordinance had on minority communities.

In 2015 the Supreme Court held that "disparate-impact claims are cognizable under the [FHA]," following the previous interpretations of the U.S. Department of Housing and Urban Development (HUD) and all 11 federal courts of appeals that had ruled on the issue. Texas Dep't of Hous. & Cmty. Affairs v. Inclusive Communities Project, Inc., 576 U.S. 519 (2015). However, HUD and the 11 courts of appeals have not all applied the same criteria for determining when a neutral policy that causes a disparate impact violates the FHA. In an attempt to harmonize disparate impact analysis across the country, HUD finalized regulations in 2013 that established uniform standards for determining when such practices violate the act. Yet, instead of adopting the 2013 HUD standards, the Inclusive Communities court adopted its three-step burden-shifting test for disparate impact claims under the FHA. On remand, the federal district court held that the Inclusive Communities plaintiffs had not proven a prima facie case of disparate impact under the new standard announced by the U.S. Supreme Court. Inclusive Communities Project, Inc. v. Texas Dep't of

Hous. & Cmty. Affairs, 2016 WL 4494322 (N.D. Tex. 2016).

(iii) Failure to Accommodate

Under the FHAA, a refusal to make reasonable accommodations in rules, policies, practices, or services, when such accommodations may afford handicapped persons an equal opportunity to use and enjoy their dwellings, constitutes discrimination. In Howard v. City of Beavercreek, 276 F.3d 802 (6th Cir. 2002), the Sixth Circuit examined the FHAA's accommodation provision and determined that, to prove that a particular accommodation is "necessary" under the Act, a disabled person must show that, but for the accommodation, he will likely be denied an equal opportunity to enjoy the housing of his choice. In this case, the plaintiff sought a variance from the City of Beavercreek to build a six-foot high fence on his property. The plaintiff alleged that the variance was necessary because he suffered from post traumatic stress disorder, which prevents him from using and enjoying his property without the fence. The court upheld the city's denial of the variance, concluding that it did not constitute a violation of the FHAA because even if the variance could be regarded as a reasonable accommodation for the plaintiff's disability, the city's denial was not likely to deny the property owner the right to live in housing of his choice, and thus did not violate the FHAA. Following this holding, the Sixth Circuit explicitly held in Smith & Lee Associates, Inc. v. City of Taylor, 102 F.3d 781 (6th Cir. 1996), that under the FHAA, the plaintiff bears the burden of demonstrating that the desired accommodation is necessary to afford equal opportunity.

(iv) Occupancy Restrictions

The FHAA provides an exception for land use regulations aimed at proscribing the maximum occupancy permitted in a particular size or type of dwelling. Typically, these "maximum occupancy restrictions" cap the number of occupants per dwelling in relation to available floor space, or the number and type of rooms. These restrictions are usually enacted to protect the public health and safety by preventing overcrowding; thus, these regulations apply uniformly to all residents, living in all different types of dwelling units. In City of Edmonds v. Oxford House, Inc., 514 U.S. 725 (1995), the Supreme Court examined this exemption when reviewing the merits of a declaratory judgment action initiated by the City of Edmonds. The city sought a declaration that its single-family residential zoning provision limiting the maximum number of unrelated occupants of single-family residents did not violate the FHAA prohibition against handicap discrimination. At issue was the city's refusal to make a reasonable accommodation for a group home that would house more than five unrelated recovering alcoholics and drug addicts. The Supreme Court held that the zoning provision governing areas zoned for single-family dwelling units—which defined family as persons related by genetics, adoption, marriage, or any group of five or fewer unrelated persons—sought to define what constitutes a family unit, not the maximum number of occupants that a dwelling unit could house. In accordance with this interpretation, the court concluded that the ordinance did not fall within FHAA's absolute exemption for total occupancy limits, which applied only to numerical ceilings.

(v) Duty to Affirmatively Further Fair Housing

In 2015, HUD promulgated a landmark rule intended to give teeth to the Fair Housing Act's requirement that state and local governments that receive federal assistance "affirmatively further" fair housing. Affirmatively Furthering Fair Housing (AFFH), 80 Fed. Reg. 42272–01 (July 16, 2015). As the Department noted, the rule sought to give shape to the statute's "affirmatively further" requirement that, while previous acknowledged, had been largely ignored. Under the AFFH Rule, state and local governments that receive certain federal funds are required to produce an Assessment of Fair Housing (AFH) through which program participants identify and evaluate fair housing issues, factors contributing to fair housing issues, and also address how to integrate fair housing into local planning processes.

On July 23, 2020, HUD announced the issuance of a new Affirmatively Furthering Fair Housing (AFFH) regulation, called "Preserving Community and Neighborhood Choice" (PCNC) regulation, a final rule that took effect 30 days after it is published in the Federal Register. It replaced the 2015 AFFH rule. Controversy surrounds the adoption of the PCNC due to lack of public notice and comment.

Strong opponents to the regulation, including the American Bar Association, assert that PCNC redefines the very meaning of fair housing, stripping away virtually all requirements for program participants to meaningfully fulfill their fair housing obligations, while removing any consequential oversight by HUD. A resolution before the ABA House of Delegates in February 2021 explained, "With the PCNC rule in effect, program participants will no longer be required to conduct any sort of fair housing planning. Thus, there will be no need for participants to identify fair housing goals, develop plans to accomplish those goals or to maintain records documenting such efforts. Program participants will not be required to gather, let alone evaluate data, analysis or public input regarding segregation, integration, discrimination, and systemic racism within their jurisdictions. Any actions taken by program participants that have the effect of perpetuating segregation both racial and economic will not be used to show that they are failing to meet their AFFH obligations. HUD will not actively monitor program participants' performance regarding their compliance with the AFFH mandate." (ABA House of Delegates Resolution 112, Feb. 2021).

On January 26, 2021 President Biden issued an Executive Order announcing plans to reverse the PCNC regulation, and on June 10, 2021 HUD published a final version of a new AFFH rule, which requires state and local governments to demonstrate that they are working to address discrimination and segregation in order to be eligible for HUD funds (see, 86 FR 30779).

C. TELECOMMUNICATIONS ACT OF 1996

To facilitate the development of the burgeoning cellular/wireless industry, Congress passed the *Telecommunications Act of 1996* ("TCA"), codified at 47 U.S.C. § 151 et seq. The law was enacted "to provide for a pro-competitive, de-regulatory national policy framework designed to accelerate rapidly private sector deployment of advanced telecommunications and information technologies and services. . .by opening all telecommunications markets to competition. . ." To further this end, Congress enacted a number of substantive and procedural limitations upon the authority of state or local governments to regulate the construction of facilities for wireless communication services. In Preferred Sites, LLC v. Troup County, 296 F.3d 1210 (11th Cir. 2002), the court acknowledged that state and local governments have legitimate concerns with regard to the siting of wireless towers, including aesthetic impacts and the costs associated with the use of public rights-of-way. The court noted, however, that "Congress recognized zoning decisions by state and local governments had created an inconsistent array of requirements, which inhibited both the deployment of personal communications services and the rebuilding of a digital technology-based cellular telecommunications network."

The primary limitations on local zoning authority under TCA provide that state and local regulation of the placement, construction, and modification of personal wireless facilities: (1) cannot unreasonably discriminate among providers of functionally equivalent services; or (2) prohibit the provision of wireless services in general. In Sprint Spectrum, LP v. Willoth, 176 F.3d 630 (2d Cir. 1999), the Second Circuit examined these limitations to determine the exact nature of their preemptive effect. The court asserted that the first limitation, which prevents municipalities from unreasonably discriminating among providers of functionally equivalent services, "provides localities with the flexibility to treat facilities that create different aesthetic, visual, or safety concerns differently to the extent permitted under generally applicable zoning requirements, even where those facilities provide functionally equivalent services." In other words, the court concluded that the TCA does not prohibit local governments from taking the location of a proposed telecommunications tower into consideration when deciding whether to require a more probing inquiry, and when deciding whether to approve a construction permit, even though this may result in discrimination between providers of functionally equivalent services.

With respect to the second limitation, the *Sprint Spectrum* court concluded that, although the Act prohibits local governments from regulating personal wireless service facilities in such a way as to prohibit remote users from reaching such facilities, or to prevent providers from filling gaps in their service, local governments may still refuse a construction permit if the service gap can be closed by less intrusive means. Thus, the court maintained that local governments retain the right to deny building permits for superfluous towers, and to impose reasonable conditions, such as requiring the use of an available, less sensitive site, a pre-existing structure, or camouflage before issuing a building permit.

Another important aspect of the TCA is the requirement in Section 332(c)(7)(B)(ii) that governments act on requests to "place, construct, or modify" wireless facilities "within a reasonable period of time" after the filing of such requests. To clarify what was meant by "reasonable time," in 2009 the FCC issued a ruling on what is referred to as the "Shot Clock," establishing "presumptively reasonable periods" for local action on wireless communication siting applications. See, In re Petition for Declaratory Ruling to Clarify Provisions of Section 332(c)(7)(B), 25 FCC Rcd 11157 (F.C.C. 2010); In re Petition for Declaratory Ruling to Clarify Provisions of Section 332(c)(7)(B), 24 FCC Rcd 13994 (F.C.C. 2009). The Supreme Court upheld the shot clock requirements in City of Arlington, Tex. v. F.C.C., 569 U.S. 290 (2013).

A number of updates have been issued to the "shot clock" rulings. In 2014 the FCC addressed the provision regarding when a permit was "deemed granted," stating, "After a careful assessment of the statutory provision and a review of the record, we establish a deemed granted remedy for cases in which the applicable State or municipal reviewing authority fails to issue a decision within 60 days (subject to any tolling . . .) on an application submitted pursuant to Section 6409(a) [1455(a)]. We further conclude that a deemed grant does not become effective until the applicant notifies the reviewing jurisdiction in writing, after the time period for review by the State or municipal reviewing authority as prescribed in our rules has expired, that the application has been deemed granted." See, In the Matter of Acceleration of Broadband Deployment by Improving Wireless Facilities Siting Policies, 29 F.C.C.R. 12865, 30 F.C.C.R. 31, 2014 WL 5374631 (F.C.C. 2014).

In 2018, another Order was issued to help promote the deployment of small wireless facilities (5G), providing the following timeframes for decisions:

(i) Review of an application to collocate a Small Wireless Facility using an existing structure: 60 days.

(ii) Review of an application to collocate a facility other than a Small Wireless Facility using an existing structure: 90 days.

(iii) Review of an application to deploy a Small Wireless Facility using a new structure: 90 days.

(iv) Review of an application to deploy a facility other than a Small Wireless Facility using a new structure: 150 days. See, In the Matter of Accelerating Wireless Broadband Deployment by Removing Barriers to Infrastructure Investment; WT Docket No. 17–79; WC Docket No. 17–84 Declaratory Ruling and Third Report and Order.

The TCA also requires the decision of the municipality must be in writing and supported by substantial evidence in the written record (§ 332(c)(7)(B)(iii)). In T-Mobile South, LLC v. City of Roswell, 574 U.S. 293 (2015), the Court held that this provision requires localities to provide the reasons for such denials in writing; however, those reasons do not have to appear in the written denial letter as long as they appear in some other written record, are sufficiently clear, and are provided or made accessible to the applicant essentially contemporaneously with the written denial notice.

Despite the controversy in communities and in the literature regarding electromagnetic field emissions (EMFs) from wireless communications facilities, the TCA expressly preempts state and local government regulation of the placement, construction, and modification of personal wireless service facilities on the basis of the environmental effects of radio frequency emissions to the extent that such facilities comply with the FCC's regulations concerning such emissions. § 332(c)(7)(B)(iv).

D. THE RELIGIOUS LAND USE AND INSTITUTIONALIZED PERSONS ACT

The Religious Land Use and Institutionalized Persons Act (RLUIPA), 42 U.S.C. § 2000 et seq., adopted in 2000 contains five substantive provisions with respect to land use regulations. The statute prohibits government from taking action that will create a "substantial burden" on the right of an individual to exercise religion freely, absent a showing that the action is the "least restrictive means" of furthering a "compelling government interest." By its terms, RLUIPA only applies where a substantial burden is imposed: (1) in connection with a federally-funded activity; (2) where the burden affects interstate commerce; or, (3) with respect to land use decisions, where the burden is imposed in the context of a scheme whereby the government makes "individualized assessments" regarding the property involved. The general prohibition prevents governments from implementing a land use regulation in a manner that imposes a substantial burden on the religious exercise of a person, including a religious assembly or institution, unless it can be demonstrated that the action is the least restrictive means of furthering a compelling governmental interest. 42 U.S.C. § 2000cc(a).

RLUIPA also protects against the unequal treatment between religious and nonreligious assemblies and institutions. 42 U.S.C. § 2000cc(b)(1). The statute further prohibits discrimination "against any assembly or institution on the basis of religion or religious denomination," 42 U.S.C. § 2000cc(b)(2), and it prevents governments from totally excluding religious assemblies from a jurisdiction. 42 U.S.C. § 2000cc(b)(3)(A). Lastly, RLUIPA prohibits governments from unreasonably limiting "religious assemblies, institutions, or structures within a jurisdiction." 42 U.S.C. § 2000cc(b)(3)(B).

Prior to the enactment of RLUIPA, courts across the country were already sensitive to the effects that local land use regulations could have on an individual's right to exercise their religion. For example, in State ex rel. Lake Drive Baptist Church v. Village of Bayside Bd. of Trustees, 12 Wis. 2d 585 (Wis. 1961), the Lake Drive Baptist Church brought an action in mandamus to compel the village to rezone their land and issue a building permit, so that it could build a new church to house its congregation. While the court acknowledged that villages and cities have the power to zone with respect to churches pursuant to their power to regulate land use, it also asserted that this power can only be exercised to promote the general welfare. In striking down the ordinance, the court held that any land use regulation that imposes a substantial burden on the exercise of religion is inconsistent with the promotion of general welfare, and thus cannot be considered a valid exercise of the police power.

In State ex rel. Wisconsin Lutheran High School Conference v. Sinar, 267 Wis. 91 (Wis. 1954), however, the same court refused such relief. There, the plaintiff, a private, non-profit religious corporation, brought suit to compel the city building inspector to issue a permit for construction of a private high school, with appurtenant athletic grounds and facilities. The plaintiff argued that the ordinance, which forbid the erection of private high schools, but permitted the construction of public high schools, violated his constitutional right to exercise his religion. The Supreme Court of Wisconsin rejected the claim, concluding that the ordinance was valid because it rested upon a permissible classification. The court asserted that the "essential differences between government and governed are so great that the two are in different classes *per se* at any time when governmental functions are involved." The court concluded, "no ordinance is void by reason of discrimination, alone, merely because it gives a preference to the government, acting in its governmental capacity, which it withholds from private corporations or individuals."

Landmark preservation ordinances have also been attacked on constitutional grounds where they have had the effect of preventing religious groups from altering or demolishing their places of worship. For example, in First Covenant Church of Seattle v. City of Seattle, 120 Wash. 2d 203 (Wash. 1992), the church sued the city, alleging that the city's ordinance designating the church as a landmark structure, and placing specific controls upon the church's ability to alter its exterior façade, violated its right to freely exercise its religion, as guaranteed by the federal and state Constitutions. After finding that the exterior and interior of the church were "freighted with religious meaning" that would be understood by those who viewed it, thus making the maintenance of the façade a form of protected speech, the court concluded that the regulations at issue violated the Constitution by impermissibly infringing on its free expression. Under RLUIPA, a zoning regulation includes a landmarking law. 42 U.S.C. § 2000cc–5(5).

Zoning ordinances that seek to prohibit churches from operating homeless shelters on their premises have also run into constitutional challenges. In First Assembly of God of Naples v. Collier County, 20 F.3d

419 (11th Cir. 1994), writ denied, 513 U.S. 1080 (1995), members of the First Assembly Church of Naples, and residents of a homeless shelter that operated on the church premises, brought an action challenging the enforcement of the county's zoning regulations, which forced the closure of the shelter. The Eleventh Circuit concluded that the enforcement of the ordinances, which were neutral and of general applicability, did not prevent the church from practicing its religion, and therefore did not violate the free exercise clause of the First Amendment.

In a similar case, Daytona Rescue Mission, Inc. v. City of Daytona Beach, 885 F.Supp. 1554 (M.D. Fla. 1995), the Daytona Rescue Mission Church, which had sought and was denied a permit to operate a food bank and homeless shelter under the city zoning code, alleged that the zoning code violated the church's rights under the Constitution. The district court held that the zoning code did not violate its rights under the Constitution's free exercise clause. The court based its determination on the fact that the provisions in question were neutral and generally applicable, and worked to advance significant government interests: specifically preserving the city's zoning code and regulating food banks and shelters. As the court noted, "the City Code regulates conduct, not religious beliefs." After the enactment of RLUIPA, the Second Circuit, in Fifth Avenue Presbyterian Church v. City of New York, 293 F.3d 570 (2d Cir. 2002), found that the church had demonstrated a likelihood of success in establishing that its provision of outdoor sleeping space for the homeless effectuates a sincerely held religious belief and is therefore protected under the Free Exercise Clause.

Following the enactment of RLUIPA in 2000, courts continue to focus on the specific burdens that such ordinances place on religious institutions, and the governmental interest that is furthered through their enactment, in determining whether or not the specific regulations violate the Constitution. In Elsinore Christian Center v. City of Lake Elsinore, 270 F.Supp.2d 1163 (C.D. Cal. 2003), the Elsinore Christian Center brought an action against the city and five members of the city council, challenging the city's refusal to issue a conditional use permit. The court held that the city's denial, which prevented the church from operating on land being used by a tenant as a food market in an economically blighted area, placed a "substantial burden" on religious exercise within the meaning of RLUIPA. In reaching this conclusion the court stated that, even if the city's justification could be considered "compelling," lack of evidence showing that the decision was the least restrictive means of furthering its interests was fatal to its case.

In another case decided by the Seventh Circuit, Civil Liberties for Urban Believers, Christ Center, Christian Covenant Outreach Church v. City of Chicago, 342 F.3d 752 (7th Cir. 2003), an association of area churches and five individual churches sued the City of Chicago to challenge an ordinance requiring special use approval to operate a church center in commercial and business areas, and limiting operation of them in manufacturing areas, alleging that the regulation violates RLUIPA and the First Amendment. The Seventh Circuit held that the ordinance did not impose a "substantial burden" on religious exercise within the meaning of RLUIPA, nor did it violate the Act's nondiscrimination provision. The court reached this conclusion after finding that the restrictions did not render the use of real property for religious purposes in the city "impracticable" or discourage the construction of churches within city limits. Thus, because the record showed that the regulation was motivated by legitimate considerations involving land use, and that the ordinance placed churches on equal footing with nonreligious assembly uses, the court concluded that the ordinance did not violate the free expression clause of the First Amendment. Defining exactly what constitutes a religious exercise under RLUIPA continues to be the subject of litigation. Educational activities such as schools, retreat centers and camps, and social services facilities that allow organizations to carry out their closely held religious beliefs have enjoyed protection under the statute. See, e.g., Westchester Day School v. Village of Mamaroneck, 504 F.3d 338 (2d Cir. 2007), and DiLaura v. Township of Ann Arbor, 112 F. App'x 45 (6th Cir. 2004).

The scope of RLUIPA is generally well settled with some courts finding it extends to environmental regulations, Fortress Bible Church v. Feiner, 694 F.3d 209 (2d Cir. 2012) and sewage requirements. United States v. County of Culpeper, 245 F.Supp.3d 758 (W.D. Va. 2017). Other courts have refused to extend RLUIPA to things such as fire codes, Petra

Presbyterian Church v. Village of Northbrook, 489 F.3d 846 (7th Cir. 2007) and accessibility requirements under the Americans with Disabilities Act, Anselmo v. County of Shasta, 873 F.Supp.2d 1247 (E.D. Cal. 2012).

According to a 2020 report published by the Civil Rights Division of the U.S. Department of Justice on the 20th Anniversary of RLUIPA, the number of RLUIPA land use cases handled by the Department is growing. Since its enactment, the Justice Department opened 148 formal land-use investigations, they have filed 25 RLUIPA land use lawsuits, and they have filed 29 *amicus* briefs involving RLUIPA's land use provisions. The report also contains a summary of many of the lawsuits the DOJ has been involved with in the last twenty years. See, https://www.justice.gov/crt/case-document/file/1319186/download. The statistics are a clear indication that the federal government is actively engaged in prosecuting local governments for failure to comply with the statute. In fact in December 2016, as a result of reported perceptions that municipal, county, and other state and local officials were insufficiently familiar with the land use provisions of RLUIPA, and that litigation could be avoided if local officials were better informed of their obligations under RLUIPA early in the process, the Civil Rights Division sent a letter to mayors and other municipal officials highlighting the requirements of RLUIPA. See, https://www.justice.gov/crt/page/file/918596/download. This is particularly important to local governments because under 42 U.S.C. § 1988(b) the prevailing party in a RLUIPA lawsuit may, in the discretion of the court, be entitled to reasonable attorney's fees, which has led to million dollar plus costs to municipalities who found themselves on the losing end of RLUIPA litigation.

The DOJ published a full statement with Q & A about the land use provisions in RLUIPA in 2018. It is an excellent resource and it contains citations to key RLUIPA cases. See, https://www.justice.gov/crt/page/file/1071251/download.

E. CIVIL RIGHTS ACT

The Civil Rights Act of 1866, passed pursuant to congressional authority under the Thirteenth Amendment to eliminate the badges and incidents of slavery, was followed over a century later by the Civil Rights Act of 1968, 42 U.S.C. § 3601 et seq., which includes provisions designed to assure fair housing practices in the United States. Section 1983 of the Civil Rights Act authorizes a cause of action where an individual or a municipality (see, Monell v. Department of Social Services, 436 U.S. 658 (1978)) violates a constitutional right. Section 1983 claims are a popular litigation strategy as prevailing parties are entitled to recover attorneys fees. Cloutier v. Town of Epping, 714 F.2d 1184 (1st Cir. 1983), invoked the protections of the Civil Rights Act to challenge town policy that allegedly discriminated against mobile home parks and apartment developers. The First Circuit concluded that the defendants cannot be held liable under Section 1983 of the Civil Rights Act unless the constitutional wrong complained of was committed pursuant to official policy.

Although Section 1983 of the Civil Rights Act does not specifically provide for immunity, courts have found an implied common law immunity for the legislative acts of local legislative bodies. This extends to land use agencies and officials who are protected with absolute immunity from Section 1983 liability when they function in an adjudicatory capacity. In Kaahumanu v. County of Maui, 315 F.3d 1215 (9th Cir. 2003), the operator of a commercial wedding business, and a pastor of a church who conducted some of the ceremonies arranged by the wedding operator, brought action against the county council and its members under Section 1983 of the Civil Rights Act after the council denied it a conditional use permit to conduct a commercial wedding business on tropical beach-front residential property. The Ninth Circuit held that the council's denial of the conditional use permit was an administrative act, rather than a "legislative" act, and thus, council members were not entitled to absolute legislative immunity under Section 1983. In reaching this determination the court focused on the fact that the denial did not change the county's comprehensive zoning ordinance, or the underlying policies, and stressed that the decision affected the applicants only, and not the general welfare of the public at large.

A holding by the Third Circuit, in United Artists Theatre Circuit, Inc. v. Township of Warrington, 316 F.3d 392 (3d Cir. 2003), accords with the First and

Ninth Circuits' analysis of the Civil Rights Act, as it is applied in the land use context. In this case, the owners and operators of movie theaters brought a Section 1983 action against the township and its supervisors for alleged due process violations after the board allegedly delayed approval for the construction of a new theater so that it could obtain a voluntary impact fee offered by a competing developer. With regard to the plaintiff's substantive due process claims, the court observed that the "core concept" of due process is "protection against arbitrary action," and that "only the most egregious official conduct can be said to be 'arbitrary in the constitutional sense.' " Thus, in determining whether an official action was arbitrary in the constitutional sense, the court asserted that the appropriate standard is whether or not the action "shocked the conscious."

F. OTHER AREAS OF FEDERAL INVOLVEMENT

While is it impossible to catalogue all federal laws that have some type of pre-emptive effect, the Federal Railway Safety Act has been held to preempt all local railroad safety legislation (except state law in an area where the Secretary of Transportation has not issued a regulation or order, and stricter state law is necessary). See, CSX Transportation, Inc. v. City of Plymouth, 86 F.3d 626 (6th Cir. 1996) (holding that a local ordinance prohibiting trains from obstructing streets for more than five minutes was preempted by the federal act).

Local regulation of television satellite dishes and antennas was specifically preempted by FCC regulation because of widespread aesthetic concerns, particularly in suburban communities, when satellite receiving dishes became popular in the 1970s and thereafter. 47 C.F.R. § 25.104 et seq. See, Loschiavo v. City of Dearborn, 33 F.3d 548 (6th Cir. 1994) (holding that the FCC regulation precluding enforcement of zoning restrictions regulating satellite dishes created a private right of action under 42 U.S.C. § 1983); but see, Camco Cable Services, Inc. v. City of Lauderhill, 13 F.Supp.2d 1329 (S.D. Fla.1998) (holding that the federal regulation protecting the right of antenna users to receive satellite signals does not confer a federal right upon a cable services company, and therefore does not confer standing to bring § 1983 action).

The National Manufactured Housing and Safety Standards Act, 42 U.S.C. §§ 5401–5426, has been held to preempt city ordinances imposing greater safety requirements for mobile or manufactured homes. See, Scurlock v. City of Lynn Haven, Florida, 858 F.2d 1521 (11th Cir. 1988). However, the act does not preempt zoning of mobile home locations. See, King v. City of Bainbridge, 276 Ga. 484, 577 S.E.2d 772 (2003).

The Stewart B. McKinney Homeless Assistance Act, 42 U.S.C. § 11301 et seq., which requires federal agencies to make surplus and underutilized federal property available to lease to organizations wishing to provide housing for homeless persons, preempts local zoning ordinances. See, United States v. Village of New Hempstead, New York, 832 F.Supp. 76 (S.D.N.Y.1993).

CERCLA (Comprehensive Environmental Response, Compensation and Liability Act) has been held to preempt conflicting state or local regulation ("conflict preemption"). See, e.g., United States v. Denver, 100 F.3d 1509 (10th Cir. 1996) (finding that a EPA order requiring the site owner to do on-site solidification of soils contaminated by radioactive waste preempted a local zoning ordinance which prohibited the maintenance of hazardous waste).

§ 4. STATE CONTROL

As discussed above, the federal government has intervened through statutes and other regulations to limit local control over certain types of land uses. State governments may also play a significant role in limiting or restricting local decision-making control in certain areas including, but not limited to: mining, agricultural uses, group homes, day-care centers, and the siting of power plants. Examples of how states may control or impact local land use decisions follow.

A. MINING

One aspect of local land use planning in which states have been particularly active is mineral extraction and other mining activities. The State of New York, for example, has sought to regulate mining activities throughout the state pursuant to The Mined Land Reclamation Law. The New York Court of Appeals, in Gernatt Asphalt Products, Inc. v. Town of Sardinia, 87 N.Y.2d 668 (N.Y. 1996), examined the preemptive nature of the law and concluded that, although the Act prohibits municipalities from enacting ordinances that directly relate to the operation of extractive mines, it does not prohibit municipalities from enacting ordinances which regulate general land use within the municipality, notwithstanding their incidental effect on mining. The court held that the town was not preempted from determining that mining should not be a permitted use of land within the town, and from enacting zoning amendments in accordance with that determination. In fact, the court asserted that such a change would be perfectly consistent with the town's authority to regulate land use generally within its borders. In states such as New York, the state agency charged with administration of the law may retain other permit approval powers that impact a local government's ability to eliminate mining within their jurisdiction.

Somewhat related to the preemption issues in the mining cases is the subject of hydrofracking which is addressed in Chapter 9.

B. AGRICULTURE

Agricultural uses are also a frequent target for statewide preemptive legislation. For example, the State of North Carolina passed a number of statutes in an effort to limit local discretion with regard to the siting and operation of various agri-businesses. The Supreme Court of North Carolina examined the preemptive effect of the Swine Farm Siting Act and the Animal Waste Management Systems component of existing statewide regulations in Craig v. County of Chatham, 565 S.E.2d 172 (N.C. 2002). In this case, a county agri-business council challenged ordinances enacted by the county board to regulate the operation, construction, and expansion of swine farms in the county. The Supreme Court of North Carolina held that, although the enactment and operation of a statewide law does not necessarily prevent a county from regulating in the same field, local regulation in the area will be excluded if it can be shown that the legislature intended to preempt the entire field. Here, the court found that the State of North Carolina created a complete and integrated system for swine farm regulation in the state, thereby preempting county regulation of swine farms. In support of this conclusion the court also noted that the county failed to show that its more stringent regulations were somehow needed to protect the health of local residents.

Right-to-farm laws are another technique employed by states to prevent nuisance-type lawsuits against farmers for the impacts of routine farming operations that may become inconsistent with changing community character as surrounding farmland is converted to residential development. These laws typically provide that established farming operations are not nuisances as a matter of law. While popular, an Iowa right-to-farm law that contained a nuisance immunity provision was found facially unconstitutional in Bormann v. Board of Supervisors in and for Kossuth County, 584 N.W.2d 309 (Iowa 1998), cert. den., 525 U.S. 1172 (1999), because the court determined that it resulted in a statutorily imposed easement on neighboring landowners forcing them to bear the burden of an activity that otherwise would have been a nuisance, and that this amounting to an uncompensated taking of property.

The topic of urban agriculture is discussed in Chapter 9.

C. GROUP HOMES

A number of states have sought to limit local decision-making authority over the siting and construction of group homes for the mentally ill. Pursuant to New York Mental Hygiene Law § 41.34, a municipality may request a hearing before the Commissioner of Mental Health to voice its objections concerning the establishment of a group home in the community. The commissioner must sustain the municipality's objection if it is determined that "the nature and character of the area in which the facility is to be based would be substantially altered as a result of establishment of the facility." Where there is no evidence to show that the facility will "substantially alter" the nature and character of the surrounding community, the commission may override the municipality's objections. In Jennings v. New York State Office of Mental Health, 90 N.Y.2d 227 (N.Y. 1997), the Mayor of the City of Albany challenged the determination of the Commissioner of Mental Health approving a new supervised community residence for individuals with mental illness in an area that already had several community residences. The Court of Appeals rejected the mayor's objections finding that the evidence supported the commissioner's conclusion that the additional facility, which would house 10 mentally disabled adults, would neither result in an over concentration of similar facilities in the area nor substantially alter the nature and character of the neighborhood.

§ 5. GEOGRAPHIC INFORMATION SYSTEMS AND TECHNOLOGY IN LAND USE

The advent of computerized mapping and the global positioning system (GPS) has resulted in a powerful tool for land use practitioners, Geographic Information Systems (GIS). Information from a GIS database can take the form of charts, graphs, tables, and spreadsheets and provide information in ways that could not be accomplished through the use of traditional maps. These charts and graphs provide information to help solve geographic challenges, or problems involving spatially related information. For example, a municipality can now overlay soil data on top of a traditional map and a zoning map to identify areas that may not be well suited for particular development. Currently, 42 states have laws relating to GIS, the majority of which establish a statewide system or clearinghouse for the exchange of GIS data between governmental entities.

The most important part of a GIS is the accuracy of the data it relies upon. Information that is out of date or inaccurate can have a significant impact on the reliability of the end product. For example, a pond or river that was plotted using GPS after the spring thaw might not represent the same pond or river in late August. Land use lawyers need to be familiar with GIS technology so that, where appropriate, they may find expert witnesses in GIS for trials to enable important GIS data to be admitted into evidence.

GIS information can be a persuasive tool in court. The U.S. Marine Corps was able to use the technology to show a lack of alternatives for placement of military housing in Surfrider Foundation v. Dalton, 989 F.Supp. 1309 (S.D. Cal. 1998). Having the GIS "map" admitted in court can fall under one of several hearsay exemptions depending on how the information is used, such as computer generated records, business records, or public records.

The use of GIS and computerized mapping by municipalities is becoming routine. These maps not only represent a benefit to municipal employees and boards by eliminating the need to pour through non-electronic maps, but access to the system through freedom of information laws may also help the community at large. For example, a corporation wishing to build around pre-existing gas/electric lines that may already be mapped on a municipal GIS database, could save thousands of dollars and months of time in locating the ideal building site if the municipal data is accessible to the private developer. GIS data will also contribute to the information available to environmental justice advocates and will empower communities to address disparate impacts of land use decision-making.

Recent litigation has focused on whether municipally-owned GIS datasets are considered "records" and therefore obtainable by the public under state freedom of information laws. Municipalities are at times reluctant to turn over GIS databases to the public (and private sector) due to the fact that there has been a significant public investment in developing the GIS system. The Connecticut Supreme Court in Director, Information Technology of the Town of Greenwich v. Freedom of Information Commission, 874 A.2d 785 (Conn. 2005), held that the town improperly denied a citizen request for electronic GIS data based upon unfounded homeland security concerns, and that the GIS data did not qualify under the "trade secret" exemption to disclosure.

Another growing area in technology and land use revolves around the use of drones. Drones are being used to help in land surveying and drones can be employed to monitor and assist in zoning enforcement, as well as in more sophisticated mapping than the earlier GIS technology. In Singer v. City of Newton, 284 F.Supp.3d 125 (D. Mass. 2017) aspects of a local ordinance regulating drones was struck down as preempted by FAA regulations. In 2020 the FAA published a fact sheet on small unmanned aircraft systems (https://www.faa.gov/news/fact_sheets/news_story.cfm?newsId=22615). Legislation has been proposed in Congress to, among other things, designate lower airspace for the use of civil unmanned aircraft systems (UAS), to provide for the privacy rights of property owners, and to authorize state, local, and tribal governments to enact reasonable restrictions on a UAS within 200 feet of the ground or a structure.

States are starting to enact regulations that will soon impact local land use and planning regulation over autonomous vehicles. See, Petruzzi, Anthony, "Automotive Autonomy: Why Planning Authorities Must Begin to Consider How to Transition Into a Driverless World," ___ The Urban Lawyer ___ (2021).

CHAPTER 7

SMART GROWTH AND OTHER FLEXIBLE LAND USE STRATEGIES

§ 1. INTRODUCTION

"Smart Growth" admits of no clear definition. It provides a popular label for a growth strategy that addresses current concerns about traffic congestion, disappearing open space, non-point source pollution, the high cost of housing, higher local property taxes, longer commutes, and the diminishing quality of community life. To achieve smart growth, government must take two related actions. The first is the designation of discrete geographical areas into which private market growth pressures are directed. The second is the designation of other areas for recreation, conservation, and environmental protection.

Smart Growth attempts to reign in the ill effects of sprawling land use patterns, which result gradually as the land use blueprint contained in the municipal zoning ordinance is built out, one project at a time. If local governments are to revise their basic blueprint and accomplish smarter growth, how should they proceed? State law provides numerous planning tools for municipalities to use in designating growth and conservation areas. The principal among these, of course, is the comprehensive plan, the ideal document to account for the rational allocation of land use. Local comprehensive plans usually include a statement of goals and objectives regarding the community's physical development and describe the specific actions to be taken to provide for the long-range growth and development of the locality.

Local plans, properly drafted to accomplish smart growth, recommend and lead to the adoption of a host of land use techniques that are capable of creating smarter, less wasteful, and more economically-efficient development patterns. These include, among others, a temporary moratorium on development, followed by the adoption of any of a number of land use controls: cluster zoning, performance zoning, overlay zoning, floating zones, traditional neighborhood zoning, planned unit development zoning, and the transfer of development rights. In addition, comprehensive plans can guide the creation of capital budgets and the funding of infrastructure (water, sewer, roads, lighting, sidewalks, and schools) in areas where denser development is needed and the purchase of open space or development rights in areas where land should be preserved.

Comprehensive plans can, in fact, be quite detailed, incorporating maps, graphs, and studies that can locate designated growth areas precisely and spell out the techniques to be used to encourage development in those areas. This authority is highly elastic and can be stretched to fit all development contexts, from urban and suburban to rural, where communities wish to control growth. Growth control measures, including goals, objectives, and techniques contained in the comprehensive plan—then adopted into a variety of local laws—were validated over thirty years ago by the New York Court of Appeals in Golden v. Planning Bd. of Ramapo, 30 N.Y.2d 359, 334 N.Y.S.2d 138, 285 N.E.2d 291 (N.Y. 1972).

In *Golden,* the town adopted a comprehensive plan and zoning law that restricted the growth of development until the town could meet the resulting increased pressure on the infrastructure. The developers argued that the phased development controls were intended to prohibit subdivisions and restrict population growth, which is not authorized under the zoning enabling legislation. New York's highest court disagreed, holding that "phased growth is well within the ambit of existing enabling legislation." The court further held that Ramapo was not acting to close its borders to growth, but was trying to prevent the negative effects of uncontrolled growth. It found that Ramapo's zoning was not in violation of the Federal or State Constitutions because a rational basis for phased growth exists where "the existing physical and financial resources of the community are inadequate to furnish the essential services and facilities which a substantial increase in population requires."

§ 2. MORATORIA

A moratorium on development suspends the right of property owners to obtain development approvals while the community takes time to consider, draft, and adopt land use plans or rules to respond to new or changing circumstances not adequately dealt with by its current laws. At the local level, moratoria figure into growth management and smart growth by giving communities experiencing growth pressures time to rethink their land use plan and laws and adopt a new, smarter approach that more properly manages growth.

A moratorium can be used by a community just prior to adopting its first comprehensive plan and zoning law or before undertaking a comprehensive revision of its plan and zoning. The moratorium prevents developers and property owners from rushing to develop their land under current land use rules that the community is in the process of changing. By so doing, it helps to accomplish the purpose of the new rules by giving them the broadest possible applicability and preventing development that is inconsistent with them. Moratoria are also used to prevent development for a time while the government agency decides whether to acquire land for a public use or until capital improvements are made, as in the *Golden* case.

A moratorium can be seen as the most extreme land use action that a regulatory agency can take, because it suspends completely the rights of all affected owners to use their property. In this light, regulators are advised to precede the adoption of a moratorium by findings that confirm the necessity of this action. What are the conditions that mandate the imposition of a moratorium? Are there no available alternatives less burdensome on property rights? Why are the existing land use plans and ordinances not adequate? What recent circumstances have occurred that justify the adoption of the moratorium? How serious and urgent are these circumstances?

What hard evidence is there to document the necessity of the moratorium? Does the regulatory agency, in fact, have the legal authority to declare a moratorium? For how long? Under what circumstances?

Recall that local governments get their authority to enact land use law from their state legislatures. In many states, the courts have held that the delegation of land use control—the authority to adopt plans, zoning, and development regulations—carries with it the implied power to adopt moratoria. Some states, however, restrict this power. New Jersey statutes, for example, limit moratoria to matters involving an imminent threat to the public health and their duration to no more than six months. Statutes in California, Minnesota, Montana, and Utah also limit the duration of development moratoria. Moratoria must be adopted in compliance with the formal provisions of law for zoning amendments, in most states, and localities that rush to adopt them bypassing such steps (such as publishing a public notice and holding a public hearing) risk having the moratorium invalidated by the courts. See, Droste v. Bd. of Cty. Comm'rs of Pitkin, 159 P.3d 601 (Colo. 2007).

The Maryland-National Capital Park and Planning Commission adopted subdivision regulations that prevented development of some land for up to three years by placing those lands in a reserve for schools and other public buildings, and for parks, playgrounds, and other public purposes. The effect of the law was to prevent all development, including grading, vegetative removal, or "any use whatsoever." Landowners filed suit claiming that the reservation of their land was an unconstitutional taking without just compensation. The Court of Appeals of Maryland held that the law stripped the landowners of all reasonable use of their property for the three-year period and was tantamount to a taking of property without compensation as required under the Fifth Amendment. Maryland-Nat'l Capital Park and Planning Comm'n v. Chadwick, 286 Md. 1, 405 A.2d 241 (Md. App. 1979). The court noted, however, that the ruling was narrow and not intended to invalidate reservations or moratoria of more limited duration and severity.

The Texas Supreme Court held that Chapter 212 of the Texas Local Government Code prohibits local governments from applying moratoria to violate developers' vested rights. See, City of Lorena v. BMTP Holdings, LP, 56 Tex. Sup. Ct. J. 1115, 409 S.W.3d 634 (Tex. 2013).

A 32-month moratorium was attacked by affected landowners as a taking, but upheld by the United States Supreme Court in Tahoe-Sierra Preservation Council, Inc. v. Tahoe Regional Planning Agency, 535 U.S. 302 (2002). The Tahoe Regional Planning Agency adopted a moratorium on development in the Lake Tahoe region in response to issues with the clarity of the lake. The agency needed time to consider the best approach to regulating development that threatened the pristine condition of Lake Tahoe, the region's principal environmental and economic asset. Developers challenged the moratorium as a regulatory taking. Specifically, the developers argued that even a temporary taking of the present right to develop the land was, on its face, a taking in violation of the Constitution. The Court held that a moratorium is not a per se taking and should be evaluated based on the particulars of the case such as "the character of the regulation, the public interest to be achieved, the extent to which it interferes with the owner's investment-backed expectations, and how severely they are affected by the regulation." The Court held that the agency's 32-month moratorium was not unreasonable and served the interests of all parties involved.

§ 3. TIMING AND AVAILABILITY OF PUBLIC FACILITIES

A little understood dimension of local land use control is the relationship between zoning and capital improvements. Zoning prescribes where development is to go and how much of it there is to be in any given place. As land is developed according to the zoning law and map, new homeowners and business operators need public services including water, sewer, transportation, schools, libraries, firehouses, police protection, etc. The cost of most of this infrastructure is borne either by the new residents and business owners who pay the developer for installing on-site improvements, or by the taxpayers of the community, who must bear the cost of public services not subsidized by higher levels of government. By adopting detailed plans for infrastructure construction and expansion, and coordinating such plans closely with the provisions of zoning, the community can control how much development will occur in any given part of the community and thereby limit its capital facility and public service costs.

In Golden v. Planning Bd. of Ramapo, 30 N.Y.2d 359, 334 N.Y.S.2d 138, 285 N.E.2d 291 (N.Y. 1972), New York's highest court, while holding that it would not countenance growth controls as a form of exclusion, ratified an 18-year growth control plan adopted by a single suburban community in the New York metropolitan area. The town combined provisions in its comprehensive plan—property tax exemptions, an 18-year municipal infrastructure budget and build out plan—with variances for hardships caused and a number of other novel techniques to create an unprecedented growth management regime. Over the objections of a strong dissent and lamenting the lack of a state legislated regional plan, the high court found implied powers in the state zoning and subdivision enabling laws for such a plan.

In response to a rapid increase in the number of housing units sprawling throughout the community, the City of Petaluma, California, adopted a moratorium on development and then adopted resolutions to control the housing development growth rate. The resolutions were termed the "Petaluma Plan" and extended over a five-year period. The plan limited the number of new dwelling units to 500 per year and established a "greenbelt" to control urban expansion. The city argued that the plan was intended to ensure reasonable and orderly development over the five-year period while the petitioner claimed that the actual purpose of the plan was to close city borders to unwanted growth. In Construction Industry Ass'n of Sonoma County v. City of Petaluma, 522 F.2d 897 (9th Cir. 1975), the landowners claimed that the plan was arbitrary and unreasonable and in violation of the Due Process Clause of the Fourteenth Amendment. The Ninth Circuit Court of Appeals held that the ordinance was a valid exercise of the police power. The court noted that "public welfare" was broad enough to cover "Petaluma's desire to preserve its small town character, its open spaces and low density of population, and to grow at an orderly and deliberate pace."

The City of Livermore enacted an ordinance that conditioned the issuance of residential building permits on the availability of educational, sewage disposal, and water supply facilities. In Associated Home Builders of the Greater Eastbay, Inc. v. City of Livermore, 18 Cal. 3d 582, 135 Cal. Rptr. 41, 557 P.2d 473 (Cal. 1976), developers challenged the constitutionality of the ordinance claiming that it sought to stop population growth within the city. The superior court agreed with the developers and issued a permanent injunction. The Supreme Court of California reversed and held the ordinance was valid. The court noted that the test is not whether there is a compelling state interest, but rather if the ordinance is "reasonably related to the welfare of the region affected by the ordinance." Because the developer-plaintiffs did not prove that the ordinance lacked a reasonable relationship to the regional welfare, the court could not find the ordinance to be unconstitutional.

In Steel Hill Development, Inc. v. Town of Sanbornton, 469 F.2d 956 (1st Cir. 1972), a developer sought to develop land in a rural community of New Hampshire for conventional and cluster housing to be sold as vacation homes—uses that were permitted by local land use controls when the land was purchased. Prior to final approval by the town, zoning amendments placed 70 percent of the developer's property in the Forest Conservation District and increased the minimum lot size to six acres from less than one acre, reducing the allowable density considerably. The developer challenged the ordinance as unconstitutional because it bore no rational relationship to the health, safety, morals, or general welfare of the community in violation of the state zoning enabling statute. The developer also alleged that the zoning constituted a compensable taking and that it was a violation of the Equal Protection Clause of the Fourteenth Amendment. The district court held for the town and the court of appeals affirmed.

The Sixth Circuit Court of Appeals upheld a slow growth ordinance that prohibited residential development unless developers won a lottery for a resident dwelling allotment in Schenck v. City of Hudson, 114 F.3d 590 (6th Cir. 1997). The court also reasoned that the ordinance was rationally related to the City's legitimate concerns regarding demographics.

The decisions in *Ramapo*, *Petaluma* and *Schenck* show that timed and sequential growth ordinances will be upheld as long as they are within the authority of enabling legislation, serve to promote the public welfare, possess legitimate features designed to permit orderly growth, and do not give rise to unconstitutional exclusion. Within the ambit of the public welfare are restrictions aimed at promoting orderly growth, a rural environment, a small town atmosphere, and quiet family neighborhoods. Decisions such as these, however, give rise to the question of whether regional or state planning should be utilized to control and direct urban growth. The dissenting opinion in *Ramapo* argues that such decisions should not be left to individual localities. The *Petaluma* opinion points out that if every municipality in the region surrounding Petaluma were to adopt a plan such as the Petaluma Plan, the impact on the housing market would be substantial. This is a serious consideration and illustrates the desirability of planning on an area-wide scale.

Municipalities sometimes attempt to control sprawl and to direct growth by denying developers permission to connect to, or use, existing public facilities. In Dateline Builders, Inc. v. City of Santa Rosa, 146 Cal. App. 3d 520, 194 Cal. Rptr. 258 (Cal. App. 1 Dist. 1983), developers challenged the land use board's denial of a certificate of compliance to a developer for a proposed development outside of the city limits. The developer appealed to the city council and the denial was affirmed. The city was trying to encourage compact development and found that the developer's plans were inconsistent with its General Plan. The developer appealed to the courts alleging that the city could not use denial of sewer hook-up as a planning device for property outside the city limits. The California Court of Appeals held that it was a valid exercise of the police power because the development was not consistent with the plan. State courts differ in their views on this matter. Some hold that public utilities have a duty to serve development as it occurs, others grant utilities greater discretion. The quandary of determining whether to service development is eliminated when capital planning for public facilities is carefully coordinated with comprehensive planning, zoning, and development regulations.

§ 4. STATE GROWTH MANAGEMENT LEGISLATION

A. IN GENERAL

The legislatures of all 50 states have developed statewide approaches to managing growth and development. The adoption of the zoning and planning enabling acts, in the first instance, evidences a policy of delegating much of the responsibility for managing private land development to the local or county level of government. What is known as "state growth management legislation" refers to additional statutes that provide further guidance to, or impose limitations on, local land use authority. Even under these statutes, local governments play a significant, if somewhat more tethered, role in land use regulation.

Growth management statutes have been enacted to create fairer, more efficient, or more environmentally sound land use patterns. Much of the attention in the literature is focused on state statutes that define urban growth boundaries or that provide for state or regional plans, which local comprehensive plans must consider or with which they must conform. But other approaches exist that guide or limit local land use authority in the interest of achieving better results. These include, for example, statutes that create regional land use review boards to which specified local decisions can be referred, affordable housing goals and mandates, regional agencies that exercise extraordinary power over a single area, state agency power over regional impact projects, and programs designed to obtain local compliance with one or more state growth management objectives. With continuing population pressures and the persistence of urban sprawl, it is likely that state statutes will continue to be adopted that attempt to influence, if not replace, local hegemony in this field. For the foreseeable future, however, it is not likely that the central role of local governments will be replaced.

B. REGIONAL PLANNING

The positions of scholars and advocates on the issue of regional planning differ greatly. Three popular views are that regional planning agencies should preempt local land use authority to the extent necessary to serve regional interests; that regional agencies should be set up to mediate inter-local matters in the region's best interest; and that localities should be encouraged to form intermunicipal land use compacts to meet their own needs, which are increasingly interdependent and regional in nature. Some states have adopted enabling acts to form regional agencies that may or may not preempt some aspect of local control. Others provide funding or assistance to facilitate the formation of voluntary regional councils or agencies, often for the purpose of securing federal transportation or planning funds.

The Standard City Planning Enabling Act, promulgated by the Hoover Commission in 1928, provided for regional planning by authorizing local planning commissions to petition the governor to establish a regional planning commission and to prepare a master plan for the region's physical development. Provisions were included in the planning enabling act for communication between the regional and municipal planning commissions with the objective of achieving a certain degree of consistency between local and regional plans. In 1968, the Douglas Commission, appointed by President Johnson, issued its Report on Urban Problems, Building the American City, which reinforced regional planning. The Commission recommended that each state create a state agency for land use planning and prepare state and regional land use plans. In other words, regional consciousness has been with us since the early days of American zoning.

Much of the country, at one time or another, has been brought within the jurisdiction of some form of regional planning organization due to a variety of influences. The most powerful of these was the promise of funding for regional efforts under housing, water, and public works programs of the federal government. Predominant among these organizations were voluntary regional councils of government, multi-state river basin compacts, and regional economic development organizations.

With few exceptions, these regional bodies have stopped far short of preemptive land use planning and regulation. They have become, however, effective vehicles for communication, education, collaboration, and networking. Among their most significant contributions is the effect they have of educating local land use officials. In these regional bodies, local representatives learn about the common problems and mutual dependence of localities that share the same economic or housing market area, or that have regulatory power over river basins and watersheds that cannot be protected without intermunicipal cooperation.

C. URBAN GROWTH AREAS

Several states have adopted statutes that create urban growth areas. These statutes aim to achieve the essential goal of smart growth: to contain growth in defined and serviceable districts. They are guided by various objectives, including the creation of cost-effective centers, preservation of agricultural districts, promotion of affordable housing, protection of significant landscapes containing critical environmental assets, and the preservation of open lands for the future. Not all of these state growth management statutes are regional in nature. Maine requires local land use plans to identify areas suitable for absorbing growth within their borders and other areas for open space protection. Minnesota authorizes, but does not require, localities to designate urban growth areas in local and county comprehensive plans. Oregon and Maryland take a more direct approach, requiring the creation of growth and preservation districts and taking effective action to see that local governments conform their regulatory activities to established state land use objectives.

The Maryland statute, adopted in 1997, establishes priority-funding areas and denies state agency funding for growth-related projects outside those designated areas. See Md. Code Ann., State Fin. & Proc. § 5–7B–02 (2000). The state makes it clear that it will not fund growth-inducing projects in rural areas not served by water and sewer systems. This is an incentive-based program intended to slow down the conversion of agricultural and rural lands and to create growth areas that are serviceable in a cost-effective manner. The Town of Hadley, Massachusetts, adopted a rate-of-growth amendment to protect the agricultural character of the community by limiting the number of building permits that may be issued to a developer of lots held in common ownership each year. The town's commitment to this rate-of-growth amendment was challenged in Zuckerman v. Town of Hadley, 442

Mass. 511, 813 N.E.2d 843 (Mass. 2004). The court held that, absent exceptional circumstances, restrictions of unlimited duration on a municipality's rate of development, and not for the purpose of conducting studies or planning for future growth, do not support the general welfare and are unconstitutional.

The Oregon growth management statute, adopted in 1973, is the most directive of its kind. It creates a state agency known as the Land Conservation and Development Commission, articulates a number of statewide land use planning goals, requires local governments to adopt comprehensive plans that contain urban growth boundaries, and requires local plans to be approved by the Commission. The statute also created the Metropolitan Service District (Metro) to supervise the intermunicipal urban growth boundary in the greater Portland area. In 1979, the statute was amended to create the Land Use Board of Appeals (LUBA) to review local land use decisions. See O.R.S. Ch. 197 (2005).

Goal 14 of the Oregon land use planning statute—the urbanization goal—classifies land into three categories: rural, urbanizable, and urban. Rural lands are agricultural, forest, or open space lands, or other land suitable for sparse settlement, with few public services. Urbanizable lands are to be contained within an urban growth boundary and are deemed suitable for future urban uses: lands that can be served by infrastructure and that are needed for the expansion of an urban area. Urban areas are within or adjacent to existing cities with concentrations of population and supporting public facilities and services. The statute provides for the orderly conversion of rural land to urban, based on the consideration of a number of factors, including the need to accommodate population growth through the provision of housing, jobs, and infrastructure. In Hildenbrand v. City of Adair Vill., 217 Or. App. 623, 177 P.3d 40 (Or. Ct. App. 2008), the court reinforced the Land Use Board of Appeals' requirement to consider a variety of factors before extending the growth boundary, including surveying the current availability of vacant and underdeveloped lands within the boundary.

Litigation under this regime has not attacked its legality, but mainly the validity of particular planning decisions that affect individual parcels. For example, in Haviland v. Land Conservation and Development Commission, 45 Or. App. 761, 609 P.2d 423 (Or. App. 1980), landowners whose property was just beyond the urban growth boundary challenged the boundary established by the City of Medford and Jackson County under Goal 14 of the state urban growth program. Upon review of the record, the Land Conservation and Development Commission (LCDC) held that the city and county did not violate the state planning goals and that the newly-established boundary was consistent with the standards contained in Goal 14. Petitioners appealed and the Court of Appeals of Oregon affirmed the LCDC's ruling. The court noted that its review was limited to whether the LCDC's findings were supported by evidence in the record and not whether the court would have decided the matter differently. Not only did the court find that all of the criteria in Goal 14 were considered by the regulators, but that the new urban growth boundary included more land than was necessary to meet the needs of the estimated future population.

§ 5. SMART GROWTH TECHNIQUES

A. CLUSTER ZONING

Normally, land is subdivided and developed in conformance with the dimensional requirements of the local zoning ordinance. Zoning usually requires that the entire parcel be divided into lots that conform to minimum lot sizes and that buildings on subdivided lots conform to rigorous set-back, height, and other dimensional requirements. Using state authority to cluster the development permitted under the local zoning ordinance, a locality can allow or require allowable development to be placed on a portion of the parcel and the rest to remain undeveloped open space. Cluster development can be used to reduce the cost of housing, to preserve critical environmental features, to provide diversity in subdivision development, to reserve land for recreational purposes, or simply to preserve open space.

New Hampshire, like many other states, permits cluster development and encourages its use as an innovative land use control. N.H. Rev. Stat. Ann. § 674:21. Under this authority, the Town of Peterborough, New Hampshire, adopted a cluster development provision in its zoning code which seeks to "permit greater flexibility in the design of housing projects; discourage development sprawl; facilitate the economical and efficient provision of public services; [and] preserve more usable space, agricultural land, recreational areas, and scenic vistas." Code of the Town of Peterborough, New Hampshire, § 245–26(A). Peterborough permits residential clustering as a special exception in its General Residence and Rural Districts and as-of-right in its Retirement Community District. The maximum number of dwelling units permitted in a clustered development may not exceed the density allowed in the zoning district where the parcel is located. The town's cluster development provision requires that a minimum of 30 percent of the total land area be dedicated as common open space. To ensure that the open space remains undeveloped, title to the open space must be deeded to a neighborhood association, the town, or to a conservation organization. The regulations require that the development be situated so as to minimize alteration of the parcel's natural features and to protect the surrounding landscape and the character of adjacent development.

In some localities, clustering is limited to parcels with particular natural resource characteristics such as wetlands, valuable viewsheds, agricultural soils, or steep slopes. Montana enacted provisions to encourage cluster development based on findings that agricultural land is being taken out of production; farmers are being forced to sell their land to generate income; and that cluster development could facilitate farmland preservation while reducing government infrastructure and services. Mont. Code Ann., § 76–3–509 (2002).

In response to an increasing number of housing developments, the South Brunswick, New Jersey, Planning Board adopted a cluster zoning ordinance that was challenged in Chrinko v. South Brunswick Twp. Planning Bd., 77 N.J. Super. 594, 187 A.2d 221 (N.J. Super. L. 1963). The purpose of this innovative provision was to provide a method of development of residential land that will preserve desirable open spaces, school sites, recreation and park areas, and land for other public purposes. The plaintiffs claimed that the ordinance was enacted to benefit the developer and not to accomplish the stated purpose of the zoning enabling statute. The court held that giving developers the option of using cluster zoning reasonably advanced the legislative goal of providing for open space even if the developer derives an incidental benefit—such as lower costs of development for street and utility installation.

B. PERFORMANCE ZONING

Performance zoning establishes standards used to measure the impact of development projects on neighboring parcels and controls those effects by imposing conditions on project approval that limit these external effects. In DeCoals, Inc. v. Board of Zoning Appeals of City of Westover, 284 S.E.2d 856 (W.Va. 1981), the city's zoning ordinance used performance criteria to control the impacts of development in industrial zones. It provided that industrial operations must not be permitted that allow dust of any kind to escape beyond the limits of the property, and noise is to be muffled so as not to be objectionable, using two objective standards to define "objectionable." The court upheld these industrial performance standards against a substantive due process challenge. A court in Florida, however, invalidated a noise standard that prevented noises that are "plainly audible," as unconstitutionally vague. See, Easy Way of Lee County, Inc. v. Lee County, 674 So.2d 863 (Fla. App. 1996).

A more expansive view of performance zoning emerged in the early 1970s in Bucks County, Pennsylvania. The Bucks County model regulated development not by using traditional dimensional and use standards but by reference to performance standards that measure the impact of a development on a particular site and area. In Bucks County, all types of housing were permitted in all zoning districts but were regulated by their impacts and benefits, such as impervious coverage, stormwater runoff, retained open space, and the protection of wetlands, watercourses, and other natural resources they affected. Each development was governed by performance standards such as an open space ratio, building volume, transportation impacts, impervious coverage, and landscaping. Dense buffering was required between incompatible uses, and a site capacity calculation was used to limit development impacts on each parcel and its surroundings. Traffic impact analyses were used, density transfers were allowed to prevent hardships, and bonus densities were allowed to encourage affordable housing. This type of performance based, standard driven zoning has not caught on generally, but its legacy is observable in environmental impact requirements and techniques such as overlay zoning used in some states and localities.

C. OVERLAY ZONING

Overlay zoning is a flexible zoning technique that allows a municipality either to encourage or to discourage development in certain areas. An overlay zone is defined as a mapped overlay district superimposed on one or more established zoning districts. A parcel within the overlay zone will thus be simultaneously subject to two sets of zoning regulations: the underlying and the overlay zoning requirements.

The overlay district is most often thought of, and is sometimes defined, as a technique for conserving a fragile natural resource area such as a pine barren, wetland, watershed, or tidal basin. Overlay districts, however, have broad application in a variety of contexts. They can be used, for example, to accomplish the redevelopment or rehabilitation of deteriorated neighborhoods. Within a designated redevelopment overlay district, developers can be given a variety of incentives to redevelop contaminated or substandard properties, to rehabilitate substandard structures, preserve historic properties, or to provide needed community facilities or affordable housing. Overlay districts can, at the same time, be used to further the development and conservation objectives of the community. For example, the locality can adopt a conservation overlay district in one or more environmentally constrained areas and a development area overlay district along a transportation corridor to provide for greater and more cost-effective development patterns. A simple strategy for achieving smart growth in a community is to identify one or two conservation overlay zones and one or two development overlay zones and implement them at the same time.

Albuquerque, New Mexico, created a Historic Overlay Zone and an Urban Conservation Overlay Zone as a means of preserving areas that have high historic value. Areas in the Historic Overlay are suitable for preservation for historical, architectural, or cultural reasons. Areas in the Urban Conservation Overlay have "distinctive characteristics that are worthy of conservation." For both types of overlay district the ordinance requires that the city council identify the area's distinctive characteristics and general preservation guidelines. Specific development guidelines must be adopted by the landmarks and urban conservation commission, which must also issue a certificate of appropriateness before any development activity begins. An application for an Urban Conservation Overlay can be made only by property owners in the area where the overlay is applied. Fifty-one percent of those property owners must agree in writing to the application before it can be submitted. Albuquerque, NM, Zoning Ordinance § 14–16–2–28.

The Ninth Circuit Court of Appeals upheld the establishment of a Senior Mobilehome Park Overlay District, which prohibited the conversion of mobile home parks with a significant amount of space reserved or intended for senior use in Putman Family P'ship v. City of Yucaipa, 673 F.3d 920 (9th Cir. 2012). The purpose of the overlay district was to preserve affordable and independent housing for the City's senior population. The court held that the Fair Housing Act provides for a "senior exemption"; therefore, the ordinance did not interfere with the purpose of the Act.

The Upland Preservation Overlay district adopted by Brookfield, Wisconsin, is intended to preserve "all significant woodlands, wildlife habitat areas, areas of rough topography and related scenic areas." In addition to maintaining "the natural beauty of the city," the overlay is intended to control erosion and sedimentation and to maintain water quality. The ordinance contains a deed restriction on subdivision plats prohibiting the erection of structures, the removal of vegetation, and any filling or excavating of land within the overlay, which runs with the land in perpetuity. Brookfield, WI, Municipal Code § 17.96.

Limington, Maine, includes an Endangered Species and Critical Areas Overlay in its zoning ordinance to protect plants, fish, and animals in areas identified by the state as habitat for endangered species and for certain waterfowl, wading birds, and shorebirds, as spawning areas for Atlantic salmon, and as deer wintering areas. Except for non-intensive recreational uses, new structures and uses within the overlay require a conditional use permit. A report by a wildlife biologist on the probable effects of the proposed use on habitat and species may be required as part of the permit application. Limington, ME, Zoning Ordinance § 6.6.1.

In Franchise Developers, Inc. v. City of Cincinnati, 30 Ohio St. 3d 28, 505 N.E.2d 966 (Ohio 1987), the Supreme Court of Ohio upheld the denial of a permit for a Wendy's restaurant in a commercial neighborhood designated for preservation and enhancement. The city council had adopted an overlay zone, called an environmental quality district, with special standards designed to prevent businesses from locating in designated urban neighborhoods where the characteristics of the environment are of significant public value and are vulnerable to damage by development permitted under conventional zoning. The court found support for the denial in the city's adopted Urban Design Plan, which provided that fast food restaurants were not appropriate in this district. By reading the underlying zoning provisions, the standards of the environmental quality district, and the adopted plan together, the court found that the property owner was put on notice of the restriction and that the restriction, plan, and ordinance accomplished a valid public purpose of preserving the quality of this urban neighborhood.

Alachua County, Florida, designated the Cross Creek area as a "special study area." The county commissioners subsequently adopted an amendment to the Alachua County Comprehensive Plan creating specific development guidelines for the area. The guidelines categorized parcels within the area as either wetland zones, exceptional upland habitat zones, hammock zones, or active use zones. Each zone had specified development requirements. In Glisson v. Alachua County, 558 So.2d 1030 (Fla. App. 1990), affected property owners challenged the regulations arguing that the county was exercising eminent domain under the guise of its police power. The court held that regulations were not facially unconstitutional and did not constitute a taking because landowners were not denied all beneficial use of their land, and the amendment was a valid exercise of the police power to address conservation concerns.

D. FLOATING ZONES

A floating zone permits uses—such as an office complex, a research laboratory, or multi-family housing—that the community wants to encourage. It is first added to the zoning ordinance as a zoning district, but the zoning map is not amended immediately to pinpoint where the authorized land use can exist. Such a zone is said to "float" until it is affixed to a qualifying parcel of land, either upon the application of the parcel's owner or upon the initiative of the local legislature. Upon approval, the parcel is rezoned to reflect the new use and becomes a small zoning district; its development is governed by the use, dimensional, and other provisions of the floating zone.

Floating zone laws contain a number of provisions intended to mitigate the impact of development on the surrounding area. Normally, for a parcel to be eligible for rezoning under a floating zone, it must be of a sufficient size to ensure that the development can be fitted properly into its surroundings. An owner who requests that the zone be applied to a particular parcel must demonstrate that a variety of impacts will be properly handled, such as traffic and site access; water and sewer service; design continuity; effect on natural resources; visual and noise impact; preservation of open space; and the effect on nearby property values.

The purpose of adding one or more floating zones to a community's zoning law is to add flexibility to that law, enabling it to accommodate new land uses, but in a controlled fashion. As a community's needs change, uses that are not readily accommodated by the adopted zoning law may be desired by local leaders. These uses may be unique and have a relatively significant but manageable impact on their surroundings. Local officials may be unclear as to where such uses should best be accommodated and where developers would prefer to locate them to ensure that they are successful economically.

Floating zones allow developers some needed flexibility in locating sites and determining how new land uses can be designed and buffered to fit into their surroundings. In some communities where affordable housing is desired, for example, a multi-family district may be created by the legislature but not located on the zoning map. This allows developers the maximum flexibility to scout out sites and design developments that mix housing types, tenures, and costs to accomplish the municipality's objective of producing affordable housing while requiring the project to fit properly into the neighborhood. Similarly, a community may want to create an office park but may not want to limit its location, in order to give developers ample opportunity to find a site best suited to current market needs.

The floating zoning technique was upheld in New York and Maryland, but it was invalidated in Pennsylvania as constituting spot zoning and as not being in accord with the comprehensive plan. Rodgers v. Village of Tarrytown, 302 N.Y. 115, 96 N.E.2d 731 (N.Y. 1951); Huff v. Board of Zoning Appeals, 214 Md. 48, 133 A.2d 83 (Md. 1957); Eves v. Zoning Board, 401 Pa. 211, 164 A.2d 7 (Pa. 1960). In the *Rodgers* case, New York's highest court confirmed the municipality's authority to adopt floating zones. The village board of trustees passed two zoning amendments in 1947 and 1948. The first created a new district for garden apartments with boundaries that were to be fixed by later amendment of the zoning map when such district was applied to properties in the village. The second ordinance applied the new district to the defendant's property. The plaintiff neighbors claimed that the first ordinance was invalid because it set no boundaries for the new district and made no changes on the zoning map. The court held that "the 1947 amendment was merely the first step in a reasoned plan of rezoning, and specifically provided for further action on the part of the board." The court also stated that the "two amendments, read together as they must be, fully complied with the requirements of the Village Law and accomplished a rezoning of village property in an unexceptional manner." The court noted that "changed or changing conditions call for changed plans, and persons who own property in a particular zone or use district enjoy no eternally vested right to that classification if the public interest demands otherwise. Accordingly, the power of a village to amend its basic zoning ordinance in such a way as reasonably to promote the general welfare cannot be questioned."

In a similar holding, a Missouri court upheld a floating zone against allegations that it amounted to an improper delegation of legislative authority, was lacking in uniform regulations, failed to define standards for project approval, and constituted spot zoning. The court stated that there were uniform restrictions within the floating zone, general standards to be considered, and that the fact that spot zoning might occur in a particular circumstance would not invalidate the zoning in general. Treme v. St. Louis County, 609 S.W.2d 706 (Mo. App. 1980).

In Fasano v. Board of County Commissioners of Washington County, 264 Or. 574, 507 P.2d 23 (Or. 1973), property owners challenged the rezoning of neighboring property from single-family to planned residential, which allowed the development of a mobile home park. The mobile home park, as a planned residential use, was available to the landowner, upon application, as a floating zone. The court invalidated the planned residential zone, holding that it was not in conformance with the comprehensive plan.

E. TRADITIONAL NEIGHBORHOOD ZONING

Traditional Neighborhood Development (TND) is a zoning mechanism that has emerged in recent years as an alternative to conventional zoning. TND zoning districts are friendlier than conventional zoning to environmental conservation, pedestrian movement, and compact development. This device is similar to Planned Unit Development, but is focused more closely on achieving traditional urban spatial relationships.

New urbanists, sometimes called neo-traditionalists, point out that, under conventional zoning and subdivision laws, most traditional neighborhoods found in existing urban areas can no longer be replicated. The corner drugstore or deli in a residential neighborhood is not allowed, apartments cannot exist above stores, and houses cannot be built close to the sidewalk, nor cars parked in garages that front on alleys that children use as playgrounds. If cookie-cutter subdivisions are the result of standards contained in zoning and subdivision ordinances, the new urbanists ask, why can't such regulations be modified to create different, more flexible neighborhoods? Their lament is that traditional Euclidian zoning (the type of rigid separation of use zoning adopted in Euclid, Ohio, and sustained by the U.S. Supreme Court in Euclid v. Ambler Realty (1926)), prevents the very land uses that traditional neighborhoods contained and that the new urbanists seek to restore.

One such approach is to adopt a new zoning district, often referred to as a Traditional Neighborhood District, designated on the zoning map as a TND zone. This allows for the development of mixed-use neighborhoods where housing types are varied, retail and commercial services are available within walking distance of residences, public green space is provided, visual and recreational amenities exist nearby, and pedestrian and bicycle travel is actively encouraged. Houses in such a neighborhood district can be allowed on smaller lots, retail and commercial uses can be mixed with residential uses, a variety of housing types can be allowed, and accessible open space can be created and dedicated to the use of all the neighbors.

Traditional Neighborhood Districts have been enacted by local governments in several states, without express enabling legislation. Some states, especially those whose courts have narrowly interpreted the requirement that zoning provisions must be uniform within zoning districts, may need to pass TND enabling statutes before localities will attempt its use. TND enabling legislation in Connecticut, Pennsylvania, and Wisconsin provides support and guidance for local TND regulations. Under Wis. Stat. § 66.034(3), cities and villages may enact the TND as a zoning district designation, an overlay zone, a floating zone, or as a modified approach to PUDs. The Belmont, North Carolina, Traditional Neighborhood Development Law,

§ 4.11.1 et seq., states that its purpose "is to minimize traffic congestion, suburban sprawl, infrastructure costs, and environmental degradation." The ordinance contains design standards for public and civic areas and privately constructed or rehabilitated structures.

F. PLANNED UNIT DEVELOPMENT ZONING

Planned unit development (PUD) zoning provisions permit large lots to be developed in a more flexible manner than is allowed by the underlying zoning. PUD ordinances may allow developers to mix land uses, such as residential and commercial, on a large parcel and to develop the parcel at greater densities, and with more design flexibility, than is otherwise allowed by the underlying zoning district. PUD provisions often require developers to compensate for the impacts of their projects by setting aside significant and usable open space, providing infrastructure needed to service the development, or offering other community facilities and services. PUD ordinances typically leave the underlying zoning in place and offer an alternative to landowners to develop the site in accordance with the PUD provisions.

A developing community that anticipates receiving a rezoning or site plan application for the development of a large shopping mall or discount warehouse could use a mixed-use PUD law to negotiate significant design and use changes in the development. Instead of ending up with another faceless commercial strip, the community may use its

PUD provisions to provide the leverage, incentives, and process necessary to encourage the development of a better commercial project, reinforced by the addition of some residential uses, community facilities, and attractive landscaping and building design.

The same community, faced with the prospect of one or more large residential developments, could avoid the proliferation of single-lot subdivisions or uniform condominium developments by using PUD provisions to provide for some on-site shopping and services for homeowners. This can be accomplished by adopting a residential PUD provision that allows mixing a variety of housing types and styles with some neighborhood commercial uses. Through design flexibility and control, an appropriate neighborhood can be created, properly serviced by infrastructure and appropriately landscaped and designed to protect surrounding areas from its impacts.

An urban community could adopt a PUD ordinance as a means of attracting developers of unique large lots. By offering a mix of land uses and flexible design options, developers are free to create a project that is economically and environmentally viable for the site. See, e.g., New Haven, C.T. Zoning § 65. In a similar way, a rural community could adopt PUD provisions, in advance of development, as its way of indicating the areas that are appropriate for mixed-use and more intense development.

The flexibility that comes with enacting a PUD plan for designated areas is demonstrated in the case of Cole v. District of Columbia Zoning Commission,

210 A.3d 753 (D.C. 2019). Petitioners complained about the excessive height approved for a portion of the site, even though the heights of buildings approved on other portions of the site were lower. The court found that the plan specifically contemplated "height step downs" to mitigate any adverse effects of building height. Accordingly, the decision of the Zoning Commission was affirmed.

Although PUD development is designed for large-lot development, this does not necessarily mean that its use is limited to communities with one or more large lots that are under single ownership. The PUD provisions can be drafted to present an opportunity to the owners of several medium-sized or smaller lots to work together to combine ownership and take advantage of the PUD development option.

G. TRANSFER OF DEVELOPMENT RIGHTS

Where authorized by state law to do so, localities can provide for the transfer of the right to develop property under current zoning provisions from one part of the community to another. This technique, called transfer of development rights or TDR, is often used to preserve critical environmental areas, farms and forests, or valuable open spaces. A 1997 survey of 3,500 local governments and a review of planning literature found 112 TDR programs in 107 communities. As of 2003, an additional 30 programs have been discovered (See Rick Pruetz, Beyond Takings and Givings (Arje Press 2003)). The programs have been established in rural communities and in some of the country's largest cities, including New York and Chicago.

There are three basic elements to a TDR program: the sending district, the receiving district, and the TDR credits themselves. The sending district consists of the area to be protected from development. The receiving district is located where additional density can be absorbed and supported with existing or expanded infrastructure and services. The TDR credits are a legal representation of the abstract development rights that will be severed from property in the sending district and grafted onto property in the receiving district. The TDR credits are traded in a free market, although a TDR bank may be established to facilitate exchanges. When a TDR credit is purchased from a property owner in the sending district, that property owner records a deed restriction prohibiting development on the property. The TDR credit can then be applied to property in the receiving district as a density bonus.

In Chesterfield Township, New Jersey, for example, the TDR ordinance allows for the shifting of development pressure from agricultural, environmentally sensitive, or open space areas of the township to villages designated for growth. The program allows the township to maintain its rural character while encouraging planned development and minimizing potential conflicts between farmers and non-farming neighbors.

The Long Island Pine Barrens in New York is another example. This TDR program was created under state legislation adopted in response to bitter division among stakeholders regarding future development over the fragile Pine Barrens aquifer. The plan establishes receiving districts into which development credits may be transferred. Developers who own land in these receiving districts may purchase credits from landowners in sending districts. Each purchased credit allows the developer to build one housing unit over that permitted by the receiving district's zoning. In this TDR program, a 52,500-acre sending district and a 47,500-acre receiving district were established that crossed the jurisdictions of three towns and two villages. The receiving areas in this program are structured to provide a demand for credits in the receiving sites that exceeds the number of credits created in the sending sites by a ratio of 2.5 to 1. This ratio was calculated to create sufficient competition to insure an active market for the development credits in the sending districts.

Where state zoning enabling acts are broadly construed by the courts, local TDR programs can be established under them. Several states (e.g., Florida, Georgia, Illinois, Kentucky, Maryland, New York, Pennsylvania) have adopted specific TDR enabling acts. State enabling acts must be read very carefully to determine precisely how and for what purposes local TDR laws may be enacted. In City of Hollywood v. Hollywood, Inc., 432 So.2d 1332 (Fla. App. 1983), the court found that protecting the aesthetic value of a pristine coastal area was a legitimate public purpose and that transferring the right to residential development was a reasonable method of accomplishing that objective. A similar result was reached when the New Jersey Pinelands TDR program was attacked (Gardner v. New Jersey Pinelands Comm'n, 125 N.J. 193, 593 A.2d 251 (N.J. 1991)) and when a Florida TDR law was challenged in Glisson v. Alachua Cty., 558 So.2d 1030 (Fla. App. 1990). An early challenge that the new TDR development pattern violated the uniformity requirement of the zoning enabling act was also unsuccessful. Dupont Circle Citizens Ass'n v. District of Columbia Zoning Comm'n, 355 A.2d 550 (D.C. App. 1976), cert. den., 429 U.S. 966 (1976). Similarly, a challenge that TDR constitutes legal spot zoning was rejected by the court in Fur-Lex Realty v. Lindsay, 81 N.Y. Misc. 2d 904, 367 N.Y.S.2d 388 (Sup. Ct. N.Y. Cty. 1975).

TDR has also been applied to assist with the preservation of historic landmarks. In Penn Central Transp. Co. v. New York City, 438 U.S. 104 (1978), the city's landmark commission denied Penn Central's request to develop in the airspace above Grand Central terminal. The city's zoning ordinance offered the terminal's owner the right to transfer the right to build over the station to nearby properties: an early transfer of development rights scheme. Penn Central challenged the restriction on development as a taking and argued that the grant of TDR rights did not constitute adequate compensation. The Supreme Court found no taking using a multi-factor balancing test for determining whether a taking has occurred. The Court has not had the opportunity to rule whether, if a taking is found, transfer of development right credits can be considered as compensation. State courts differ as to whether TDR credits provide adequate compensation for a regulatory taking. In Aptos Seascape Corp. v. Santa Cruz County, 138 Cal. App. 3d 484, 496, 188 Cal. Rptr. 191, 197 (Cal. App. 1 Dist. 1982), the availability of such credits was found to preclude a finding that a taking occurred. An Arizona court, however, held that TDR credits did not constitute compensation. Corrigan v. City of Scottsdale, 149 Ariz. 553, 720 P.2d 528 (Ariz. App. 1985), aff'd in part and vacated in part, 149 Ariz. 538, 720 P.2d 513, cert. den., 479 U.S. 986 (1986).

H. FORM-BASED ZONING

There is a growing trend toward replacing conventional zoning with form-based zoning. The latter concentrates on the appearance of mixed-use buildings and street scapes and attempts to achieve a predictable, livable, and aesthetically pleasing building and neighborhood development. Conventional zoning, on the other hand, concentrates on use regulation within fixed districts combined with dimensional specifications for building heights and placement on lots subject to minimum sizes.

In the smart growth era, the space between conventional zoning and form-based codes has been filled with many of the zoning techniques discussed in this chapter. Together, these land use regulatory options provide a full tool box of strategic options for communities with varying needs to consider.

Zoning that conforms with form-based codes aims to improve aesthetics, protect the environment and public health and safety, enhance walkability and reduce dependence on personal vehicle use, increase property values, promote energy conservation, and, generally, improve the environment. As such, along with other techniques described in this chapter, form-based zoning is an antidote to sprawl and its consequences.

There is little evidence of successful litigation challenging the authority of local governments to adopt form-based zoning or of the techniques it employs. The seminal case of Euclid v. Ambler Realty Co., 272 U.S. 365 (1926) and basic due process standards support the devices and objectives of form-based requirements. The case law upholding other smart growth strategies creates a high barrier to facial challenges of form-based provisions. Euclid's presumption of validity, deferential attitude, and its heavy burden of proof on challengers to zoning heighten that barrier.

The "purpose in view" of zoning, dating back to the Standard Zoning Enabling Act (SZEA) itself, and the specific land use regulations authorized by that Act support most of the features of the form-based model. These include, inter alia, height restrictions suitable in the context, the character of construction, open space requirements, prevention of overcrowding, provision of adequate light and air, and the exclusion of noxious or offensive land uses and structures. The SZEA makes it clear that the details of zoning must be designed with a "view to conserving the value of buildings and encouraging the most appropriate use of land throughout [the] municipality." This aligns with the stated purposes of form-based codes and other smart growth regulations and is reinforced by *Euclid's* presumption of validity.

CHAPTER 8

HOUSING AND URBAN REDEVELOPMENT

§ 1. INTRODUCTION

This Chapter addresses the interplay between the private and public sectors regarding the provision of housing and the redevelopment of urban areas. Land use law encompasses many of the techniques used by municipalities to influence these matters: to ensure that safe and sanitary housing is available and affordable to all income groups, to stimulate the redevelopment of blighted or undeveloped neighborhoods, and to provide infrastructure to serve urban populations. Demography, employment, housing, and infrastructure are all subjects of land use planning, zoning, and land use regulation.

Comprehensive plans normally analyze and deal with demographic trends. Planners recommend that communities maintain a balanced mix of households with respect to age and income and are concerned, for example, when either high-income households leave or moderate-income households cannot afford to live locally. In many older cities, official land use plans hope to reverse the flight of affluent households—along with their purchasing power and contribution to the tax base. In some high-cost suburban areas, the lack of affordable housing can cause labor shortages which, in turn, prejudice the location of retail, service, and manufacturing businesses in the locality.

Land use plans often contain recommendations for the local legislature regarding these trends such as promoting the revitalization of one or more neighborhoods to attract higher income households or zoning more land for high density housing to cure an affordable housing problem. Plans also contain strategies to improve public transportation in urban neighborhoods to serve a host of mixed-use land uses and other initiatives intended to ensure safe and livable housing conditions.

The practice of housing and urban redevelopment law involves many other influences, normally thought of as outside the scope of land use law as a regulatory regime. Municipalities and developers rely on a large number of state and federal grants, subsidies, mortgage programs, tax deductions, and tax credits, for example, to implement their land use goals.

§ 2. URBAN REDEVELOPMENT

A. HISTORY

State and federal laws authorize and enable urban cities and villages to designate and redevelop blighted and underdeveloped neighborhoods. The classic example is urban renewal, which was funded by the federal government beginning in the 1950s and authorized by state legislation prescribing the conditions under which renewal could take place. State legislation empowered certain municipalities to create urban renewal agencies to manage the redevelopment process. These agencies, at the behest of their municipal governments, then studied and designated areas in need of renewal, adopted discrete plans for their redevelopment, acquired property using the power of eminent domain (condemnation), demolished buildings, and cleared the land—preparing the way for redevelopment projects. Urban renewal agencies then designated quasi-public redevelopment companies, or private land developers with proven track records, to carry out development projects in conformance with the urban renewal plan. Although the federal funding that fueled the urban renewal enterprise has disappeared as such, lawyers and planners continue to use traditional urban redevelopment tools and a host of new ones to stimulate the revitalization of moribund urban neighborhoods.

B. THE POWER OF CONDEMNATION

(i) Introduction

One of the most intriguing questions in this area of law is why one person's private property can be taken under the power of eminent domain and conveyed to redevelopment companies or private developers for redevelopment purposes. The Fifth Amendment allows government to take title to private property for a public use and requires that just compensation be paid to the property owner ("nor shall private property be taken for a public use without just compensation"). At issue is the critical matter of whether distressed cities, when specifically authorized by state legislation, can carry out programs to increase jobs, strengthen their tax bases, revitalize neighborhoods, and stabilize property values by condemning the land of private property owners who are not willing to sell to the government at a negotiated price.

The role of the courts in reviewing the propriety of land condemnations is threefold: to be sure the condemning authority followed the procedures required by the state eminent domain law; to be sure the purpose for which the property is taken is a public one; and to see that just compensation is paid. Just compensation is defined as the price a willing buyer would pay a willing seller at the time of the condemnation.

(ii) Public Use

In the 1954 U.S. Supreme Court case of Berman v. Parker, 348 U.S. 26 (1954), the question was whether the petitioner's non-blighted department store could be condemned by the District of Columbia renewal authority to carry out its urban renewal plan for a blighted neighborhood. The Court noted that the public uses for which property may be taken under the power of eminent domain are coextensive with the police power of the state. Since the public welfare which justifies governmental intervention is broad and inclusive, the power to condemn title to land can be employed to stem blight and deterioration, redevelop underdeveloped areas, and increase the economic productivity of an area: all legitimate police power objectives. The *Berman* court noted that the role of the judiciary in determining whether the power of eminent domain is being exercised for a public use is an extremely narrow one. The Court deferred to the urban renewal authority in the District of Columbia, which had decided that area-wide blight could only be cured by an area-wide solution and, thus, it was necessary to take the plaintiff's building whose existence and use did not conform to the urban renewal plan.

The advocates of urban renewal won a short-lived victory in *Berman*. The inequities and questionable results of slum clearance and redevelopment came under fierce attack only a few years after the decision. The critics held that urban renewal fostered segregation, led to the demolition of historic buildings, dislocated the urban poor, and wasted government resources. With the passage of the Housing and Community Development Act of 1974, federal urban renewal planning and project grants were folded into the special revenue sharing formula of the Community Development Block Grant program. The disappearance of dedicated urban renewal funding and a number of other categorical funding programs for urban areas added to the sense of ambivalence about the ability of cities to revitalize themselves.

This ambivalence has not curtailed the use of the power of eminent domain to take blighted and underdeveloped property and commit it to redevelopment. Many challenges have been brought against condemnation schemes that take title to moderately blighted or underdeveloped properties so that commercial or industrial developers can acquire title to the land and develop commercial centers, mixed-use marina complexes, shopping plazas, light industrial parks, and other, more intensive, job-producing developments.

Courts have not set aside these arrangements even when the funds used to pay the owners of the condemned land come from the private company that is selected to redevelop the area. In Sun Co. v. City of Syracuse Indus. Dev. Agency, 209 A.D.2d 34, 625 N.Y.S.2d 371 (N.Y.A.D. 4th Dept. 1995), various oil refining and manufacturing companies challenged the Industrial Development Agency for condemning their properties to further a waterfront redevelopment master plan for an 800-acre area on the south shore of Onondaga Lake known as "oil city." The area was located next to several low-income neighborhoods in Syracuse where a disproportionately large percentage of welfare recipients, jobless, and poverty-level households resided. The court found that the purpose of the taking was to accomplish a proper use and that this determination was not without a proper foundation, nor suspect because the funds used to pay the petitioners were provided by the private redevelopment company selected to revitalize the area. The petitioners' motion for leave to appeal was denied by the New York Court of Appeals in 1997. Mobil Oil Corp. v. City of Syracuse Indus. Dev. Agency, 89 N.Y.2d 811, 657 N.Y.S.2d 404, 679 N.E.2d 643 (N.Y. 1997).

In Kaur v. New York State Urban Dev. Corp., 15 N.Y.2d 235, 933 N.E.2d 721, 907 N.Y.S.2d 122 (N.Y. 2010), the NYS Urban Development Corporation condemned the plaintiff's gas station in order to permit the expansion of Columbia University, a private educational institution. The Court of Appeals of New York held that the exercise of the power of eminent domain in this case to benefit the private university was supported by sufficient showing of public use, benefit, and purpose.

In Kelo v. New London, 545 U.S. 469 (2005), petitioners challenged the taking of their modest homes in an "underdeveloped" portion of a state-designated distressed city for the purpose of carrying out an area-wide, mixed-use waterfront redevelopment plan. The petitioners found it particularly objectionable that title to their modest single-family homes was to be leased by the New London Development Corporation—the condemning authority—to a private redevelopment company, in part to construct luxury housing. In a 5–4 decision, the Court held that the purpose for the taking was a legitimate public use, clearing the way for the Corporation to condemn title from nine individual owners who held onto 15 parcels of the 115 private lots in the redevelopment area. The majority noted: "For more than a century, our public use jurisprudence has wisely eschewed rigid formulas and intrusive scrutiny in favor of affording legislatures broad latitude in determining what public needs justify the use of the takings power."

The dissent worried that this precedent was overly broad and would allow condemning authorities too much latitude in justifying "so-called" public interests for the primary purpose of promoting private economic interests. Where state legislatures do not step in to limit such condemnations, state courts may by determining that they do not carry out a truly public use. In 99 Cents Only Stores v. Lancaster Redevelopment Agency, 237 F.Supp.2d 1123 (C.D. Cal. 2001), for example, a federal district court in California invalidated the condemnation of a store to accommodate the interest of an adjacent Costco's expansion plans; it found that the redevelopment agency's only purpose "was to satisfy the private expansion demands of Costco." In Bailey v. Myers, 206 Ariz. 224, 76 P.3d 898 (Ariz. App. 2003), the state court held that the taking of a brake shop for a hardware store to advance economic development lacked the requisite public use. Donald Trump's attempt to get the Casino Reinvestment Development Authority in New Jersey to condemn the parcels of a few landowners who had refused to sell to expand his hotel and casino was thwarted by the state court; it found that the Authority had given Trump a blank check regarding future development on the site. Casino Reinvestment Development Authority v. Banin, 320 N.J. Super. 342, 727 A.2d 102 (N.J. Super. L. 1998). In Sw. Ill. Dev. Auth v. Nat'l City Envtl., L.L.C. 199 Ill. 2d 225, 768 N.E.2d 1 263 Ill. Dec. 241 (Ill. 2002), cert. den., 537 U.S. 880 (2002), the city condemned a property owned by one private developer and subsequently conveyed the land to a new private developer to build a parking lot open to the public. Illinois' highest state court found that the state agency improperly utilized its eminent domain power for a private use.

(iii) Just Compensation

"Just" compensation does not mean enough money to reestablish your home or business; the standard is whether the authority paid the price that a willing buyer would pay a willing seller at the time of the condemnation. Since the properties taken are often in declining or underdeveloped areas, this price can be quite modest. The fact that many area-wide redevelopment projects displace numerous property owners, often with modest resources, who are not able to find suitable locations to live or reestablish their businesses, has not altered the favorable judicial attitude toward the use of eminent domain in the interest of renewal, redevelopment, higher tax bases, and more jobs for struggling cities and older suburbs. Some legislatures, on the other hand, are paying increased attention to these consequences and considering legislation to protect property owners from the harsher consequences of the redevelopment process.

C. MODERN PUBLIC/PRIVATE PARTNERSHIPS

The disappearance of federal funding for urban renewal projects changed, but did not stop the process of developing partnerships between local public agencies and private development companies. Through zoning, planning, capital projects, condemnations, and with the use of state and federal grants and tax benefits, urban redevelopment projects are proceeding apace. In financially distressed cities and villages, market forces are insufficient to attract developers to redevelop aging downtowns, industrial waterfronts, multi-family neighborhoods, underdeveloped sites, and deteriorating infrastructure. In these places, a more intense partnership is needed, one that joins the public sector, using resources uniquely available to it, and the private sector with its debt and equity financing and development competence.

Developers, to be attracted to work in urban places where the market is less than robust, look for municipal administrations that are proactive regarding land development. Developers will invest in urban areas, purchasing land and risking capital, only where they are convinced that the municipality can deliver financial resources and supportive infrastructure needed to make the project work practically and financially.

Regarding particular redevelopment areas and large sites, developers will ask whether the municipality has committed itself to a clear master plan with defined objectives and design standards. They are attracted when the municipality has drawn the boundaries of redevelopment districts, given them name identities, specified how they should be redeveloped, and identified the resources they can bring to the bargaining table.

Constitutional and state legislative standards prevent state and local governmental agencies from giving land, infrastructure, and other public assets to private entities or providing special tax benefits or exemptions to them. Under some state statutes, however, when the purpose of these incentives is the provision of affordable housing, job creation, or the redevelopment or economic development of certain designated areas, such benefits may be provided to the private sector. The purpose of these incentives is to induce the private sector to create benefits for the public that are not financially feasible without public assistance.

In Geisler v. City of Wood River, 383 Ill. App. 3d 828, 892 N.E.2d 543, 322 Ill. Dec. 906 (Ill. Ct. App.), cert. den., Geisler v. City of Wood River, 229 Ill. 2d 666 (Ill. 2008), the city entered into an economic incentive agreement with a developer pursuant to the Illinois state statute, 65 ILCS5/8–11–20. The developer planned to demolish a regional shopping center. The agreement provided that the city would use its share of the state general sales tax to cover some of the developer's costs. City residents argued that the agreement violated state statutes and that the new tax imposed on Business District Two did not conform to the uniformity requirement in the Illinois state statute. The court held that the developer agreement was valid; however, the new tax on Business District Two was invalid because the proposed district violated the requirement that the business district be contiguous with surrounding parcels.

Through the use of local development corporations, industrial development agencies, enterprise communities, or empowerment zones, a municipality can offer the developer financial incentives such as Brownfield Liability Relief, Brownfield Tax Credit, and Real Property Tax Relief including Payment in

Lieu of Taxes and Tax Increment Financing. Industrial Development Agencies can acquire land by eminent domain, issue tax-exempt bonds to provide low cost financing, and participate in sale and lease back arrangements to create eligibility for partial exemption from real property taxes for development companies.

Using more traditional land use authority, localities can also provide incentives to private entities by adopting regulatory plans for high density, mixed-use areas within their boundaries, offering incentive zoning for developers to build pursuant to those plans or using floating zoning districts, special use permits with clear standards and regulations, or other techniques to implement those plans. These same agencies and laws can be used to guide the developer, streamline the project review process, and waive requirements that are otherwise applicable under existing zoning and development standards.

§ 3. HOUSING AND REDEVELOPMENT SUBSIDIES

The Department of Housing and Urban Development (HUD) is a cabinet-level agency in the Executive Branch of the Federal Government. Congress created HUD through the Department of Housing and Urban Development Act of 1966. In creating HUD, Congress recognized that the sound development of communities and metropolitan areas in our nation is essential for our nation's general welfare and security. In the Act's declaration of purposes Congress stated:

> in recognition of the increasing importance of housing and urban development in our national life, . . . establishment of an executive department is desirable to achieve . . . assistance for housing and for the development of the Nation's communities; to assist the President in achieving maximum coordination of the various Federal activities . . . ; to encourage the solution of problems of housing, urban development, and mass transportation through State, county, town, village, or other local and private action . . . ; to encourage the maximum contributions that may be made by vigorous private homebuilding and mortgage lending industries . . . ; and to provide for full and appropriate consideration, at the national level, of the needs and interest of the Nation's communities and of the people who live and work in them. 42 U.S.C. § 3531.

The principal federal program relied on by communities for urban redevelopment today is the HUD-administered Community Development Block Grant Program (CDBG), through which the federal government provides general funds to state and local governments to be used to improve housing and community conditions for low-and moderate-income persons and families. Other important programs include the HOME Investment Partnership Program, through which state and local governments are eligible for grants to be used for the exclusive purpose of creating affordable housing for low- and moderate-income families; the HOPE VI Program, which provides funds to public housing authorities to demolish or revitalize severely distressed public housing projects; and the Section 8 Tenant Based Assistance Program, which provides rental assistance to very low-income families.

There are a number of tax credits that are provided by both federal and state governments to those who redevelop urban areas. Tax credits are powerful incentives that can significantly reduce a taxpayer's net tax liability. The Rehabilitation Tax Credit is provided by the federal government and it is applied to the expenses incurred in the rehabilitation of a qualified building or certified historic structure. The Low-Income Housing Tax Credit can be claimed by taxpayers who own residential properties that they rent to low-income individuals.

The Empowerment Zone/Enterprise Community (EZ/EC) program, established in 1993, is a federal initiative designed to create self-sustaining, long-term economic development in areas of deep poverty and unemployment. The EZ/EC program is modeled after certain state enterprise zones and provides financial incentives to individuals to rejuvenate economically depressed areas within designated geographic locations. The EZ/EC's financial incentives seek to address these issues and fund revitalization strategies that provide business assistance, train and educate area residents, improve access to healthcare, and develop transportation. Designated rural and urban communities are eligible to receive tax incentives, performance grants, and loans.

§ 4. HOUSING REHABILITATION AND HOUSING STANDARD CODES

Other municipal approaches to housing and neighborhood revitalization include initiatives to rehabilitate deteriorated housing and establish housing repair and maintenance standards. Some of the federal programs listed above provide direct grants, subsidies, or tax credits to those who acquire and rehabilitate substandard housing. Some local programs encourage squatters in abandoned buildings to improve them by legalizing their tenancies and providing them with financial and technical assistance. Through the adoption of housing codes, local legislatures specify the facilities and services that landlords must provide, the level of maintenance required, and the maximum numbers of people who can occupy dwellings. Judicially created and state-adopted warranties of habitability provide defensive mechanisms that protect tenants from eviction for nonpayment of rent when physical conditions in multi-family buildings are unsafe.

New York City adopted the first urban housing code in 1901: the Tenement House Act. Housing codes aim to ensure that multi-family buildings are safe, sanitary, and efficient. The housing code, like a number of other techniques used to maintain livability and redevelop cities, is not traditionally thought of as a land use technique, but is one of a growing list of tools that community leaders use to accomplish their land use planning objectives.

Land use students may remember Javins v. First National Realty Corp., 428 F.2d 1071 (D.C. Cir. 1970), from their first-year property class and that, at common law, no warranties with respect to property condition are implied by courts in conveyances, including leases. The landlord in *Javins* brought an action against tenants for failure to pay rent. The tenants posited a novel argument: they withheld payment of rent because the landlord had violated its warranty of habitability through poor maintenance resulting in approximately 1,500 violations of the District of Columbia housing code. In finding for the tenants, the *Javins* court found that "a warranty of habitability, measured by the standards set out in the Housing Regulations for the District of Columbia, is implied by operation of law into leases of urban dwelling units covered by those Regulations and that breach of this warranty gives rise to the usual remedies for breach of contract, including the withholding of rent." The *Javins* case illustrates that urban cities, in their struggle to remain livable, do have authority to regulate housing conditions, to enforce housing code standards, and to force building owners to repair, where the funds are available.

In Moore v. City of Detroit, 159 Mich. App. 199, 406 N.W.2d 488 (Mich. App. 1987), landlords challenged the authority of the City of Detroit to adopt a nuisance abatement ordinance to address the growing number of vacant and abandoned buildings in the city and the negative impact of the deteriorating structures on surrounding property values. To abate the nuisance effect of the abandoned buildings, the ordinance allowed families to move in and repair them for their own use. The new tenants were allowed to secure title through delinquent property tax proceedings or by bringing quiet title actions. The court held that the city ordinance was properly enacted under the police powers and did not deprive the building owners of a property interest in violation of due process.

§ 5. PROTECTING GROWTH DISTRICTS FROM COMPETITION

Urban redevelopment, housing rehabilitation, and housing codes are palliatives that deal with a larger problem. In many urban areas, private market pressures operate as a centrifugal force: the conditions at the urban core repel capital investment and affluent households outward. The underlying tension in land use policy and lawmaking is the tension between the principle of centered growth and the realities of the market. Can localities use their land use authority to tug at the momentum of the market? Can zoning be used to prevent competition with businesses in downtowns, main streets, and waterfronts in which they invest to keep people from moving away or to bring them back in? Do commercial property owners in developed districts have standing to sue adjacent municipalities for zoning land in ways that accommodate their competitors? How much control do individual localities have over external market and political forces that frustrate their carefully conceived land use plans? These are major policy issues that land use law attempts to address.

The typical problem is evidenced by Mason City Center Associates v. City of Mason City, Iowa, 671 F.2d 1146 (8th Cir. 1982), involving a city policy of discouraging outlying shopping centers within its boundaries in order to preserve its core central business district. The city refused to rezone land on its outskirts for shopping center development while approving redevelopment of the downtown area by another developer. This was attacked as a restraint of trade but the federal circuit court upheld a lower court decision that found the zoning actions of Mason City constitutional.

In Swain v. County of Winnebago, 111 Ill. App. 2d 458, 250 N.E.2d 439 (Ill. App. 1969), the issue was whether business owners in downtown Rockford, Illinois, had standing to sue Winnebago County for rezoning 145 acres of agricultural land in an area outside, but adjacent to, the city to accommodate a regional shopping center that would compete with their businesses. The plaintiffs claimed that the rezoning was not properly approved by the board and that it was arbitrary and had no relationship to promoting public health, safety, or welfare. The court held that the plaintiffs did not have standing to sue and that increased competition was not sufficient to confer standing on them. The court noted that it was not the function of the county zoning ordinance to provide economic protection to the plaintiffs and that business owners who sue for the single purpose of preventing competition have no actionable injury.

In Juster Associates v. City of Rutland, Vermont, 901 F.2d 266 (2d Cir. 1990), the city was sued for supporting one mall developer and opposing another in a permit proceeding before state environmental agencies. The city had entered into an agreement with the favored shopping mall developer who had agreed to provide low-income housing, transportation, and cultural facilities, and not to recruit existing downtown businesses to move to the mall. The federal appeals court affirmed the trial court's dismissal of the complaint, holding that no violation of federal antitrust statutes occurred since consumers would not be harmed by the city's actions.

Federal statutes prevent private individuals, including land developers, from being penalized under anti-trust statutes for exercising their First Amendment rights to petition the government to take actions that benefit them and disadvantage their competitors. In Miracle Mile Associates v. City of Rochester, 617 F.2d 18 (2d Cir. 1980), the court held that a developer was immune from anti-trust liability where it aggressively petitioned federal and state agencies to require a competitor to comply with environmental regulations.

A city ordinance that allowed existing billboards to continue but banned new ones was upheld in City of Columbia v. Omni Outdoor Advertising, Inc., 499 U.S. 365 (1991). Omni alleged that the city was engaging in anti-trust behavior constituting a restraint on trade in violation of the Sherman Act.

The court held in favor of the city and ruled that it was immune from anti-trust damage actions of this type.

§ 6. BROWNFIELD REDEVELOPMENT

Another method of promoting proper urban redevelopment is encouraging the reuse of "brownfields." In many communities, former industrial properties—polluted by prior use—blight the urban landscape and present formidable barriers to redevelopment. Generally known as "brownfields," these properties are abandoned, idle, or under-used industrial and commercial facilities where expansion or redevelopment is complicated by real or perceived environmental contamination and federal and state laws that impose significant liabilities on prior, present, and future owners. Nationwide, there are nearly 500,000 brownfields.

Because brownfields are often contaminated from past operations, they present economic and public policy challenges to their host communities. Developers are often reluctant to engage in redevelopment efforts because of the liability that may be imposed upon them under the Comprehensive Environmental Response, Compensation and Liability Act (CERCLA, 42 U.S.C. § 9601 et seq.). CERCLA and similar laws adopted by many states impose strict, joint, and several liability upon an owner or operator of a site where contamination is present, regardless of whether that person caused the pollution. See, e.g., Tanglewood East Homeowners v. Charles-Thomas, Inc., 849 F.2d

1568 (5th Cir. 1988). Consequently, a developer could be liable for millions of dollars of remediation costs simply by purchasing a brownfield site. This potential liability causes many brownfields to lie fallow. As a means to encourage their redevelopment, a number of states have enacted statutes to reduce liability and have created programs that provide financial incentives to redevelopers.

These state programs are important for several reasons. First, by encouraging the remediation of contaminated properties, the environmental threat presented by them is eliminated, thereby protecting the health of the community. Second, when redeveloped, the formerly abandoned sites generate tax revenue for the community. Third, by developing brownfield sites, which are typically located in urban areas, some development pressure is removed from outlying greenfields. Fourth, communities can use brownfields to meet various planning objectives such as the creation of affordable housing or additional commercial development.

Under its Land Recycling Program, the State of Pennsylvania provides grants to communities to create inventories of their brownfields. In 1993, New Jersey created the Environmental Opportunity Zone Act (EOZA), N.J. Stat. Ann §§ 54.4–3.150 et seq., which permits municipalities to designate certain contaminated properties as environmental opportunity zones. Once such properties are designated, they are eligible for the abatement of local real property taxes for up to 15 years, which helps redevelopers pay the cost of required remediation.

§ 7. EXCLUSIONARY ZONING

A. THE EXCLUSIONARY NATURE OF ZONING

Zoning is exclusionary by nature. Since its inception, zoning has separated land uses by excluding from particular districts all uses except those that are expressly permitted. The exclusionary effect of zoning presents several important issues. Are there any uses that a zoning ordinance may exclude entirely? Are there some that cannot be excluded for one reason or another? If zoning cannot exclude truly harmful uses—by eliminating or confining boiler factories, rendering plants, other types of heavy industry, or automobile junkyards, for example—then how can it truly protect its residents? If zoning is permitted to be exclusionary with respect to certain land uses, then how broadly can this principle be applied? Carried to the extreme, zoning's exclusionary effect could be extremely damaging to broader state interests and property rights. What happens, for example, if suburban zoning ordinances prevent the construction of multi-family housing or impose building standards that greatly increase housing costs? If the effect of these is to exclude a significant portion of the state's population, can such zoning be valid?

B. THE DEFINITION OF "FAMILY" AS EXCLUSIONARY

Zoning ordinances typically include a section of definitions that explains the technical terms used in subsequent provisions. Many ordinances define "family" for the purpose of limiting the types of households that may live in "single-family" housing. In many communities this is vastly important, since the majority of the land is zoned for single-family development. When such definitions allow any number of persons who are related by blood, marriage, or adoption to constitute a family, but limit the number of unrelated persons living together as a single household, legal problems arise.

Some courts simply hold that such distinctions have no place in the zoning ordinance—that land use regulations should be limited to what uses are permitted and not define who should live in permitted types of housing. In Des Plaines v. Trottner, 34 Ill. 2d 432, 216 N.E.2d 116 (Ill. 1966), for example, the Illinois court struck down a provision that defined a family as one or more persons each related to the other by blood, adoption, or marriage, together with the relatives' spouses and including domestic servants, but not more than one permanent guest, living together as a single household. The court found the ordinance objectionable because it was not based on a specific type of use but sought to inquire into the relationship of the occupants.

The U.S. Supreme Court in Belle Terre v. Boraas, 416 U.S. 1 (1974), upheld a village ordinance that restricted the occupancy of single-family dwellings to families that include any number of individuals related by blood, marriage, or adoption (excluding servants) but only two unmarried people living together as a single housekeeping unit. The Court found no violation of federal constitutional principles in such discrimination, reckoning that the purpose of the law was to accomplish a legitimate public purpose: "A quiet place where yards are wide, people few, and motor vehicles restricted are legitimate guidelines in a land use project addressed to family needs." The Court did not agree with the plaintiffs that the exclusion of a larger number of unrelated people living together in a communal arrangement interfered with the right to travel, the interests of interstate commerce, the right of privacy, or the interests of an open and egalitarian society. Nor did it find that equal protection rights were violated, noting that lines are routinely drawn by legislatures that create classes and treat those classes differently. These are valid, according to the Court, as long as the distinctions are not arbitrary or unreasonable.

In More v. City of East Cleveland, 431 U.S. 494 (1977), East Cleveland enacted a housing ordinance that only allowed a few categories of related family members to occupy the same dwelling; specifically the ordinance prohibited two first cousins from living in the same home. The U.S. Supreme Court held that the regulation was an intrusive regulation on the family and family living arrangements.

In McMinn v. Town of Oyster Bay, 66 N.Y.2d 544, 488 N.E.2d 1240, 498 N.Y.S.2d 128 (N.Y. 1985), New York's highest court invalidated a zoning provision that defined family as "any number of persons related by blood, marriage, or legal adoption, living and cooking on the premises together as a single, non-profit housekeeping unit," or "any two (2) persons not related by blood, marriage or legal adoption, living and cooking on the premises together as a single, nonprofit housekeeping unit, both of whom are sixty-two (62) years of age or over." According to the court, "Manifestly, restricting occupancy of single-family housing based on the biological or legal relationships between its inhabitants bears no reasonable relationship to the goals of reducing parking and traffic problems, controlling population density, and preventing noise and disturbance." These legitimate goals, including the goal of preserving the character of a single-family zone, cannot be achieved through such a narrow definition of family. The court also reasoned that *Belle Terre* was not controlling because the Oyster Bay ordinance contained more restrictive age limitations.

The New York approach was rejected by the Missouri Court of Appeals in City of Ladue v. Horn, 720 S.W.2d 745 (Mo. App. E.D. 1986). The case involved an unmarried couple living together in a large house with their teen-age children from earlier marriages, a household configuration not included in the local definition of family. The court rejected the federal constitutional arguments, relying on *Belle Terre v. Boraas*, and also rejected arguments under state law, finding "a governmental interest in marriage and in preserving the integrity of the biological or legal family."

C. ZONING THAT PRECLUDES AFFORDABLE HOUSING

Since local governments derive their power to adopt zoning and land use controls from the state, devices that tend to exclude various groups of households from living in the community are problematic. How can the state's police power, delegated to local governments, be used by them to exclude such populations? Zoning provisions that require all housing to be built on large lots, or that require houses to exceed a certain size tend to produce costly housing and to exclude lower- and moderate-income households. Zoning ordinances that do not permit multi-family housing can have the same effect.

(i) The "Fair Share" Requirement

In Appeal of Girsh, 437 Pa. 237, 263 A.2d 395 (Pa. 1970), the Pennsylvania court invalidated the total exclusion of apartments from a municipality. The town was zoned for single- and two-family residential as well as industrial and commercial use. Apartment buildings were not affirmatively provided for in the zoning, but were permitted upon the approval of a variance. When the plaintiff sought a building permit to construct an apartment on land zoned for single-family construction, the permit was denied because multiple dwellings were not allowed in the zone. The court noted that the township cannot take action to allow only certain types of homeowners to reside within its borders.

The leading case on the subject of exclusionary zoning is Southern Burlington County NAACP v. Township of Mount Laurel, 67 N.J. 151, 336 A.2d 713 (N.J. 1975) (Mount Laurel I). In this case, the NAACP challenged the township's zoning ordinances as invalid because they had the effect of excluding low- and moderate-income persons from the community. The zoning was primarily for large lot and low density residential development. There was no multi-family or mobile home zoning. The New Jersey Supreme Court agreed with the NAACP and held that because the right to housing is a fundamental right and the zoning had an exclusionary effect, it was a violation of due process and equal protection. The court held that Mount Laurel should take action to amend its zoning to provide for low- and moderate-income persons.

Southern Burlington County NAACP v. Township of Mt. Laurel, 92 N.J. 158, 456 A.2d 390 (N.J. 1983) (Mount Laurel II), was decided eight years later. The Supreme Court of New Jersey revisited the issue because the township had not made changes to its exclusionary zoning provisions. The court held that municipalities must remove all zoning, subdivision, and exaction ordinances that are not necessary for the protection of the health and safety of the community. In essence, municipalities were required to eliminate all barriers that stand in the way of providing their fair share of low- and moderate-income housing.

In 2008, the New Jersey state agency, the Council on Affordable Housing ("COAH"), promulgated the revised Third Round Rules, which were challenged and invalidated by the Appellate Division. The rules had three components for a fair share allocation of housing responsibility to a local government. The lawsuit focused on the third component, a "growth share" standard under which low- and moderate-income housing was required to be built as a percentage of actual residential growth. In a 3–2 opinion by the NJ Supreme Court, In re Adoption of N.J.A.C. 5:96 & 5:97 by New Jersey Council on Affordable Housing, 215 N.J. 578, 74 A.3d 893 (N.J. 2013), the court agreed with the opponents of the rule that local governments could avoid meeting their constitutionally mandated housing obligations by manipulating their residential growth or simply deciding to have no such growth.

The courts in New York have exhibited a forceful judicial policy regarding affordable housing: "What we will not countenance, then, under any guise, is community efforts at immunization or exclusion." Golden v. Planning Bd. of Town of Ramapo, 30 N.Y.2d 359, 285 N.E.2d 291, 334 N.Y.S.2d 138 (N.Y. 1972). In Berenson v. Town of New Castle, 38 N.Y.2d 102, 341 N.E.2d 236, 378 N.Y.S.2d 672 (N.Y. 1975), a landowner attacked as exclusionary a suburban town's zoning law that contained no provision for the development of multi-family housing in any zoning district in the jurisdiction. The Court of Appeals found the town's law to be exclusionary, stating that "[t]he primary goal of a zoning ordinance must be to provide for the development of a balanced, cohesive community which will make efficient use of the town's available land." The court held that "in enacting a zoning ordinance, consideration must be given to regional [housing] needs and requirements" and that "[t]here must be a balancing of the local desire to maintain the status quo within the community and the greater public interest that regional needs be met." The *Berenson* case held that developers have standing to challenge zoning laws that exclude more affordable types of housing since their rights cannot realistically be separated from the rights of nonresidents, in search of a comfortable place to live.

(ii) Large Lot Zoning

Attacks have been made on zoning provisions that require large minimum lot sizes. What is reasonable and not exclusionary in nature cannot be defined with mathematical precision. Zoning provisions that require three- or even five-acre minimum residential lot sizes have been upheld. Factors that courts use to support the upholding of large-lot zoning include the need to prevent overcrowding and an undue concentration of people; the burden on public facilities including schools, fire and police services, streets, and water and sewer systems; the fact that there are other zones with smaller minima; the rural and occasionally historic character of the area; the desire to promote tourism; and compatibility with the socio-economic situation and existing uses prevailing in the community.

Factors that courts cite in invalidating large-lot zoning include the lack of a reasonable relationship to the police power; a size which is so large and reduces the overall value of the land so much that the court regards it as confiscatory; a tendency for the lot sizes to be exclusionary and to serve private interests; the fact that the town is in the onward path of suburban development; and the fact that the result would be to exclude low-income people from living there. The validity of large-lot zoning is likely to vary depending on the size of the lot, the circumstances of the community or area involved, and the hostility, or lack of it, to large-lot zoning in a particular jurisdiction.

New York's highest court sustained a minimum lot size requirement in Robert E. Kurzius, Inc. v. Incorporated Village of Upper Brookville, 51 N.Y.2d 338, 414 N.E.2d 680, 434 N.Y.S.2d 180 (N.Y. 1980). The Village of Upper Brookville appealed a lower court ruling that its five-acre minimum lot size for single-family residences was invalid under *Berenson*. The Court of Appeals sustained the zoning in the absence of any showing that the village had failed to consider regional housing needs and that such needs were unsatisfied. The court held that there was no evidence that the zoning law was enacted with an "exclusionary purpose," implying that a showing of such a purpose would be an additional rationale for finding a zoning law unconstitutionally exclusionary.

(iii) Minimum Building Size

Similar attacks have been brought against zoning provisions that require houses to exceed minimum building size requirements. The general rule remains in most jurisdictions that a minimum size requirement that can be reasonably related to health considerations is valid. Modern courts have shown a tendency to look with skepticism at such requirements, however, because substantial variations in the size of the family make such requirements less meaningful in terms of mental health considerations and because some ordinances provide for different minimum requirements in different districts.

In Lionshead Lake, Inc. v. Wayne Township, 10 N.J. 165, 89 A.2d 693 (N.J. 1952), a minimum house size requirement was upheld as valid because preserving the character of the community was a valid objective and house size could achieve that goal. This was true even where the plaintiff demonstrated that the township was in the path of development. This New Jersey doctrine matured in Home Builders League of South Jersey, Inc. v. Township of Berlin, 81 N.J. 127, 405 A.2d 381 (N.J. 1979), where plaintiffs attacked a minimum floor area requirement. Even where such a provision can be shown to be reasonably related to a legitimate state interest, it can be invalidated if its adverse consequences become too severe. In this case, however, the town was unable to establish that the ordinance achieved a legitimate state interest since it failed to show what public purpose was served by it other than achieving economic segregation. The Supreme Court of New Jersey affirmed the lower court's holding that the ordinance was invalid.

D. MOBILE HOMES AND MANUFACTURED HOUSING

Most efforts to exclude mobile homes totally from a multi-use community have been held unconstitutional; but courts generally permit the separate classification of mobile homes and the restriction of them to certain zones because of their adverse impact on neighborhood development and property values, their minimum storage capacity for items of personal property, and the fact that aesthetically they are less pleasing. See, e.g., Duckworth v. Bonney Lake, 91 Wash. 2d 19, 586 P.2d 860 (Wash. 1978). In Yurczvk v. Yellowstone Cty., 319 Mont. 169, 83 P.3d 266 (Mont. 2004), the state's highest court held that the county zoning regulation, allowing only permanent and continuous dwelling in District 17, was invalid because this regulation prohibited mobile homes and had no real bearing on the public health, safety, morals, or general welfare of the community.

The bulk of the litigation involving zoning and mobile homes, or manufactured housing, deals with the issue of whether such dwellings can be confined to parks or special districts and excluded from single-family zones. In Town of Glocester v. Olivo's Mobile Home Court, Inc., 111 R.I. 120, 300 A.2d 465 (R.I. 1973), the owner of a mobile home park challenged a city ordinance that limited the number of mobile homes in any one park to 30. The Rhode Island court noted that the test used to determine whether an ordinance is a legitimate exercise of the police power is whether there exists a reasonable relationship between the ordinance and protecting the public health, safety, morals, and welfare. The court held that the limitation of 30 mobile homes per park was not a valid exercise of the police power, but was more likely intended to protect the community's tax base, which is not a proper basis for such a limitation.

§ 8. AFFORDABLE HOUSING AND ENVIRONMENTAL JUSTICE

A. INCLUSIONARY ZONING

Local governments may, and in some states must, include in their comprehensive plans the consideration of regional needs, including housing, and to respond to the present and future housing needs of the community, including affordable housing. The comprehensive planning studies of the community may identify a particular housing need for senior citizens, young families, or other special population groups. Local governments in various states have used their zoning authority to encourage the development of housing for all types of households: senior citizens, middle-income families, homeless families, employees of the municipality, volunteer firefighters, farm workers, and first-time homebuyers.

Municipalities have authority to adopt zoning measures that encourage private developers to provide a wide variety of housing types. These can include multi-family housing of a variety of types, factory-constructed and modular homes, accessory houses and apartments, in-fill elderly cottages, and clustered housing on smaller lots, with party walls and with other cost efficiencies.

To ensure that housing is provided for low- and moderate-income households, some communities simply require that all residential developments in certain zones contain a percentage of housing affordable to them. Developers of 20 or more residential units in San Jose, California are required by local ordinance to provide 20% of their units at an affordable cost, meaning no more than 30% of income for low and moderate income households. Options to provide the required units off-site are provided and a density bonus is provided for developers who provide the affordable units on site. In California Bldg. Indus. Assn v. City of San Jose, 61 Cal. 4th 435 (2016), petitioners argued that the ordinance constituted a regulatory taking and a violation of the unconstitutional conditions doctrine. The court disagreed, holding that, "[As] a general matter, so long as a land use regulation does not constitute a physical taking or deprive a property owner of all viable economic use of the property, such a restriction does not violate the takings clause," and that there can be "no valid unconstitutional conditions takings claim without a governmental exaction of property, and the ordinance . . . does not effect an exaction." The U.S. Supreme Court issued a denial of certiorari.

The City of Napa enacted an inclusionary housing ordinance requiring developers of all new residential construction to set aside 10% of the new units for affordable housing. The Home Builders Association brought an action against the city alleging that the ordinance was facially invalid as a taking. In Home Builders Association of Northern California v. City of Napa, 90 Cal. App. 4th 188, 108 Cal. Rptr. 2d 60 (Cal. App. 1 Dist. 2001), the court found that creating affordable housing was a legitimate state interest and that the ordinance "substantially advanced" that governmental interest. The court also rejected the plaintiff's argument that the set asides were unconstitutional exactions constituting a taking of the developers' property without just compensation.

The apparatus required to carry out such inclusionary schemes can be somewhat complicated. Municipalities can establish income guidelines defining "moderate-income," for example, maintaining waiting lists of income-eligible households, not issuing certificates of occupancy until developers have placed deed restrictions on affordable units requiring them to be occupied by eligible moderate-income households over time, and requiring that units be sold or leased to target households.

Where state law permits them to do so, communities can encourage developers to provide affordable housing by allowing them additional houses if they promise to make a percentage of them available to certain types of households in need of affordable accommodations. State law can go further and require communities to provide affordable housing. In New Jersey, the legislature adopted the Fair Housing Act of 1985 to provide for the development of low- and moderate-income housing under local zoning (N.J. Stat. Ann §§ 52:27 D–301–

329). It established the Council on Affordable Housing (COAH) to implement the statute's fair share plan, based on an extensive statewide housing study and allocation formula. The COAH determines the fair share of each locality and reviews and certifies local fair share housing plans. Such plans are prepared and submitted by municipalities throughout the state. If a local government fails to submit such a plan, or if the plan does not merit COAH certification, the locality is particularly vulnerable to developer challenges. If a developer of affordable housing is denied approval to build in a locality without a certified plan, the court is likely to mandate the rezoning of the developer's land to a higher density allowing the construction of affordable housing.

The city of Austin, Texas amended its zoning ordinance to add a bonus density incentive for affordable housing. (§ 25–1–720). It establishes a voluntary density bonus for residential developments where at least 50% of units are affordable to residents making 60% median family income or below or where at least 20% of units are affordable to residents making 50% or below. Rental units have a minimum affordability period of 40 years and owner-occupied units have a minimum affordability period of 99 years.

In Connecticut, the state legislature adopted the Affordable Housing Land Use Appeals Act of 1990, which expressly reverses the burden of proof when a municipality denies a developer's application to construct affordable housing (Conn. Gen. Stat. § 8–

30g). Under the Act, a municipality that denies a developer's application to construct affordable housing carries the burden of proving that its action is justified by showing that it was "necessary to protect substantial public interests in health, safety . . . and such public interests clearly outweigh the need for affordable housing." Connecticut communities in which at least 10% of the housing stock is affordable to low- and moderate-income families are exempt from the application of this burden-shifting statute.

Under the Chapter 40B Housing Program in Massachusetts, developers may override restrictive local zoning bylaws in order to increase the number of affordable homes in municipalities where less than 10% of the housing is defined as affordable using HUD's definitions of low- and moderate-income households.

Another method of increasing affordable housing is to allow owners and developers in single-family zoning districts to add a dwelling unit within a single-family home or to an accessory building, like a garage, or even as a free-standing unit on the lot. Originally called accessory apartments, such units are now referred to as Accessory Dwelling Units or ADUs. Some municipalities are amending provisions of single-family zoning districts to permit three or four units in such districts and some are permitting small multi-family buildings on lots in single-family zones.

Allowing the owners of existing single-family homes and developers of vacant lots in single-family zones to add one or more dwelling units allows for more affordable housing by spreading the cost of land, infrastructure, design, and permitting costs among two or more units. The potential of this strategy to increase needed housing supply is great, since the typical American municipalities have zoned from 75–90% of their land single-family.

In 2020, Portland, Oregon added a Better Housing by Design component to its comprehensive plan, zoning code, and zoning map. In addition to greater ADU flexibility in its single-family zones, it zones more land for multi-family zoning, scaled to the neighborhood. The zoning allows the market to dictate number of units with the number of dwellings determined by developers and the market they want to reach.

Portland's zoning amendments immediately followed the adoption of the "middle housing" law by the state legislature in 2019. Middle housing is becoming a popular term describing a range of housing types that stand between single-family and larger multiple family buildings: the so called "missing middle" in most zoning ordinances. The Oregon law requires larger cities and counties to allow duplexes, triplexes, quadraplexes, cottage clusters, and townhouses in all single-family zones. The law specifies that all cities must allow the development of "[a] duplex on each lot or parcel zoned for residential use that allows for the development of detached single-family dwellings." The Oregon law also voids provisions in recorded title instruments filed after its effective date that allow the development of a single-family dwelling on the property but prohibit the development of middle housing or an accessory dwelling unit.

B. HOUSING AND ENVIRONMENTAL JUSTICE

This subsection focuses its coverage of the broad, critical, and complex issue of environmental justice on its affordable and fair housing dimensions. Fair housing includes affordable housing, but is broader in scope and purpose. Fair housing prohibits discrimination against protected groups in the leasing and sale of housing as well as zoning.

The federal Fair Housing Act of 1968 (Pub. L. 90–284) prohibits discrimination in housing based on disability, race, color, religion, national origin, sex, and familial status. The statute bars state and local governments from enacting or enforcing land use and zoning laws, policies, practices, and decisions that discriminate against persons because of a protected characteristic, such as race, national origin, or disability.

In Texas Department of Housing and Community Affairs v. Inclusive Communities Project, 576 U.S. 519 (2015), the U.S. Supreme Court held that the disparate impact liability standard applied in Title VII of the Civil Rights Act also applied to claims brought under the Fair Housing Act (FHA). Petitioners alleged that statewide criteria for distribution of federal Low Income Tax Credits encouraged the development of subsidized housing in predominantly black urban areas while simultaneously discouraging development in predominantly white suburban areas, thus leading to continued racial segregation in the Dallas metropolitan area. The Court found that disparate impact liability was "consistent with the FHA's central purpose" of eradicating discrimination, particularly noting the discriminatory effects of local zoning laws. While the Court's decision was a victory for fair housing advocates, it limited the potential exposure of local zoning authorities in several significant ways that have proved difficult barriers for plaintiffs to overcome in subsequent cases.

Environmental justice poses a major challenge for local governments to correct the segregation of minorities caused by ubiquitous single-family zoning. In some communities, early zoning ordinances segregated blacks by designating specific districts where they were allowed to live. Baltimore, Md., Ordinance 692 (May 15, 1911). In Buchanan v. Warley, 245 U.S. 60, 82 (1917), the Supreme Court found a similar ordinance in Louisville, Kentucky to be unconstitutional not because it was discriminatory against blacks, but because it restricted the rights of white property owners to sell.

After these laws were declared unconstitutional, *de facto* segregation continued due to the high cost of developing and purchasing single-family houses on individual lots with discrete infrastructure. This had an obvious disparate impact on households of color, which were disproportionately of low and moderate income.

Federal Housing Administration (FHA) and private bank redlining of neighborhoods in which households of color lived under this zoning, beginning in the 1930's, prevented homeowners in those neighborhoods from qualifying for mortgage insurance and mortgage loans. The FHA and banks' underwriting criteria specifically considered the presence of blacks in such neighborhoods too great of a risk to insure and provide mortgages. Further, 1936 FHA mortgage insurance eligibility standards favored loans to properties with deed restrictions prohibiting occupancy by African Americans where enforceable by eviction pursuant to court order in suits brought by neighbors. (1936 FHA Underwriting Manual.)

In 1948, the U.S. Supreme Court in Shelley v. Kraemer, 334 U.S. 1 (1948) held that restrictive covenants enforced by state courts violate the equal protection of law guaranteed by the 14th Amendment. The holding did not invalidate restrictive covenants as such, but only their enforcement by state courts. Despite the Court's ruling in *Shelly*, FHA officials declared in 1949 that insuring mortgages in an interracial community is a "bad risk."

While redlining wasn't the beginning of racial segregation, the practice solidified it and caused systemic underinvestment in targeted neighborhoods by banks and mortgage lenders. The original redlined maps show that the neighborhoods deemed bad risks already had less vegetation, greater concrete coverage, and more pollution than white neighborhoods that were not redlined. The unavailability of homeownership and underinvestment in neighborhoods led to further deteriorating conditions and cheap land, which attracted government sponsored roads and highways, public- and private-housing complexes, and private industry that was unwanted or unaffordable elsewhere.

Today, many of the formerly redlined neighborhoods are characterized by distressed property conditions and the absence of amenities such as parks, street trees, and other landscaping. In a 2020 study of over 100 such neighborhoods, showed that nearly all of them are now between 5 to 12°F hotter during heat waves than non-redlined nearby neighborhoods. People who live in these urban heat islands are at increased risk during extreme heat events.

Greater sensitivity to systemic racism is causing some communities, through planning and land use regulation, to mitigate some of the effects of racial discrimination and redlining. These include tree preservation ordinances, requiring green roofs and cool roofing materials, use of less pavement and pervious pavement, reduced parking surfaces, more landscaping and the provision of open space.

In Portland, Oregon, a zoning overlay district applied to lower income neighborhoods was used to designate where these types of mitigating measures are required. Montgomery County, Maryland, requires all amendments to its zoning code to be reviewed using a legislated racial impact study. Some communities are reviewing zoning and development proposals using Health Impact Assessments to identify and mitigate the social determinants of health due to poor housing and neighborhood conditions.

CHAPTER 9

LOCAL ENVIRONMENTAL LAW AS A LAND USE ISSUE

§ 1. INTRODUCTION

Environmental law, as studied in most law school classes, involves an examination of federal statutes such as the Clean Water Act and the Clean Air Act, adopted in the early 1970s. During the next decade or so, over a dozen additional federal laws were adopted and a new era of environmental cleanup and pollution prevention was underway. Uniform standards were created, aggressive enforcement practices were adopted, and federal and state agencies were employed to preserve threatened natural resources and to protect the public health.

As a result, federal agencies have successfully reduced pollution that emanates from "point sources," such as smokestacks and water pipes. Point source pollution enters navigable waters and air currents that cross state lines and are within Congress's power to regulate in the interests of interstate commerce. Most environmental damage today, however, is caused by "nonpoint source" pollution that results from land uses that are the legal responsibility of municipal governments. Federal attempts to influence local land use control in the interest of abating nonpoint source pollution have been thwarted by a variety of legal, political, and practical obstacles, not the least of which is the Tenth Amendment, which reserves to state legislatures the authority to regulate such local matters.

The focus of law school environmental law courses on the federal government as the standard-setter and steward of a healthy environment obscures the importance of the role that local governments can and do play in environmental protection. Local governments in most states have been delegated primary responsibility for determining how private land is developed and conserved. It is the legislative and regulatory actions of those governments that dictate how much of the land is covered with impervious surfaces, how many miles of roads are built, how many septic systems, sewer plants, and water systems are created, and where buildings and improvements are located. These actions determine how much "nonpoint source" air and water pollution occurs. Local land use decisions greatly affect the watersheds, waterways, and other biological resources in areas that are rich in natural resources as well as in areas where environmental assets are scarce.

§ 2. ADVENT OF LOCAL ENVIRONMENTAL LAW

During the last two decades, there has been a remarkable but little noticed trend among local governments to adopt laws that protect natural resources and lessen environmental pollution. These local environmental laws exhibit a number of forms. They include local comprehensive plans expressing environmental values, zoning districts created to protect critical environmental areas, environmental standards contained in subdivision and site plan regulations, and stand-alone environmental laws adopted to protect particular natural features such as ridgelines, wetlands, floodplains, stream banks, existing vegetative cover, and forests. Local governments have creatively used a variety of traditional and modern powers that their state legislatures have delegated to them to address locally occurring environmental problems.

As earlier chapters demonstrate, our nation's legal system gives local governments a key, if not the principal, role in land use regulation. Local governments may adopt master plans, zoning ordinances, and a variety of community-building regulations that provide for their future development. Comprehensive zoning began as a mechanism for protecting public health and safety by separating incompatible land uses from one another. In its application, zoning became design-oriented, focusing on the layout of streets and highways, the location of public buildings, the ability of fire trucks and firefighters to reach and fight fires, the size and bulk requirements that protect property values, and the infrastructure connections that create a workable community.

Subdivision and site plan regulations emerged to complement zoning and to help localities implement their physical plans. Such regulations initially concentrated on the creation of safe intersections, the fluid movement of vehicles, the siting of buildings, the prevention of off-site impacts such as flooding, and the adequacy of road width, curbs, and sidewalks. In Golden v. Planning Board of Town of Ramapo, 30 N.Y.2d 359, 334 N.Y.S.2d 138, 285 N.E.2d 291 (N.Y. 1972), the leading state court case sustaining local growth management ordinances, New York's highest court referred to subdivision control as a mechanism "to guide community development . . . , while at the same time encouraging the provision of adequate facilities for the housing, distribution, comfort, and convenience of local residents."

In their inception, regulatory tools such as zoning, and the regulation of subdivision and site plan development, were not designed to protect natural resources from degradation. An early case that demonstrates the early judicial antipathy to local environmental regulation is Morris County Land Improvement Co. v. Township of Parsippany-Troy Hills, 40 N.J. 539, 193 A.2d 232 (N.J. 1963). The Supreme Court of New Jersey invalidated a county zoning provision that severely restricted the development of swampland that served as a natural flood control system for the Passaic River Valley. The provisions limited land uses to hunting and fishing preserves and wildlife sanctuaries, which the court labeled as "nonproductive" land uses. The court found that the regulations were so severe that they constituted a taking of the owner's property under the Constitution. The court characterized swampland protection as an attempt to achieve a public benefit, rather than to prevent the owner from harming the area through the destruction of valuable wetlands.

A different perspective on the importance of wetlands, and their protection, is evident in a Wisconsin case decided in 1972, Just v. Marinette County, 56 Wis. 2d 7, 201 N.W.2d 761 (Wis. 1972). In *Just*, the plaintiffs purchased 36.4 acres of lakefront property with the intention of subdividing the land and selling individual parcels. Under the county-adopted shoreland zoning ordinance, the property was placed in a conservancy district and classified as wetlands. The plaintiffs argued that the restrictions were an unconstitutional taking of their land without just compensation. The county argued that wetland regulation of this type was a valid exercise of the police power needed to prevent the degradation of valuable natural resources. The court agreed with the county and held that the ordinance was constitutional, stating that "The shoreland zoning ordinance preserves nature, the environment, and natural resources as they were created and to which the people have a present right." The court recognized that a landowner has "no absolute and unlimited right to change the essential natural character of his land so as to use it for a purpose for which it was unsuited in its natural state and which injures the rights of others."

How local land use regulation complements federal and state environmental regulation is evident in the legal system's approach to protecting water quality. The drinking water serving most homes and businesses in many communities comes from groundwater wells, and much of the surface water pollution in her community is due to nonpoint source pollution, caused by surrounding development and land uses. The Clean Water Act (CWA) effectively regulates neither of these. It is limited in its reach. Non-navigable waters, groundwater, and nonpoint sources of water pollution all fall outside the statute's regulatory scope. Federal authority, therefore, can only go so far, leaving many gaps to be filled by the states and the municipalities to which they delegate power to regulate land use. State and local regulations can go beyond the limits of the CWA, reaching isolated wetlands and intrastate waters, groundwater, and the sources of nonpoint source pollution.

With respect to regulating non-point source pollution, States often defer to local governments to regulate the land use causes of such disturbances. State laws concentrate on issuing and enforcing permits for point source pollution and the construction and maintenance of on-site wastewater facilities and larger wastewater plants.

Local governments have the authority to fill the gaps in the nation's water law regime. Local land use laws can include aquifer and watershed overlay zoning, open space provisions in land use plans, urban growth boundaries, designated priority areas for growth, designated water conservation areas, creation of rain gardens and sedimentation ponds, cluster development requirements to avoid development in vulnerable watershed areas, sedimentation controls of surface mining operations, special limitations on water use in subdivisions that exceed recharge levels, density bonuses for water conserving features in residences, aquifer protection districts, required wetland creation, use of pervious cover and detention ponds, adoption of EcoDistricts with provisions that lower per capita water consumption, use of a green building checklist including water conservation measures, adoption of tree preservation ordinances and Urban Tree Canopy goals, mandatory well testing provisions, stormwater management fees with incentives to reduce impervious coverage, local water conservation and permitting laws, and public nuisance laws.

These laws are adopted by local governments to fit the unique circumstances of each one, demonstrating the difficulty that a remote state or federal legislature might have in legislating to protect water quality and other public values. Many of the local solutions mentioned here are not within the regulatory authority of the federal government and beyond the reach of the power that state legislatures have given their state water, health, and environmental conservation agencies.

§ 3. AUTHORITY

Whether local governments have the authority to adopt laws to protect natural resources and prevent environmental pollution depends on the scope of power they have been delegated by their state legislatures and also on how state courts interpret their delegated authority. Some state courts have adopted rules of strict construction and others interpret local authority more broadly.

One of the original purposes for delegating zoning authority to municipal governments was to "encourage the most appropriate use of the land." This language was contained in the model act formulated in the 1920s, the Standard Zoning Enabling Act, which served as the basis for state zoning enabling acts in most of the states, and it is found in the enabling acts of many states still today. When state courts interpret local legal authority broadly, this language may be sufficient to justify the adoption of land use controls designed to protect the environment. In some states, state legislatures have adopted special legislation authorizing local governments, for example, to protect the physical and aesthetic environment, control development in floodplains, prevent soil erosion, or require local governments to conduct environmental impact reviews before approving development proposals.

An example of how the interplay of state legislative delegation and state court interpretation works to empower local governments to adopt creative environmental legislation is found in South Carolina, where the constitution authorizes the legislature to provide for "the structure and organization, powers, duties, functions and responsibilities of the municipalities . . . by general law." S.C. Const. Art. VIII, § 8. The constitution says that "[t]he provisions of [the] Constitution and all laws concerning local government shall be liberally construed in their favor," and that any powers granted local governments by the constitution and laws "shall include those fairly implied and not prohibited by [the] Constitution." S.C. Const. Art. VIII, § 17.

This broad grant of local authority was statutorily implemented by the South Carolina Legislature by provisions such as the following: "All counties of the State ... have authority to enact regulations, resolutions, and ordinances ... respecting any subject as appears to them necessary and proper for the security, general welfare, and convenience of counties or for preserving health, peace, order, and good government in them." S.C. Code Ann. § 4–9–25 (1976). State legislation provides that the powers of a municipality shall be liberally construed in favor of the municipality, and the specific mention of particular powers shall not be construed as limiting in any manner the general powers of such municipalities. S.C. Code Ann. § 5–7–10 (1976).

Local governments in South Carolina derive their express zoning and planning powers from the South Carolina Local Government Planning Enabling Act. S.C. Code Ann. § 6–29–310–1200 (1976). Under the Act, comprehensive land use plans must include, but are not limited to, seven elements: (1) population, (2) economic development, (3) natural resources, (4) cultural resources, (5) community facilities, (6) housing, and (7) land use. S.C. Code Ann. § 6–29–510 (1976). All zoning and land use regulations must be in accordance with the comprehensive plan. S.C. Code Ann. 6–29–720(B) (1976). The Act also authorizes specific zoning techniques such as cluster development, floating zones, and planned development districts. S.C. Code Ann. § 6–29–720(C) (1976). However, it makes clear that "any other planning and zoning techniques may be used." S.C. Code Ann. § 6–29–720(C) (1976). When making revisions to the zoning ordinance, the municipality is authorized to consider "the protection of ... ecologically sensitive areas." S.C. Code Ann. § 6–29–710 (1976).

Based on this authority from the state, the Town of Mount Pleasant adopted a local environmental review ordinance. Mount Pleasant, S.C. Code of Ordinances § 156.054 (1996). The purpose of the ordinance is to provide a basis for assessing the impacts of significant development proposals on the "town's overall environment and infrastructure, natural ecology, and economic, historic, social, and related public resources." Mount Pleasant, S.C. Code of Ordinances § 156.054(A) (1996). The ordinance requires an impact assessment for development projects that meet certain thresholds. The town planning director reviews the impact assessment and may conduct independent field investigations for verification. If negative impacts are identified, the town council determines whether the impacts are "acceptable and in the public interest." Mount Pleasant, S.C. Code of Ordinances § 156.054(G) (1996). If not, the council has the authority to request the developer to mitigate negative impacts. This local law provides its local boards extensive authority to review and condition land development projects so that their adverse impacts on the environment are minimized.

In other states, local governments are required, rather than allowed, to conduct environmental impact reviews of any action they might take that could affect the environment. California, New York, and Washington state statutes, for example, require local land use agencies to impose mitigation conditions on the development projects that they approve to protect the environment.

How this requirement works to insinuate environmental values into the day-to-day business of approving developments is evident in a Washington state case, Moss v. City of Bellingham, 31 P.3d 703 (Wash. Ct. App. 2001). In *Moss*, a developer planned to purchase 79 acres and develop a 172-lot subdivision in the City of Bellingham. The parcel contained steep slopes and ridges and two creeks, among other features that physically limited its development. Pursuant to the state mandated environmental review process, the developer submitted an environmental checklist to the City of Bellingham. The developer then submitted an extensive environmental assessment at the request of the local planning and development commission, together with a number of mitigation measures to reduce the environmental impact of the project. Following the commission's determination that the project, as mitigated, would not have an adverse impact on the environment, local citizens sued, claiming that the developer should be required to submit a full environmental impact statement. The court deferred to the commission's determination of no environmental impact, stating that the petitioners were unable to show that it was clearly erroneous.

Dillon's Rule historically has been an obstacle to claim that local governments enjoy broad and flexible land use authority. Merriam v. Moody's Executors,

25 Iowa 163 (1868). It holds that municipalities are not sovereign entities but merely instrumentalities of states and that the legal powers delegated to them by state legislatures are to be narrowly construed. Since 1868, the rule has been seriously eroded. State constitutional amendments, home rule provisions, state enabling statutes, and case law have diminished the effect of Dillon's Rule as it pertains to the authority of local governments to adopt and enforce land use regulations in the vast majority of states.

The law in two generally conservative states demonstrates the demise of Dillon. In Alabama, the court's holding in Ryan v. City of Bay Minette, 667 So.2d 41, 43 (1995) states:

> Zoning is a legislative matter, and, as a general proposition, the exercise of the zoning power should not be subjected to judicial interference unless clearly necessary. In enacting or amending zoning legislation, the local authorities are vested with broad discretion, and, in cases where the validity of a zoning ordinance is fairly debatable, the court cannot substitute its judgment for that of the legislative authority.

State legislation in Arkansas, Ark. Code Ann. § 14–43–602(b) (2011) states that "The rule of decision known as 'Dillon's Rule' is inapplicable to the municipal affairs of municipalities." The legislation defines "municipal affairs" to mean "all matters and affairs of government germane to, affecting, or concerning the municipality or its government except" certain state affairs "subject to the general laws of the State of Arkansas."

The remainder of this chapter discusses additional local laws that protect the environment, dividing them somewhat arbitrarily into those that accomplish the protection of water resources and those that protect the land itself.

§ 4. WATER RESOURCE PRESERVATION

A. AQUIFER/GROUNDWATER SUPPLIES

Some localities use their environmental authority to protect drinking water aquifers by imposing additional regulatory standards on development projects proposed in such areas. The aquifer protection ordinance of Wallingford, Connecticut, for example, prohibits certain land uses in order to protect its groundwater resources. Landowners are not allowed to conduct businesses that use hazardous chemicals, or to use their land for solid waste disposal facilities, junk yards, septage lagoons, hazardous waste drum storage areas, bulk storage piles, surface impoundments, road salt storage, or pipelines that transmit oil, gasoline, or other hazardous materials. Other less dangerous land uses are allowed but carefully controlled, such as above-ground chemical and fuel storage, underground fuel storage, dry cleaning, and new or enlarged manure, fertilizer, pesticide, and herbicide storage sites. Wallingford, CT, Zoning Ordinances § 4.12 (1985). In Connecticut Resources Recovery Auth. v. Planning and Zoning Comm'n of Wallingford, 225 Conn. 731, 626 A.2d 705

(Conn. 1993), the Supreme Court of Connecticut upheld the Wallingford Zoning Ordinance § 4.12 as a valid exercise of police power because the regulation is rationally related to the protection of groundwater and the community's public health, safety, and welfare.

An early zoning case illustrates that aquifer protection has long been a legitimate objective in land use regulation. In De Mars v. Zoning Commission of Town of Bolton, 142 Conn. 580, 115 A.2d 653 (Conn. 1955), the Town of Bolton, Connecticut, adopted amendments to its zoning districts in the community. The amendments were made to meet the challenges caused by a sudden increase in the demand for housing in the town, which put pressure on the residential water supply. Increasing the lot size would lower the total number of new households that would need water and provide a larger area for septic systems, reducing the prospects of water contamination. Property owners objected claiming that the town could only amend the regulations if there was a substantial change in the circumstances and conditions since the adoption of the regulations. In upholding the amendments as valid, the court noted that zoning authorities have liberal discretion, which can only be overruled when used unfairly, without proper motive, or for an invalid purpose. The court held that the purpose of the amendments, protecting the drinking supply, was not so unrelated to providing for the health, safety, and welfare to be deemed unreasonable or unfair. Note that the Connecticut Supreme Court mentions that one of the purposes of zoning under the state zoning enabling act is to "encourage the most appropriate use of land." At this early stage, the motivation for the local law was to protect the health of the town residents, rather than environmental protection per se.

In Quick v. City of Austin, 7 S.W.3d 109 (Tex. 1998), the City of Austin, by way of referendum, adopted an ordinance to protect the water quality of the Barton Creek, Barton Springs, and the Barton Springs Edwards Aquifer. The ordinance placed strict controls on the amount of impervious (i.e. non-porous) land coverage allowed in the aquifer's watershed. Impervious coverage damages the environment in several ways: it prevents percolation of rainfall into the groundwater aquifer and increases stormwater runoff and downstream flooding; in addition, the hard surfaces collect heavy metal, petroleum, and other harmful residues, which are then washed off by storms and flushed into nearby surface waters. Buildings, driveways, parking areas, basketball courts, and other paving and construction associated with land development create non-porous surfaces of this type. Land use laws that calculate a permissible percentage of impervious coverage are aimed directly at the reduction of nonpoint source pollution and maintaining groundwater recharge: clear and important environmental objectives. Property owners challenged the validity of the ordinance because it had the effect of severely reducing their property values. In upholding the validity of the ordinance, the Texas Supreme Court found "the fact that the Ordinance severely impacts some property values does not make it invalid, arbitrary, unreasonable, inefficient, or ineffective in its attempt to control water quality."

B. STORMWATER MANAGEMENT

Stormwater management is the process of preventing, controlling, and cleansing stormwater runoff so it does not harm natural resources or human health. As more land is covered with impervious surfaces, such as roads, parking lots, and buildings, there is less surface area available for stormwater to infiltrate. Where storm basins do not exist or are not adequate, stormwater finds its way to the nearest water body. Impervious surfaces not only increase the volume and velocity of runoff, but also prevent the natural processing of nutrients, sediments, and other contaminants.

Stormwater runoff can be controlled by the use of infiltration structures, such as basins, wells, or porous pavement. Conveyance structures, such as storm drains, open ditches, and channels or streams, can be used to delay or speed runoff to a receiving stream. Detention or retention structures, such as impoundment basins or ponds, can be used to store water temporarily. Stormwater management reduces flooding, erosion, and sedimentation, and aids in replenishing groundwater.

States authorize local governments to enact stormwater programs and ordinances through comprehensive plans, zoning ordinances, and subdivision and site plan regulations. Some states have set up grant programs to aid local governments in stormwater management. Some municipalities have created utility systems to fund stormwater programs. Pennsylvania cities, boroughs, townships, and counties, for example, are authorized to prepare comprehensive plans and zoning, subdivision, and land development ordinances that may provide for stormwater management. Pennsylvania Municipalities Planning Code, Act 247 as amended. The state's Stormwater Management Act of 1978 authorizes a comprehensive watershed stormwater management program based upon local implementation and enforcement.

Stormwater management can be implemented through site plan review. Pierce County, Washington, enacted a Construction and Infrastructure Regulation that includes a Site Development and Stormwater Management System. The regulation prohibits grading, filling, clearing, excavation, or creating impervious surfaces without a site development plan. The site development plan must include a stormwater drainage plan. Pierce County, Wash. Code, title 17A (1999). Because stormwater design standards "vary in different areas of the city," Wauwatosa, Wisconsin, requires the preparation, approval, and implementation of site-specific stormwater management plans for any proposed development, redevelopment, or subdivision. Wauwatosa, Wis. Mun. Code, ch. 24.59 (1973).

Mason, Ohio, requires every subdivision and land development to include a stormwater management system "such that in a 100 year storm, the rate of stormwater runoff leaving the project area at strategic points is no more after development than if the project area had remained undeveloped." Mason, Ohio, Code of Ordinances part 11, title 1, § 1119.04 (1976). The ordinance includes highly detailed submission requirements. Two distinct drainage systems must be provided: the minor system, to accommodate runoff from frequently occurring storms; and the major system—including open channels, street cross sections, low points, culvert entrances, and even downstream areas—to accommodate runoff from a 100-year storm.

C. FLOODPLAINS

Floodplain regulation was one of the first and most extensive examples of local environmental law. Development activities in floodplains can decrease their water storage capacity, increase runoff, and decrease water quality. Local floodplain regulations can limit the extension of buildings and infrastructure into the flood areas, require that such buildings are built at certain elevations, prevent the obstruction of stream channels, and prohibit the construction of chemical or other hazardous materials storage facilities.

The early movement in floodplain regulation was initiated by the federal government's adoption of the National Flood Insurance Program, which required localities to adopt and enforce floodplain management programs as a prerequisite to the eligibility of local property owners for flood disaster insurance and payments: a significant incentive.

Irvine, California, adopted a Floodplain District Ordinance for the purpose of promoting the public health, safety, and general welfare, and to minimize public and private losses due to flood conditions in specific areas. Irvine, Ca. Zoning Ordinance § 5–2–2 (2005). Its floodplain ordinance notes that the flood hazard areas of the city are subject to periodic water inundation, which results in loss of life and property, health and safety hazards, and extraordinary public expenditures. The Flood Hazard Area Ordinance adopted by the City of Detroit is aimed at maintaining stable development patterns that are not subject to the "blighting influence of flood damage." Detroit, Mich. Zoning Ordinance § 49.0102(D) (2001). The Floodplain Protection District Ordinance of the town of Penfield, New York, contains extensive provisions to protect the environment and the public from the dangers of flooding. Penfield, N.Y. Zoning Ordinance §§ 3–14(A), (F)(1–4) (1987).

In Dooley v. Town of Fairfield, 151 Conn. 304, 197 A.2d 770 (Conn. 1964), the town of Fairfield, Connecticut, amended its zoning regulations to include a "flood plain district." Additional regulations applied to development in this one district, which prohibited the excavation, filling, and removal of soil, earth, or gravel within the district. Based on the permitted uses of a floodplain district, the rezoning had the effect of reducing the landowners' property value by 75%. Landowners challenged the rezoning as a regulatory taking. The Connecticut Supreme Court held that "from the standpoint of private ownership, the change of zone to floodplain district froze the area into a practically unusable state." "[E]nforcement of the regulation amounts, in effect, to a practical confiscation of the land." The court further reasoned that although the purposes of the regulations were laudable, they could not overcome the constitutional violations. Some type of economically viable development must be permitted by such environmental regulations.

A landowner in Oklahoma was not denied all economic and viable use of his land when his 40-acre lot of agricultural land was rezoned in a floodplain zoning district subsequent to his purchase. April v. City of Broken Arrow, 775 P.2d 1347 (Okla. 1989). The Flood Damage Protection Ordinance limited development to "flood tolerant uses." The landowner challenged the ordinance as a regulatory taking and the Oklahoma Supreme Court held that, although the landowner's application to rezone the property for higher density development was denied, the property still had economically viable uses under the current ordinance because it allowed the construction of single-family residential units.

The Supreme Court of South Dakota upheld Rapid City's decision to deny a landowner's request to rezone land located upstream of a floodplain in Parris v. City of Rapid City, 2013 S.D. 51, 834 N.W.2d 850 (S.D. 2013). The landowner's property was located within the Flood Hazard Zoning District; he requested that his parcel be rezoned to allow him to build on the 500-year floodplain. The court upheld the city's refusal because it had relied on extensive historic evidence of devastating flooding in the floodplain.

The Federal Emergency Management Act (FEMA) may be consulted by local zoning and planning boards when evaluating applications for development in a floodplain overlay district. In Doherty v. Plan Bd. of Scituate, 467 Mass. 560, 5 N.E.3d 1231 (Mass. 2014), the plaintiff applied for a special permit from the planning board to construct residential dwellings on two unimproved lots on a barrier beach peninsula. The local board denied the special permit because the plaintiff failed to demonstrate that the lots were "not subject to flooding" as required under the town's zoning law. The highest state court in Massachusetts affirmed this decision reasoning that the local board may determine whether the lots were "subject to flooding" by considering the testimony of witnesses describing their observations of the inclusion of the lots in established FEMA flood zones.

D. WETLANDS AND TIDELANDS

Local wetlands regulations restrict activities such as dredging and soil disposal, construction of roads, grading and soil removal, timber harvesting, and placement of buildings and infrastructure on wetlands and their buffer areas. Wetlands exist where there is sufficient water to saturate the soil long enough to support animals and plants suited to wetland environments. In nature, wetlands often include wildlife habitat areas adjacent to watercourses, upland slopes, wooded lands, and other critical environmental features. Although development in wetland areas is regulated by federal law and by state statutes in some states, local governments may also regulate development to protect wetlands in many jurisdictions. Some local wetlands laws go beyond wetland protection and attempt to conserve habitat and surface water resources associated with wetlands. The town of Lewisboro, New York, for example, has adopted a local wetlands and watercourse law that contains extensive protections for these resources. Lewisboro, N.Y. Code § 217–1(A) (1999). The City of Concord, New Hampshire, adopted the Shoreline Protection District to maintain the quality of surface waters and groundwater, retain flood storage properties, protect wildlife habitat and feeding areas, and protect other unique natural resources. Concord, N.H. Code ch. 28 § 3–3 (2002).

In Connecticut, state law requires local governments to adopt wetlands regulations and establish wetland agencies to regulate development activities within municipally designated wetlands. Wetlands are defined as areas containing soil types "designated as poorly drained, very poorly drained, alluvial, and floodplain by the National Cooperative Soils Survey, as may be amended from time to time by the Natural Resources Conservation Service of the United States Department of Agriculture." Conn. Gen. Stat. § 22a–38(15) (2001). A local wetlands agency has the right to regulate not only the land within the established boundaries of a wetland or watercourse, but also any adjacent area where activities might occur that would "use" the wetlands in a prohibited manner. The Act prohibits property owners from carrying out a "regulated activity" on any wetland or watercourse without a permit. Regulated activities include almost all development and land use activities. The Commissioner of the State Department of Environmental Protection (DEP) may revoke the local wetlands agency's authority to regulate activity in the wetlands if the DEP determines that the local agency has failed to perform its duties. Local wetlands agencies are given the authority to adopt regulations that expand on the Commissioner's regulations, or to add to them if necessary to protect the wetlands.

In Fafard v. Conservation Commission of Barnstable, 432 Mass. 194, 733 N.E.2d 66 (Mass. 2000), a local conservation commission in Barnstable, Massachusetts, denied the plaintiffs' application to construct a pier extending through coastal wetlands into a tidal river. Plaintiffs argued that the agency acted beyond its authority because the protection of coastal resources resided in the State of Massachusetts and that the state legislature had preempted local legal authority in this arena. The highest court in Massachusetts found that only the state had the right to regulate "public trust rights" in coastal areas, but that it had properly delegated authority to local conservation commissions to preserve coastal wetlands. As a result, the court found that the local commission was authorized to protect the wetlands by restricting and regulating construction in tidal areas, including piers. The court upheld the commission's denial of the application.

In Esplanade v. City of Seattle, 307 F.3d 978 (9th Cir. 2002), the plaintiff applied to the city to develop single-family homes on navigable tidelands that were submerged completely for approximately half of the day. The City of Seattle found three major issues with the application: the size of the pilings, the design of the access to the houses, and the lack of dry land to park cars. The Third Circuit Court of Appeals disagreed with the plaintiff's inverse condemnation argument and held that the plaintiff did not have a right to develop on the land in the first place under the public trust doctrine.

§ 5. LAND RESOURCE PRESERVATION

A. EROSION AND SEDIMENTATION CONTROL

Soil erosion is a major source of nonpoint source pollution. Some erosion occurs naturally, but it is greatly accelerated by urbanization. Erosion control measures are a critical ingredient in local stormwater management plans and floodplain programs. Comprehensive wetland regulations aim to limit erosion in upland development to prevent the effects of sedimentation of wetlands, which greatly impairs their function and value to the public and nature.

Local governments can adopt regulations to prevent soil erosion and the deposit of sediments in surface waters that land development projects cause. Undeveloped land contains organic particles that are biologically and chemically active and that, when disturbed and transported to surface waters, can cause serious water quality problems. One local soil protection ordinance observes that its purpose is to safeguard persons, protect property, prevent damage to the environment, and promote the public welfare by guiding, regulating, and controlling the design, use, and maintenance of any development or other activity that disturbs or breaks the surface of soil or results in the movement of earth on land situated in the town.

In Marion Road Association v. Westport Planning & Zoning Commission, 1994 WL 592221 (Conn. Super. Ct. 1994), a neighborhood association challenged a Connecticut town planning and zoning commission's approval of a synagogue in a residential neighborhood. The association claimed that the synagogue plans did not comply with local Sediment and Erosion Control Regulations. The regulations require that developers submit a site map and a narrative describing potential impacts related to erosion and sedimentation. The record did not indicate that a proper plan was submitted, only that a conceptual plan was submitted. The court held that such a general plan was not sufficient to meet the local law requirements. "To allow applicant's 'conceptual' plan to pass muster would trivialize these requirements into a 'consciousness-raising exercise [rather] than as obligatory regulations.' "

B. STEEP SLOPES, RIDGELINE, AND HILLTOP PROTECTIONS

Ridgelines and hilltops are valuable for both their scenic and their ecological qualities. Surface runoff from ridgeline development can contaminate rivers and streams that supply drinking water downstream. Development of septic systems on ridges and hilltops can cause contamination of lower-lying properties. Buildings and roads can disrupt wildlife corridors and critical habitats. Hillsides and ridgelines are inherently unstable and care must be taken to prevent mudslides and other catastrophic movements of earth. Local laws can require that development on ridgelines and hilltop areas blend in with the natural environment and be controlled to prevent environmental damage and to preserve particularly valuable viewsheds in the community.

Steep slopes usually are associated with other environmental features such as rock outcrops, shallow soils, bedrock fractures, and groundwater seeps. Excavations or building construction can cause instability through loosening of the soil structure and the removal of trees, vegetation, and rocks. Grading, cutting, and filling—activities associated with preparation of construction sites—can compromise the stability of some slopes. Activities such as agriculture, road and railway construction, house building, and land drainage can be regulated to protect steep slopes. The town of Cortlandt, New York, adopted a local law for the purpose of preventing the "improper alteration" of steep slopes. Cortlandt, N.Y. Code § 259.1 (1992).

Provisions of this kind can be found in local ridgeline or hilltop protection ordinances throughout the nation.

The trend in local environmental law is to recognize natural connections on the land and waters by broadening the scope of natural protection laws. Steep slopes, like wetlands, are often found in association with other critical environmental features and perform multiple functions of community value ranging from providing breathtaking vistas, to harboring wildlife in their unique, horizontal ecosystems, to protecting down-slope landowners and water bodies from flooding, erosion, and sedimentation. In Harris v. Zoning Commission of the Town of Milford, 259 Conn. 402, 788 A.2d 1239 (Conn. 2002), the Connecticut Supreme Court sustained a town law that protected ridgelines in this broader context. The local law excluded wetlands, watercourses, and land with a 25 percent slope or greater from calculations used to determine how much land is developable under the zoning ordinance. The calculation was applicable only in residential districts and served to lower density in those districts by increasing the minimum lot size needed for single-family home construction. The court rejected the plaintiffs' claim that the law lacked a rational basis and violated the uniformity requirement for zoning under Connecticut law.

The City of Manitou Springs, Colorado, adopted a hillside protection ordinance to regulate development on mountain slopes and ridges and to control erosion, subsidence, and drainage. The ordinance used an equation to determine the lot sizes allowed for development of property located on designated hillsides: the steeper the slope, the larger the required lot size, and the lower the density permitted. As a result of the ordinance, a density for a proposed new development was reduced from 194 homes to 108. The affected landowners, in Sellon v. City of Manitou Springs, 745 P.2d 229 (Colo. 1987), argued that the hillside ordinance was not related to the public health, safety, and welfare and thus violated their due process rights. In holding that the ordinance was valid, the Supreme Court of Colorado noted that the ordinance responded to a legitimate state concern and that, therefore, the due process rights of the landowners were not violated. The court also noted that its role is not to determine whether the ordinance was the optimal method of achieving the public interest, only that the city's law was rational and reasonably related to preventing erosion, harmful drainage, and achieving other legitimate public objectives.

C. SCENIC VIEWS

As congestion of homes, traffic, and people has accompanied urban sprawl, a counter movement has begun, focusing on one salient symptom: the disappearance of open space—the appearance that things are too crowded. Citizens and local voters notice and complain that their communities look different. They lobby for local laws that protect views and the visual environment. Local legislatures have responded by enacting laws that protect scenic resources and assets, including open views, country roads, panoramic landscapes, tree-lined streets, stonewalls, and agricultural scenes. Local efforts to preserve scenic resources include the regulation of road construction and maintenance, land clearing, architecture, and location of utility lines and signage. Other requirements such as the maintenance of vegetative buffers, street trees, and other vegetation may be included in local scenic protection laws to minimize the visual impact of development.

Municipalities may protect specific view corridors that have particular aesthetic or economic importance to the community. The town of Vail, Colorado, has adopted a View Corridors Ordinance expressly because "[t]he protection and perpetuation of certain mountain views and other significant views from various pedestrian public ways" will "strengthen and preserve the Town's unique environmental heritage and attributes," and will "enhance the aesthetic and economic vitality and values of the Town." Focal points and prominent landmarks are protected that "contribute to the community's unique sense of place." Vail, Colo. Town Code ch. 22 § 1 (1992). In Landmark Land Co. v. City and County of Denver, 728 P.2d 1281 (Colo. 1986), the Colorado Supreme Court upheld a similarly worded ordinance as within the city's police powers. Kern County, California, adopted a Scenic Corridor District "to designate areas which contain unique visual scenic resources as viewed from a major highway or freeway wherein the siting of off-site advertising signs needs to be reviewed on a case-by-case basis." Kern County, Cal. Code § 19.74.010. The purpose of the law is "to safeguard the scenic qualities of the natural environment and the visual qualities of primary entranceways into the county."

The Upland Preservation Overlay zoning district adopted by Brookfield, Wisconsin, is intended to preserve "all significant woodlands, wildlife habitat areas, areas of rough topography and related scenic areas." Brookfield, Wis. Mun. Code § 17.96.010 (1997). In addition to maintaining the natural beauty of the city, the overlay zoning district is intended to control erosion and sedimentation and to maintain water quality. The ordinance allows local land use agencies to impose deed restrictions on subdivision plats where needed to prohibit development, the removal of vegetation, and land filling or excavating within the overlay district in order to accomplish the objectives of the law. Brookfield, Wis. Mun. Code § 17.96.070 (1997). These restrictions impose development limitations on the title to the land; they burden the subdivision developer and restrict the title of the land in the hands of the original and all subsequent purchasers of the individual parcels in the subdivision.

D. TREE AND FOREST PRESERVATION/TIMBER

Local tree preservation ordinances typically establish a permit system under which tree removal is allowed, but only upon a showing of necessity and subject to certain conditions, such as the replacement of some or all of the trees to be removed. Tree preservation ordinances may consider views, pruning, trimming, and setbacks from curbs, sidewalks, and street intersections. A number of states have adopted statutes that either require or permit local governments to adopt tree preservation laws. See, for example, Georgia, Ga. Code Ann. § 12–2–8(h)(8) (2001); Hawaii, Haw. Rev. Stat. §§ 58–1 to 58–5 (2001); Maine, Me. Rev. Stat. § 38.439–A(5) (2001); and Maryland, Md. Code Ann., Nat. Res. I § 5–1603 (2000).

Some communities have adopted ordinances to protect native tree species, or "heritage trees," such as oak, sycamore, walnut, and eucalyptus. These ordinances require reports by professional arborists and practices to be followed to preserve such specimens from development activities, including additions to single-family homes. Steamboat Springs, Colorado, has adopted a Trees and Shrubs Ordinance. The purpose of this local law is to prescribe requirements "for the protection of plants, including . . . trees, shrubs, lawns, and all other landscaping located, standing, or growing within or upon city property, including . . . any city-owned street, alley, right-of-way, or other public place or city or mountain park, recreation area, or open space." Steamboat Springs, Colo. Code § 24–1 (2002).

In Echevarrietta v. City of Rancho Palos Verdes, 86 Cal. App. 4th 472, 103 Cal. Rptr. 2d 165 (Cal. App. 2 Dist. 2001), the California court upheld a local ordinance that both provided for the protection of viewsheds and of trees themselves. The ordinance created a procedure allowing a property owner to preserve valuable views by requiring a neighbor to trim or remove trees blocking existing views. The ordinance stipulated, however, that when trees are removed, the petitioning property owner bears the cost of their replacement. The ordinance was enacted for the purpose of preserving hillsides as a natural resource and the associated scenic value to resident owners, local citizens, and visitors. The court found that the local ordinance constituted a legitimate exercise of the city's police power.

Local ordinances may regulate timber harvesting in the absence of a State law that preempts the matter. In Rancho Loo v. Devargas, 303 F.3d 1195 (10th Cir. 2002), the court held that the New Mexico Forest Conservation Act does not impliedly preempt the county Timber Harvest Ordinance that required permits to harvest timber.

The regulation of commercial timber harvesting can help maintain the ecological balance in forests while meeting present and future demand for lumber and pulp. Some factors considered by local harvesting regulations include the successional role of species regeneration, the effects of competing vegetation, and potential damaging agents such as insects and pathogens. Construction of access roads, timber products processing centers, and other permanent structures in heavily forested areas are development activities that may be regulated by timber harvesting laws. The town of Pawling, New York, adopted a Timber Harvesting Law that regulates tree clearing and harvesting to prevent sedimentation and drainage problems. Pawling, N.Y. Code §§ 45–2, 45–9 (1993).

E. WILDLIFE HABITAT PROTECTION

Habitat destruction, which can be caused by land development, is harmful to the preservation of biodiversity. Natural habitats provide resources that species need to survive: the proper temperature, water and soil conditions, sunlight, food sources, places of refuge, and safe reproduction grounds. The U.S. Fish and Wildlife Service has listed more than 1,200 species as endangered or threatened. Eighty-five percent of these listed species are threatened because of habitat degradation and loss. Poorly planned development in critical wildlife areas creates harmful land uses in close proximity to critical habitats and prevents migration of species from one suitable habitat to another. Proper land use planning can ensure the preservation of important habitat areas, open up the borders around them, and provide migration corridors sensitive to the needs of vulnerable species. While habitat protection for federally listed endangered and threatened species is better known, state and local law also plays an important role in habitat protection.

Washington State has been at the forefront. The state's Growth Management Act of 1990 implements what the Washington Department of Fish and Wildlife calls "a bottom-up approach to land use planning." It requires all counties, cities, and towns in the state to classify and designate resource lands and critical areas, including fish and wildlife habitats, and to adopt development regulations for them. The department has created detailed checklists to assess the wildlife potential of urban areas and to aid local governments in reviewing the elements of their development regulations and comprehensive plans to ensure habitat protection.

Under this state regime, Cowlitz County, Washington, adopted a Critical Fish and Wildlife Habitat ordinance to protect species and habitats of local importance including shellfish areas; kelp and eelgrass beds; herring and smelt spawning areas; and naturally occurring ponds and their submerged aquatic beds. The county law establishes performance standards and requires developers to secure permits, which may not be issued unless the standards are respected in critical habitat areas in the proposed developments. One of the law's objectives is to protect habitat and vegetated open space in contiguous blocks, and to create continuous corridors of open space and habitat areas. Native species must be used in any landscaping of disturbed, undeveloped, or buffer areas, and landscaping plans must emphasize heterogeneity and structural diversity of vegetation. Cowlitz County, Wash. Code § 19.15.130 (2001).

In Colorado, statutes provide local governments with the authority to adopt local environmental laws that protect wildlife habitat. Colo. Rev. Stat. §§ 29–20–101–107, 24–65–101–106 (2001). The purpose of the Local Government Land Use Control Enabling Act is to maintain a balance between the basic human needs of its changing population and "legitimate environmental concerns." Specifically, the Act empowers local governments

> to plan for and regulate the use of land by * * * [p]rotecting lands from activities which would cause immediate or foreseeable material danger to significant wildlife habitat and would endanger wildlife species * * * [and by] [o]therwise planning for and regulating the use of land so as to provide planned and orderly use of land and protection of the environment in a manner consistent with constitutional rights. Colo. Rev. Stat. §§ 29–20–104(1)(b), (h) (2001).

Pursuant to this authority, Summit County, Colorado, protects wildlife through its Wildlife Habitat Overlay District that "seeks to fully protect wildlife habitats * * * from the significant adverse effects of development." Summit County, Colo. Dev. Code § 4203.01 (2002). The ordinance requires that all proposals for development within the district include a special wildlife impact report that the State Division of Wildlife is to review and approve.

Additional techniques are available to local governments for wildlife habitat protection. A Florida county amended its comprehensive plan to establish Natural Resource Protection Areas to protect indigenous flora and fauna, especially the endangered Florida panther. The law allowed only agricultural land uses and single-family homes in designated habitat areas. In Florida Wildlife Federation v. Collier County, 819 So.2d 200 (Fla. App. 2002), environmental groups challenged the law on technical grounds claiming that the law did not contain sufficiently detailed standards to limit the agricultural uses in the interest of habit protection.

The court held that the plaintiffs did not carry their burden of proving that the standards were clearly erroneous.

F. AGRICULTURE AND FARMLAND PRESERVATION

Agriculture and farmland preservation are important because they help sustain healthy food sources, preserve open space, and promote biodiversity. The Supreme Court of Illinois upheld lower tax rates for land use for farming and agricultural properties adopted by Du Page County was valid as an incentive to preserve farmland and open space. See, Hoffman v. Clark, 69 Ill. 2d 402, 372 N.E.2d 74 (Ill. 1977).

The Court of Appeals of Oregon upheld the preservation of farmland defined by soil types and the history of agricultural use, rather than profitability. See, Wetherell v. Douglas Cty., 235 Or. App. 246, 230 P.3d 976 (Or. Ct. App. 2010).

In Tonter Inv. v. Pasquotank Cty., 199 N.C. App. 579, 681 S.E.2d 536 (N.C. 2009), the plaintiff purchased three tracts of land that were included in agricultural zoning districts. In these zones, the county adopted an ordinance prohibiting residential development. The law also required all structures to be located within 1,000 of a public water supply. Together, these requirements prevented the plaintiff from developing on two of his three tracts of land as residential subdivisions. The court held that the ordinances were within the county's statutorily granted zoning power, that they protected public safety and health; did not deprive the plaintiff of all uses of the land.

G. URBAN AGRICULTURE

Many zoning codes permit community gardening or urban agriculture using general definitions. Providing explicit and detailed definitions of terms, particularly for agriculture processes, helps clarify what is permitted and better promotes urban agriculture. This allows potential farmers to enter the food production field, encourages more established farmers to take advantage of more farming-friendly zoning allowances, and ultimately increases fresh, local, and affordable food production and access. The Austin, Texas Code of Ordinances (§ 25–2–7) has a section specifically defining agricultural. The code defines where processes such as aquaponics, horticulture, and indoor crop production are permitted, and what is meant and included within each of these agricultural terms. The national Healthy Food Project has a draft guide for municipalities to assist with thinking through agricultural terminology for zoning codes.

In addition, allowing greenhouses, hoop houses, and other smaller structures to assist with urban/semi-urban farming and small animal husbandry is key for effective and efficient use of a space for farming. Without flexible provisions for such structures, landlords and their farming tenants or partners will not be able to accommodate more variety, higher yielding crops and appropriate livestock on their urban land for risk of violation.

Philadelphia's zoning code (§ 14–604(9)) specifically allows agricultural structures within certain size requirements based on lot size. And, if a structure is only needed for 180 days or less, the city waives all permitting requirements. This breaks down obstacles for farmers who may want a temporary greenhouse for winter crops or small hoop houses during a frost season.

Allowing on-site sale of produce significantly improves food access for consumers and helps food producers access markets without costly transportation and "middlemen" fees. Allowing food to be grown in a wider range of zones is key, but it is exponentially more beneficial if that food can be sold and distributed to consumers just as immediately. Kansas City's Zoning Code (§ 88–312–02) allows the direct sale or donation of "whole, uncut fresh food and/or horticultural products grown in home gardens, community gardens, and land managed under a community supported agriculture model." Clarity in the zoning code itself decreases uncertainty and concern about violating zoning laws and encourages more urban agriculture and community-based food secure cities.

H. HYDROFRACKING

Hydraulic fracturing, or fracking, is a gas well stimulation and extraction technique designed for areas underlain by large shale formations found often a mile or more below the surface. Vertical fracking has been done for decades, but relatively recent technology enables directional drilling, which allows the drill stem and borehole to follow the horizontal structure of the shale formations and proceed thousands of feet to exploit gas reserves far from the wellhead. Such operations, if not properly regulated, can cause ground and surface water contamination, emit volatile organic compounds and methane and generate trips that require improved or new roads, that can cause landscape fragmentation, and that create congestion, noise, and the need for expensive road repairs: a burden to local taxpayers.

From a land use perspective, fracking operations are an industrial use that would be permitted, controlled, or prohibited by local zoning where local power is not preempted by the federal or state government. The federal government does not regulate many of the aspects of the fracking process. Oil, gas, and mining are heavily regulated by state governments, however, but the scope of state regulations varies greatly. Where they are not preempted, local governments have the opportunity to regulate natural gas extraction and to fill in the gaps in federal and state regulation. The New York Court of Appeals, for example, held that local governments have the authority to regulate fracking through zoning including the adoption of complete bans. Wallach v. Town of Dryden, 23 N.Y.3d 728 (2014). In 2015, the Department of Environmental Conservation banned fracking after conducting in-depth review of public health and environmental impacts.

In Texas, after the City of Denton banned fracking from its jurisdiction in 2014, the state legislature adopted a law preempting municipalities from prohibiting fracking. Tex. Nat. Res. Code Ann. § 81.0523 (2015). The new law, however, conceded some power to local governments. Included are the control of "aboveground activity related to an oil and gas operation that occurs at or above the surface of the ground, including a regulation governing fire and emergency response, traffic, lights, or noise, or imposing notice or reasonable setback requirements." This is a recognition of the fact that state agencies focus mostly on permitting production, while ensuring that the operation of facilities is sufficiently controlled so as to be efficient and safe for workers and the public. Allowing these above ground matters to municipal control recognizes the historically important role of local governments, which focus on the land use impacts of industrial operations.

The state legislature of Oklahoma provides local governments the right to enforce many traditional land use standards regulating oil and gas facilities. A municipality, county or other political subdivision may enact reasonable ordinances, rules, and regulations concerning road use, traffic, noise, and odors incidental to oil and gas operations within its boundaries, provided such ordinances, rules and regulations are not inconsistent with any regulation established by Title 52 of the Oklahoma Statutes or the Corporation Commission. A municipality, county, or other political subdivision may also establish reasonable setbacks and fencing requirements for oil and gas well site locations as are reasonably necessary to protect the health, safety, and welfare of its citizens but may not effectively prohibit or ban any oil and gas operations, including oil and gas exploration, drilling, fracture stimulation, completion, production, maintenance, plugging and abandonment, produced water disposal, recovery operations, flow and gathering lines or pipeline infrastructure. Okla. Stat. Ann. tit. 52 § 137.1 (2020).

An Amendment to Pennsylvania's Oil and Gas Act, commonly known as Act 13, contained a provision preempting local bans. Specifically, it limited "the extent to which [energy] companies are permitted to engage in fracking activities, ostensibly in part to protect the environment, while simultaneously preempting local ordinances seeking to prohibit or limit fracking within municipalities." In December 2013, Supreme Court of Pennsylvania held that Act 13 was unconstitutional because it violated the state constitution. Robinson Twp. v. Commonwealth of Pa., 83 A.3d 901, 913 (2013). Pennsylvania's constitution includes an Environmental Rights Amendment that was invoked for purposes of this case: "The people have a right to clean air, pure water, and to the preservation of the natural, scenic, historic and esthetic values of the environment. Pennsylvania's public natural resources are the common property of all the people, including generations yet to come. As trustee of these resources, the Commonwealth shall conserve and maintain them for the benefit of all the people." Pa. Const. art. I § 27 (1981). Based on this provision, the Court determined that statewide preemption of local bans violated the Pennsylvania Constitution.

In Morrison v. Beck Energy Corp., 37 N.E.3d 128 (2015), the Ohio Supreme Court held that local land use authority "does not allow a municipality to discriminate against . . . [fracking facilities] that the state has permitted . . . ." A concurring judge noted that "the traditional concerns of zoning laws" were not at issue and the court did not decide whether state law "conflicts with local land use ordinances that address only the traditional concerns of zoning." That remains to be decided.

State legislation in Colorado recognizes the role of local governments in regulating fracking. Colo. Rev. Stat. Ann. § 34–60–131 (2019). It requires that an application for a new drilling site include proof that "the applicant has filed an application with the local government having jurisdiction to approve the siting of the proposed oil and gas location and the local government's disposition of the application; or, [that] [t]he local government having jurisdiction does not regulate the siting of oil and gas locations." Further the statute provides that "Local governments and state agencies, including the commission and agencies listed in section 34–60–105(1)(b), have regulatory authority over oil and gas development, including as specified in that section. A local government's regulations may be more protective or stricter than state requirements." Colo. Rev. Stat. Ann. § 34–60–131 (2019).

CHAPTER 10

AESTHETIC, HISTORIC, AND CULTURAL INTEREST PROTECTION

§ 1. INTRODUCTION

Besides a method of controlling growth and regulating development, zoning can also be used as a tool to protect the aesthetic and cultural interests of a community. Today, aesthetics has permeated into many aspects of land use law that have already been discussed: housing codes, variances, smart growth, and planned development, to name a few. Notwithstanding their current prevalence, laws that addressed aesthetic and cultural interests were not considered valid subjects of regulation until the mid-1950s. Even today there are some courts that will not uphold a zoning ordinance that is based solely on aesthetic grounds.

The Supreme Court decision that opened the door for aesthetic zoning was Berman v. Parker, 348 U.S. 26 (1954). In *Berman*, local officials in Washington D.C. sought to use the power of eminent domain to take possession of undesirable structures in furtherance of an urban renewal project. Proponents of the plan argued that this was a valid exercise of the police power because it was a measure to promote the general welfare of the community. The Supreme Court agreed, stating that "the concept of public welfare is broad and inclusive. The values it represents are spiritual as well as physical, aesthetic as well as monetary. It is within the power of the legislature to determine that the community should be beautiful as well as healthy. . . ." By adopting such a broad interpretation of the public welfare, the Supreme Court established a precedent that local officials could rely on when enacting ordinances that protect aesthetic values, and set the stage for using zoning and other land use regulation tools for protecting the aesthetic and cultural resources of a given community.

§ 2. REGULATION OF SIGNS AND BILLBOARDS

The placement and appearance of signs and billboards is one of the most obvious and ever-present land use issues that invokes the virtues of aesthetic zoning. Due to recent advances in technology, traditional two-dimensional signs are losing ground to newer electronic displays, which may contain flashy designs or three-dimensional images. Although these new displays may be more effective at drawing attention to a particular message, many people consider them to be distracting and undesirable additions to the community. As a result, it is not surprising that some communities are making an effort to regulate or eliminate outdoor billboards and signs altogether. Laws that regulate the spacing and design of signs have grown in popularity in recent years, despite the fact that some courts have been unwilling to uphold some types of sign control legislation.

In jurisdictions that have rejected the general welfare justification for aesthetic zoning, the location and size of signs and billboards may still be controlled as a means of ensuring the public health and safety. A majority of courts acknowledge that improperly constructed or positioned signs may pose a health or safety hazard should they collapse or catch fire. Furthermore, it has been found that reducing the number of billboards along the highways reduces the amount of distraction to drivers and thereby promotes public safety. See, e.g., Mayor and City Council of Baltimore v. Mano Swartz, Inc., 299 A.2d 828, 268 Md. 79 (Md. App. 1973); Thomas Cusack Co. v. Chicago, 267 Ill. 344 (Ill. 1914). Some courts accept aesthetic considerations only as a side benefit, and thus, would most likely strike down a sign ordinance that is enacted solely for the purpose of achieving aesthetic objectives. Most courts do not want to be put in the position of determining whether a sign or billboard is aesthetically detrimental to a given community.

Although many jurisdictions will not uphold a sign law solely on the basis of aesthetic considerations, a recent trend has gained momentum that favors viewing aesthetics alone as a sufficient justification for exercising the police power. In State v. Diamond Motors, Inc., 50 Haw. 33 (Haw. 1967), the Supreme Court of Hawaii relied on the public welfare doctrine to uphold an ordinance, which regulated signs in an industrial area for aesthetic reasons. Like the Supreme Court in *Berman*, the court here asserted that, "beauty [is] a proper community objective, attainable through the use of the police power. In upholding the ordinance, enacted solely for aesthetic objectives, the court maintained that this view was the "more modern and forthright position." This "aesthetic alone" argument has also been successfully used in New Hampshire where the state Supreme Court upheld an ordinance restricting the use of internally lit signs after finding that it was rationally related to the municipality's legitimate, aesthetic objectives. This court also relied on the Supreme Court's "expansive view" of the police power, as handed down in *Berman*, to support its position that towns may consider, "aesthetic values, such as preserving rural charm, when passing zoning ordinances under state law." Town of Conway v. Cardiff & Co., 137 N.H. 368, 628 A.2d. 247 (N.H. 1993).

In People v. Goodman, 31 N.Y.2d 262 (N.Y. 1972), the New York Court of Appeals upheld an ordinance limiting the size of signs on beachfront buildings, finding that the state and its political subdivisions may regulate the erection and maintenance of outdoor advertising and that regulations enacted solely for the purpose of achieving aesthetic objectives are valid. Here the court held that, "it is now settled that aesthetics is a valid subject of legislative concern and that reasonable legislation designed to promote the governmental interest in preserving the appearance of the community represents a valid and permissible exercise of the police power."

Typically, when a municipality adopts a sign law solely for the purpose of advancing aesthetic goals, existing signs are allowed to continue in place until the owners have received some return on their investment. This is generally referred to as amortization of the investment. To accomplish this goal, ordinances typically will direct that all "on-site" nonconforming signs be either altered to conform to the ordinance or removed within a specified time period. For example, in Fayetteville v. McIlroy Bank, 278 Ark. 500 (Ark. 1983), nonconforming sign owners brought suit challenging a city ordinance that regulated the size, height, and placement of signs within the city, and required all on-site nonconforming signs to be altered to conform with the new law, or removed within seven years. Here, the preamble to the ordinance stated that its primary purpose was to protect the city's scenic resources, which had "contributed greatly to its economic development." The Supreme Court of Arkansas upheld the ordinance, and directed the plaintiff to remove his nonconforming signs after finding that the applicable amortization period gave him sufficient time to recoup his investments, thus making the law fair with respect to the city's property owners.

Similarly, an ordinance regulating "off-site" signs and billboards that had been fully amortized was upheld in California in National Advertising Co. v. County of Monterey, 1 Cal. 3d 875 (Cal. 1970). The court rejected the plaintiff manufacturer's unsubstantiated contentions that the signs had been repaired, thus extending their useful life, and that they could not be readily used in another location, therefore making the law unfair as applied to them. The court concluded that the removal provision of the ordinance may be applied to billboards that had fully amortized; with regard to those billboards that had not, the court asserted that, "removal should await expiration of appropriate amortization periods."

The use of the police power for the purposes of regulating the size, placement, and appearance of signs and billboards raises important constitutional issues as well. The First Amendment prohibits governments from regulating the content of speech, regardless of whether it is communicated in oral or written form. This general prohibition does not necessarily place restrictions on government's ability to regulate the time, place, and manner of the speech. The Supreme Court faced this issue in Metromedia, Inc. v. City of San Diego, 453 U.S. 490 (1981), with a city ordinance that banned off-site billboards, and permitted on-site signs, while excluding political signs altogether. While a plurality of four justices acknowledged that the purpose of the ordinance was to promote aesthetics and traffic safety valid uses of the police power they ultimately concluded that the ban on off-site, noncommercial advertising was invalid. In reaching this conclusion, the court stressed that local governments could not limit the permissible subjects of non-commercial discourse, and that the ordinance in question reached "too far into the realm of protected speech." In a concurring opinion, two justices reached the same conclusion after finding that the city failed to justify the substantial restriction on protected speech, while also failing to show how a sufficient governmental interest was promoted through the use of a partial ban.

Following the Supreme Court's decision in *Metromedia*, there was a wave of litigation challenging the constitutional validity of sign laws, leading to conflicting, and sometimes confusing, results. Although municipalities have generally interpreted the Court's decision to mean that they cannot, or at least should not, ban on-site signs altogether, many have maintained that it is within their power to regulate them by imposing setbacks, size limitations, lighting requirements, placement conditions, and by implementing permit and variance procedures, and amortization provisions. Not surprisingly, sign laws that regulate the display of political signs in this manner have been the focus of much litigation. For example, in City of Ladue v. Gilleo, 512 U.S. 43 (1994), the Supreme Court invalidated a sign law that prohibited the placement of an anti-Gulf War sign in a residential window. One major difference between *Ladue* and *Metromedia* is the nature of the communication at issue; here the Court was dealing with a sign which conveyed a political message, as opposed to the advertising sign which was subject to a commercial based regulation in *Metromedia*. In a later decision, Village of Schaumburg v. Jeep Eagle Sales Corp., 285 Ill. App. 3d 481 (Ill. App. 1996), the Appellate Court of Illinois adopted the same rationale, finding that an ordinance prohibiting the placement of more than three official on-site flags violated the First Amendment rights of an automobile dealer who had 13 oversized American flags on his lot.

The Supreme Court of the United States reviewed a local law that restricted signs, based on their content in Reed v. Town of Gilbert, 576 U.S. 155 (2015). The Town of Gilbert imposed more stringent restrictions on signs that directed the public to a meeting of a non-profit group than it did on signs conveying other messages. The court unanimously held that this local law was invalid as a content-based regulation of speech. The local law failed the Court's strict scrutiny analysis; the town could not claim placing strict limits on temporary directional signs was necessary to beautify the town while similar signs that created the same issue of distracting from the aesthetics of the town.

Although federal and state programs that have been implemented for the purposes of beautifying our nation's highways by controlling the use of billboards have been upheld as valid exercises of the states' police power to control outdoor advertising, it should be noted that the 1965 Highway Beautification Act imposes specific requirements on the states with regard to this type of regulation. Specifically, the Act requires states to pay just compensation to landowners and to owners of billboards when preexisting signs, placed along highways prior to the enactment of controls, are targeted for removal. This requirement was reiterated when the Act was amended in 1978, further specifying the compensation requirement imposed for the forced removal of certain signs.

§ 3. THE APPEARANCE OF STRUCTURES AND OTHER AESTHETIC REGULATIONS

Municipalities have also used aesthetic zoning ordinances to regulate the appearance of structures within their communities. Much like the sign laws discussed earlier, these ordinances have been upheld as a valid exercise of the police power. For example, in Saveland Park Holding Corp. v. Wieland, 269 Wis. 262 (Wis. 1955), the court upheld an ordinance requiring, before the issuance of a building permit, a finding by the village building board that the exterior architectural appeal and functional plan of the proposed structure will be in accordance with other structures in the surrounding neighborhood. In reaching this conclusion, the court found it immaterial that the village's sole objective was the protection of surrounding homes and businesses, and asserted that, "anything that tends to destroy property values of the inhabitants of the village necessarily adversely affects the prosperity, and therefore the general welfare, of the entire [municipality]."

Similarly, in Stoyanoff v. Berkeley, 458 S.W.2d 305 (Mo. 1970), the court upheld the denial of a permit pursuant to an ordinance that prevented the construction of "unsightly, grotesque, and unsuitable structures" within certain neighborhoods. The petitioner was denied a permit to construct a "highly modernistic" house within a neighborhood that contained traditional Colonial, English Tudor, and French provincial style homes. The court rejected his assertion that the law was arbitrary and unreasonable and ultimately concluded that the general welfare was promoted through the denial if it would protect property values in the surrounding area. Moreover, where an architectural review board refused to approve the construction of a one-story house that could resemble a commercial building in a neighborhood that consisted primarily of multi-story dwellings, the Ohio Court of Appeals similarly held that the authority to render such determinations was appropriate for maintaining the character of the community. Reid v. Architectural Bd. of Review of City of Cleveland Heights, 119 Ohio App. 67 (Ohio App. 1963).

In addition to regulating the appearance of certain structures, many municipalities have enacted zoning ordinances to regulate the size and appearance of lawns or yards. In People v. Stover, 12 N.Y.2d 462 (N.Y. 1963), the Court of Appeals of New York sustained an ordinance that prohibited the maintenance of clotheslines in front or side yards abutted by a street. The court acknowledged that the ordinance was enacted solely for aesthetic purposes, but ultimately concluded that it was a valid use of the police power to protect property values and the general appearance of the city. The court further rejected the plaintiff's argument that the ordinance violated a constitutional right to free speech, stating that it was of no significance that the clothesline in question was erected as a form of protest against the plaintiff's property tax assessment.

Parking lots have also been singled out and subjected to specific aesthetic zoning requirements in certain municipalities. For example, in Parking Association of Georgia, Inc. v. City of Atlanta, 264 Ga. 764 (Ga. 1994), the Supreme Court of Georgia upheld a city ordinance that required the installation of curbs, landscaping, and trees in surface parking lots, after rejecting the plaintiff's contention that the law was an unreasonable exercise of the police power. The court concluded that the regulation could be justified by "aesthetics alone," and further stressed that it could not be invalidated simply because it restricts the use of the property, diminishes its value, or imposes costs in connection therewith. Similar rationales have been adopted to uphold laws prohibiting individuals from removing trees or stone walls located on property abutting scenic highways. See, Webster v. Town of Candia, 146 N.H. 430 (N.H. 2001).

Although many jurisdictions have upheld the use of zoning ordinances as a means of protecting property values, municipalities must be careful to draft local laws and regulations that contain standards and review criteria. For example, in Piscitelli v. Township Committee of Scotch Plains, 103 N.J. Super 589 (N.J. Super. L. 1968), the New Jersey Superior Court determined that an ordinance establishing an architectural review board with unbridled review powers, to which applicants had to apply for construction or renovation permits, was an invalid exercise of the municipal police power since it usurped the power of the board of adjustment by not providing specific criteria for the review of applications. In West Palm Beach v. State ex rel. Duffey, 158 Fla. 863 (Fla. 1947), the court took issue with vague provisions that were contained in an ordinance requiring new buildings in a residential subdivision to be substantially equal in design to adjacent structures. The court invalidated the entire ordinance after finding that its standards were not sufficiently clear, thus leaving exactions to the "whim or caprice" of the building inspector. See also, Anderson v. City of Issaquah, 70 Wash. App. 64 (Wash. App. 1993). In Pacesetter Homes, Inc. v. Village of Olympia Fields, 104 Ill. App. 2d 218 (Ill. App. 1968), a zoning ordinance that created an architecture advisory committee that was given the power to make declaratory determinations with respect to the issuance of building permits, was struck down on constitutional grounds. The court found that there were no adequate guidelines or standards to govern the action of the committee in determining whether a proposed development was prohibited by the ordinance. Finally, it should be noted that such ordinances may face preemption challenges if regulation and control of this area has been vested in another body, such as a public service commission. See, Union Electric Co. v. City of Crestwood, 562 S.W.2d 344 (Mo. 1978).

§ 4. HISTORIC DISTRICTS

Besides regulating the existence of signs, billboards, and the appearance of structures, the public welfare aspect of the police power has also been relied upon by municipalities to justify the need for historic preservation district regulations. These laws have been upheld as a valid and reasonable use of the police power to achieve a legitimate end: the preservation of a community's historic treasures. See, e.g., Opinion of the Justices to the Senate, 333 Mass. 773 (Mass. 1955). Typically, the creation of a historic district is focused on the protection of historic areas consisting of multiple buildings, rather than the protection of individual structures. In this respect, the New Mexico Supreme Court, for example, upheld zoning that was focused on preserving historic architectural patterns in a particular neighborhood. Santa Fe v. Gamble-Skogmo, 73 N.M. 410 (N.M. 1964). Similarly, local governments in Nantucket, Massachusetts, and in the French Quarter in New Orleans, Louisiana, have created historic districts to protect the local architecture. Historic district regulations that are enacted solely for the purpose of preserving one historical structure within the district, such as the home of former President Abraham Lincoln, have also been upheld in some jurisdictions. See, Rebman v. City of Springfield, 111 Ill. App. 2d 430 (Ill. App. 1969).

Most of the litigation involving the creation of historic districts centers on the question of what can be considered a historically or culturally significant area worthy of this type of aesthetic zoning. Typically, historic districts are distinguished because the area in question has some sort of aesthetic values that have created a unique economic (e.g., tourism), educational, or cultural opportunity that contributes to the public welfare of the community. Generally, aesthetic considerations are seen as secondary to the cultural, educational, and economic values of these sites. See, A-S-P Associates v. City of Raleigh, 298

N.C. 207 (N.C. 1979). Any regulation that prevents commercial intrusion in these areas and, as a result, maintains the area's value, is typically considered to be an appropriate means of promoting the general welfare.

Regulations seeking to preserve unique and cultural areas through historic district designation may impose restrictions on the manner in which the property owner may maintain her property. These restrictions have been upheld despite opposition from aggrieved property owners. For example, in State of Minnesota by Powderly v. Erickson, 301 N.W.2d 324 (Minn. 1981), a property owner challenged the validity of a regulation that designated an area, encompassing his property, as an historical resource entitled to protection from impairment and destruction of an historical structure. The court concluded that, pursuant to the regulation, the government had a duty to enjoin destruction of an historical structure until all parties interested in preserving the structure had an opportunity to protect the building by appropriate legislation, or by other equitable remedies. In reaching this conclusion, however, the court noted that regulations that permanently deny an owner of an historic building the beneficial use of his property would constitute a "taking" requiring just compensation. Therefore, if those interested in the preservation of the building take no steps to acquire the building, or to provide the funds necessary for its preservation, the property owner has a constitutional right to destroy his building, or to put the property to another lawful use. Similarly, in Figarsky v. Historic District

Commission, 171 Conn. 198 (Conn. 1976), the Supreme Court of Connecticut held that the amount of an owner's loss is the basic criterion for determining whether the purported exercise of police power is valid, or whether it amounts to a taking necessitating the use of the eminent domain power, and payment of just compensation.

The establishment of historic districts as an integral part of community development is widespread today. Local efforts have been bolstered by federal legislation, such as the National Historic Preservation Act of 1966, the Historical and Architectural Data Preservation Act of 1974, and the Archeological Resources Preservation Act of 1979, as well as state legislation, which provide for the creation of commissions and committees with functions and duties in this area.

§ 5. LANDMARK PRESERVATION

Substantially similar to historic district laws, landmark preservation ordinances are typically focused on the preservation of individual landmarks, as opposed to defined areas, that are found to have some historical or cultural significance. However, they generally operate in the same way, by prohibiting the demolition or alteration of a designated landmark unless prior approval has been granted by an appropriate authority. These ordinances have been largely upheld as a valid exercise of the police power to protect and promote the general welfare, but due to the limitation and restrictions they impose on affected property owners, landmark preservation regulations often encounter regulatory takings claims as well.

Generally speaking, landmark preservation ordinances that focus on regulating the use of land will be upheld if the regulations are not so severe as to rise to the level of an uncompensated taking. However, landmark preservation ordinances seeking to dictate how property may be owned have been struck down in some jurisdictions as improper and unconstitutional. For example, in FGL & L Property Corp. v. City of Rye, 66 N.Y.2d 111 (N.Y. 1985), a plaintiff brought suit challenging the constitutional validity of a landmark preservation ordinance which applied to one 22-acre lot. The court concluded that the regulation, which directed that the lot be maintained in single ownership, and which limited the development of the property to residential condominiums, was an unconstitutional taking of private property without just compensation. The court stated that, "a municipality does not have the power to regulate the manner of ownership of a legal estate, as it is use rather than form of ownership that is the proper concern and focus of zoning and planning regulations." Thus, any ordinance that can be considered "confiscatory" as to the particular situation runs the risk of being declared invalid. See, Lutheran Church v. City of New York, 35 N.Y.2d 121 (N.Y. 1974). In Teachers Ins. & Annuity Ass'n of America v. City of New York, 82 N.Y.2d 35, 623 N.E.2d 526, 603 N.Y.S.2d 399 (N.Y. 1993), plaintiffs challenged the Landmark Preservation Committee designation of the interior of the Four Seasons restaurant as a landmark. The court upheld the law because it regulated a building that is customarily open to the public. In Lake Oswego Preservation Society v. City of Lake Oswego, 360 Or. 115, 379 P.3d 462 (2016) the Oregon legislature developed a historical designation statute which allowed the landowner to refuse the designation, and to demand its removal later if they so choose to prevent any takings issues. The issue was whether the removal powers passed to subsequent land owners. The court concluded, based on the statute, that the removal powers did not extend to subsequent landowners. The purpose of the law was to allow for historical preservation while also respecting the investment-backed expectations of the landowners. But subsequent landowners do not have investment-backed expectations considering they bought the property with knowledge of the historical designation and would furthermore trivialize the ability to actually preserve historical sights.

There are some useful solutions to these problems. Municipalities seeking to protect and preserve a particular landmark may authorize the acquisition of an easement in the façade of a structure, or provide a mechanism for interested parties to acquire the structure in fee. However, programs that encourage and promote fee title acquisition through condemnation may be impractical in many situations where the property is located in prohibitively expensive locations. In addition, because many of the architectural treasures in the United States are owned and operated by various religious institutions, efforts to landmark buildings such as churches and synagogues are often attacked as interfering with the free exercise of religion. In a hotly contested decision, the Second Circuit held in St. Bartholomew's Church v. City of New York, 914 F.2d 348 (2d Cir. 1990), that the City of New York could prevent the Episcopal Diocese from selling the rights to the air space above its vestry building located on Park Avenue. The church had been offered $50 million for the development rights, and it intended to use the money to further its mission and social programs sponsored in the community. The Supreme Court was faced with the same issue in the case of City of Boerne v. Flores, 521 U.S. 507 (1997). In this case the Catholic Church in Boerne challenged the inclusion of portions of its church in a designated historic district, citing the Religious Freedom Restoration Act (an act of Congress specifying that any regulation impacting religion must be justified by a compelling governmental interest) as its authority. The Court ultimately concluded that the Act exceeded the powers of Congress under the Fourteenth Amendment, and the case was dismissed on those grounds. Following the trial, the Catholic Diocese of Boerne negotiated an agreement with the city that would allow construction of new facilities while preserving the façade of the existing structure.

The federal government has been active in promoting landmark preservation beginning with the Antiquities Act of 1906. In 1966, Congress passed the Historic Preservation Act, and it remains in effect today. The Act authorizes the Department of the Interior to create and maintain a registry of historic places for the purpose of identifying structures and districts that are in need of preservation.

Furthermore, the Act creates an Advisory Council on Historic Preservation that is responsible for advising the President and Congress on historic preservation matters, recommending measures to coordinate activities among the various levels of government, and counseling officials on how to educate the public about landmark preservation. Although the Act requires all federal agencies to consider the effect that their proposed projects may have on existing historic sites and landmarks, the law does not impose any affirmative duties on state and local officials. Furthermore, preservation is not guaranteed in the Act even if the site is listed in the National Register. Lastly, citizens who have brought suit pursuant to the Act, for the purposes of preserving landmarks, have run into standing challenges that have prevented the courts from granting relief in many situations. See, e.g., Kent County Council v. Romney, 304 F.Supp. 885 (W.D. Mich. 1969).

Transfer Development Rights, or TDRs, have also been used in connection with landmark preservation regulations. Typically, a municipality will use TDRs to separate the right to develop property from other property rights that may be limited by a landmark preservation ordinance. For example, a landowner may agree not to demolish a landmark structure, pursuant to the applicable regulations, in return for the issuance of certificates of development rights. The development rights lessen the burden on the effected property owner because he is given the opportunity to realize the value of development rights, either by using them to build in another location or by selling them to someone else who can use them in an appropriate district. In addition, tax deductions may be offered to further induce compliance with the landmark preservation ordinance. Although proponents of TDRs assert that the landowner is fully compensated by receiving an equivalent right to develop elsewhere, opponents maintain that landmark designation amounts to inverse condemnation, and that TDRs represent only a potential for future development and should not be considered just compensation.

The New York Court of Appeals, in Fred F. French Investing Co., Inc. v. City of New York, 39 N.Y.2d 587 (N.Y. 1976), tried to resolve this issue by holding that "floating development rights" could not be evaluated until such rights were applied to a specific piece of property. The court ultimately held that the rezoning of two private parks as public parks deprived the property owners of their substantive due process rights, and that the grant of TDRs as compensation was insufficient to save the law from unconstitutionality. The court asserted that TDRs were an "abstraction," and that their real value could not be determined until some future date when they are actually applied to a specific development project. In Penn Central Transportation Co. v. City of New York, 397 N.Y.S.2d 914 (N.Y. 1977), however, the same court asserted that TDRs were "valuable" and that they provided "significant, perhaps 'fair' compensation." In concluding that the TDRs provided just compensation for the limitations that were imposed on the development of the station itself, the court relied on specific facts, namely the pecuniary benefits—for example, the massive governmental investment that had already been pumped into the railroads—and the fact that the Penn Central railroad could continue to benefit from the use of the landmark as a terminal. Moreover, the fact that these TDRs could be applied to specific parcels in other parts of the city, some which were already owned by Penn Central or its affiliates, seemed to support the court's conclusions that the TDRs had value. In Suitum v. Tahoe Regional Planning Agency, 520 U.S. 725 (1997), the Supreme Court avoided an opportunity to decide the question of whether TDRs could be considered just compensation. Before remanding the case, on the ground that the case was not ripe for adjudication, Justice Scalia, in a concurring opinion, seemed to indicate that TDRs could be considered partial just compensation to affected property owners. Justice O'Connor disagreed, saying that the credits were relevant to whether the owner's investment-backed expectations were frustrated.

§ 6. NATIVE AMERICAN GRAVESITES

While most states have laws prohibiting the excavation of gravesites, the Native American Graves Protection and Repatriation Act (NAGPRA) is the preeminent law protecting Native American gravesites. Established in 1990, it provides a number of protections to Native American burial grounds that the common law did not afford. One hundred years prior to the NAGPRA, the federal government played an active role in the destruction of Native American burial grounds; in 1868 the Surgeon General issued an order to Army personnel to collect

Native American remains for the Army Medical Museum; and in 1906 the Antiquities Act allowed buried Native American remains to be classified as "archeological resources" permitting them to be exhumed as government property. This policy of treating Native American remains as specimens or exhibits continued throughout much of the twentieth century. See, Lucus Ritchie, Indian Burial Sites Unearthed: The Misapplication of the Native American Graves Protection and Repatriation Act, 26 Pub. Land & Resources L. Rev. 71 (2005).

NAGPRA establishes a number of requirements to help preserve Native American burial remains and sites. It requires federal agencies and museums to inventory and return any funerary items and human remains it may have in their possession to the lineal decedents or to the tribe. It also contains a notification requirement for any future discoveries or remains, and it makes the trafficking of burial remains or cultural objects a crime. The discovery requirement established by NAGPRA applies only to federal and Native American lands, and distinguishes between intentional excavation and inadvertent discoveries. See, 25 U.S.C. § 3002 (1990).

CHAPTER 11

INITIATIVES, REFERENDA, MEDIATION, AND JUDICIAL REVIEW

§ 1. INTRODUCTION

Land use law involves the study of legislative and administrative processes. State legislatures delegate and withhold certain powers from municipalities. Local legislatures adopt land use plans and regulations and establish local administrative agencies that grant variances, special use permits, hear appeals from determinations of zoning enforcement officers, and approve proposals to develop sites or subdivide property and develop individual lots. What happens if local citizens, or persons aggrieved by a local land use decision, want it reviewed, modified, or reversed? In this chapter, we examine three approaches: (1) consent, initiative, and referendum—so called "direct democracy" techniques; (2) mediation of disputes among the parties themselves; and (3) review by the courts. Each of these forms of review is limited by the circumstances and the laws and practice of the particular state.

As we consider all of the options for reviewing the public body's decision, we are forced to review the nature of that decision, the characteristics of the decision-making entity, and the procedures that agencies follow. In this respect, our studies here serve as a useful review of the preceding chapters. Whether the courts will review the legality of a land use decision will depend on whether the matter is ripe, the decision final, and appeal timely. Were all administrative remedies pursued and exhausted? Was a variance requested, for example? What standards do courts use in reviewing the actions of land use agencies? Does it matter if the decision is a legislative, quasi-judicial, or administrative one? Given the courts' standards of judicial review, am I likely to prevail if I chose the judicial route? What are my alternatives to judicial dispute resolution? Do state statutes provide citizens an opportunity to vote on the matter, that is, to reconsider it via referendum? Do the procedures of the decision-making board allow us and other affected parties to mediate the matter? Once litigation has been initiated, can we still settle the dispute through mediation or other alternative methods of dispute resolution? Will we be required to do so?

§ 2. REVIEW BY THE PEOPLE

Local citizens have an opportunity to review land use decisions and even to initiate land use proposals under the law in several states. "Consent requirements" refer to state or local laws that prohibit land use decisions from going into effect unless they are consented to by the affected neighbors or parties. "Initiative provisions" allow local voters to enact land use laws themselves, and "referendum requirements" either allow or require certain land use decisions adopted by the local legislature to be subject to voter approval at the polls.

A. NEIGHBORS' CONSENT

Consent requirements most often occur in the context of issuing special permits or variances. They require that a certain percentage of neighbors within a certain distance of the affected parcel consent to the action, or they allow a certain percentage of them to overturn the permit or variance. The questions that arise when such provisions are used are whether the state and local law permits such review by the people and, if so, whether the legislature is unlawfully delegating its prerogatives to the public.

In Luger v. City of Burnsville, 295 N.W.2d 609 (Minn. 1980), the question was whether a city may condition the granting of a variance on the consent of abutting property owners. The Minnesota court held that there was no specific statutory or legislative authority in the state that permitted such conditions, and, unlike a referendum provision, the right of affected individuals to consent to official public decisions is not a power reserved to the people themselves.

The City of Chicago enacted an ordinance that required consent by the majority of neighbors on both sides of the street before the local land use agency could approve a home for the elderly. In Valkanet v. City of Chicago, 13 Ill. 2d 268, 148 N.E.2d 767 (Ill. 1958), the court held that the ordinance was unconstitutional as applied to siting the home in a zoning district that allowed apartments and multi-family housing. There was no evidence that such a use would be a nuisance in the apartment district. In fact, the city's general zoning plan provided that an apartment district was a suitable location for a home for the elderly. "The record fails to disclose a rational basis for subjecting homes for the aged to the requirement of frontage consents and is without evidence to support a conclusion that the proposed use has any different effect on the public health, welfare, safety and morals than the other permitted uses in the district."

In Cary v. City of Rapid City, 559 N.W.2d 891 (S.D. 1997), the highest court in South Dakota held that a statute allowing the public to overturn legislative rezoning by a protest vote of 40 percent of the neighbors was unconstitutional because it gave a disproportionately small number of neighbors the power to decide what is in the public interest. Minnesota's highest court held that a city improperly delegated its legislative authority to the people by permitting a variance "subject to letters of approval by all abutting property owners." The court noted that the agency could not simply avoid the political effects of granting the variance by shifting power to the neighbors. Luger v. City of Burnsville, 295 N.W.2d 609 (Minn. 1980).

B. INITIATIVE AND REFERENDUM

Constitutions of the 50 states delegate the power to legislate to protect the public health, safety, welfare, and morals to state legislatures. Zoning enabling laws are enacted by those legislatures to give localities power to control land use. In some jurisdictions, the state legislature has seen fit to give some of this legislative authority back to the people directly. At the local level, citizens may be authorized to enact land use regulations by initiative or to subject local legislative zoning decisions to their review by referendum. A referendum refers a matter decided by the local legislature to a vote of the people at the polls. Both initiative and referendum proceedings are begun, in most cases, by voter petitions, which must comply with the procedural and time prescriptions of state law.

The judicial questions that arise in this context are whether state law allows local citizens initiative or referendum rights and, when the answer is yes, whether the particular objective of the initiative or referendum is within the authority granted to citizens to act by direct democratic means. Initiative and referenda requirements, and their exercise, are referred to as "ballot box zoning." They are often used by voters in developing communities to adopt or reverse laws that slow down the rate of growth, or to oppose locally unwanted land uses such as affordable housing. Where they can take the initiative, voters can propose and adopt new zoning and land use standards for an area where unwanted growth is feared; using their referendum rights, voters can subject legislated zoning standards to popular vote and overturn provisions to which they object. Usually, state laws allow referenda upon the submission of a petition signed by a certain percentage of voters; in some states certain land use decisions by local legislatures are required to be submitted to the voters through a referendum.

A key inquiry here is often whether it matters that the decision subjected to popular vote is a legislative one, such as the adoption of a zoning law or amendment, or one that is administrative or quasi-judicial in nature, such as the issuance of a variance, special use permit, or zoning interpretation. The cases examine a range of nuts and bolts issues as well, such as whether the petitions were properly drafted, submitted in a timely fashion, signed by a sufficient number of registered voters, and properly presented to the electorate. Of concern to the courts is whether voter decisions are exclusionary, render planning efforts superfluous, or undermine the due process rights of property owners.

Referenda on land use planning and zoning decisions enacted under state planning and zoning enabling acts are prohibited in some states because they are thought to undermine the purpose of the enabling acts. In Township of Sparta v. Spillane, 125 N.J. Super. 519, 312 A.2d 154 (N.J. Super. A.D. 1973), the New Jersey court held that comprehensive zoning "might well be jeopardized by piecemeal attacks on the zoning ordinances if referenda were permissible for review of any amendment. Sporadic attacks on a municipality's comprehensive plan would tend to fragment zoning without any overriding concept." The court in Hawaii concurred in Kaiser Hawaii Kai Development Company v. City and County of Honolulu, 777 P.2d 244 (Haw. 1989). When a developer applied for a permit to begin construction of a residential housing complex, citizens protested. Although the area was zoned for residential development, a portion of the land was within a Shoreline Management Area. Citizens circulated an initiative proposal to rezone the area from residential to preservation uses only and gathered enough signatures to place the initiative on the ballot for a vote. The electorate adopted the initiative and the development plan, and zoning maps of the city were amended accordingly. The Supreme Court of Hawaii held that the state legislature does not permit land use regulation to occur through the initiative process. The court looked at the state zoning enabling act and found language that emphasizes "comprehensive planning for reasoned and orderly land use development." "Zoning by initiative" it wrote, "is inconsistent with the goal of long range comprehensive planning."

In City of Eastlake v. Forest City Enterprises, Inc., 426 U.S. 668 (1976), a developer applied to the city planning commission to rezone a tract of land from light industrial to high-rise apartment use. The commission and the city council approved the rezoning, but when put to the voters, the rezoning did not gather the required 55 percent approval. The Supreme Court of the United States considered whether an applicant's due process rights are violated when a city ordinance requires that proposed zoning changes must be approved by a 55 percent vote. The Court held that the state of Ohio specifically reserved to the people the powers of initiative and referendum and that subjecting a local land use decision of a legislative or administrative matter to voter referendum cannot be considered the delegation of legislative power; rather it is a power reserved to the people under the state constitution.

The court distinguished this requirement from one that stipulates that a percentage of nearby property owners approve setback lines or certain land uses in their neighborhood. Granting such powers to a narrow segment of the community can be attacked as a standardless delegation of power to a limited group of property owners. Similarly, in Krejci v. City of Saratoga Springs, 2013 Utah 74, 322 P.3d 662 (Utah 2013), the highest state court of Utah held that a site specific rezoning is a legislative action; therefore, it is subjected to referendum.

A local ordinance that permitted low-income housing construction and the city council's approval of a developer's site plan for the project were submitted to referendum under provisions of a city charter. The vote by the people blocking construction was challenged in City of Cuyahoga Falls v. Buckeye Community Hope Foundation, 538 U.S. 188 (2003). The Cuyahoga Falls City Charter gave voters "the power to approve or reject at the polls any ordinance or resolution passed by the Council within 30 days of the ordinance's passage." A landowner brought a suit alleging that the city violated equal protection rights and that subjecting an administrative matter such as site plan approval to the voters was an unlawful delegation of legislative approval. The Court disagreed, holding that the developer failed to prove the requisite racially discriminatory intent and that, under Eastlake, the Court made it clear that reserving referendum powers to the people is not a delegation of power and that the power of referendum covers all matters within the "realm of local affairs," including legislative and administrative actions.

The U.S. Supreme Court, in cases like *City of Cuyahoga Falls* and *City of Eastlake*, has made it clear that land use decisions made by voters under initiative or referendum provisions are as subject to attack as provisions adopted by local legislative bodies or administrative agencies. They can be invalidated upon a showing that they are arbitrary and capricious or that they violate equal protection guarantees or state or federal statutes, such as the Fair Housing Act.

§ 3. MEDIATION

When a landowner submits an application for a development permit to a local land use agency, an extended process of negotiation is initiated. The parties to this negotiation are the owner, the members of the local administrative agency with approval authority, other involved public agencies, and individuals affected by the proposed project: neighbors, taxpayers, and residents of the community. For most significant development proposals, the local decision-making process is lengthy, inflexible, and frustrating. The outcomes are unpredictable and relationships among those involved are more often damaged than strengthened.

Mediation is a voluntary, consensus-based conflict prevention and resolution strategy. It is a non-predictive method that leaves the outcomes to its participants. In essence, it is a negotiation-assisting process that works when the parties believe that settlement is a better alternative than the protracted hostility often encountered in the process of reviewing and approving controversial development projects. Mediated proceedings are usually informal and flexible, allow the parties to structure the decision-making process itself, and result in consensus-based settlements that are not binding on the participants or public bodies. When the agreement is based on the consensus of all affected parties, supported by credible facts, and consistent with regulatory standards, it can be highly influential in determining the administrative review body's decision on a development proposal.

The Consensus Building Institute (CBI) and the Lincoln Institute of Land Policy undertook a study in 1999 of mediated land use disputes based on interviews with participants in 100 cases in which a professional neutral assisted in the resolution of a land use dispute. This study indicated that 85 percent of participants had a positive view of assisted negotiation. Additionally, of respondents who participated in cases that were settled, 92 percent believed that their own interests were well served by the settlement and 86 percent believed that all parties' interests were served by the agreement reached.

Mediation has been used in recent years as a method of building consensus regarding public policies and formulating land use plans and regulations. In this context, mediation techniques assist parties with disparate interests to participate in a productive public decision-making process. In the land use field, this can involve the development of a comprehensive land use plan, the scope of an environmental impact study of a proposed project, determining how to rezone a community or a neighborhood, and coming to an agreement regarding specific development proposals advanced by a land developer during the permit issuance process.

Land use mediation of various types is authorized by statute in about two dozen states. Mediation may be authorized for very specific issues such as regional impact development projects, border disputes between local governments, or decisions on land use applications. The point at which mediation is encouraged or required varies under these laws from early in the development approval process until after a project decision is made and litigation has been initiated. At least twelve states offer some type of mediation or dispute resolution services to assist parties in the land use context. Some state mediation statutes use the word mediation but describe a process that it is not completely voluntary and is more akin to arbitration. About half of the statutes are directed to the resolution of a specific type of issue, an example being reuse of a military base. Fourteen states authorize mediation for regional planning disputes.

How local legislatures may insert mediation processes into the land use decision-making process is evident in Kucera v. Lizza, 59 Cal. App. 4th 1141, 69 Cal. Rptr. 2d 582 (Cal. App. 1 Dist. 1997). A local law in California regulated the growth and maintenance of trees in the interests of preserving the views of neighbors. Property owners whose views were obstructed by unreasonable tree growth were given the right to begin a process of review that could result in an order requiring tree pruning or removal. The local ordinance required petitioning owners to follow a four-step process: (1) written notice to and personal discussions with the adjoining owners whose trees block the petitioner's view in order to seek a mutually agreeable solution; (2) continuation of discussions through voluntary mediation; (3) if mediation is refused or fails to resolve the matter, the petitioner must present written evidence of the problem, propose restorative action, and offer voluntary, binding arbitration to determine the result; and (4) judicial action to enforce settlement where the other steps fail. A landowner subjected to this process sought a judicial determination that the municipality did not have the legal authority to regulate views and sunlight. In finding that the town did have the authority, the court did not address the validity of the mediation provisions.

In Merson v. McNally, 90 N.Y.2d 742, 665 N.Y.S.2d 605, 688 N.E.2d 479 (N.Y. 1997), New York's highest court upheld the use of an alternative "open and deliberative process" of involving neighbors and stakeholders in a decision about a proposed mining operation being reviewed by the local planning board for a special permit. Normally, developers submit applications for special permits that are evaluated by the planning board, subjected to environmental review, and then reviewed by the public at a formal public hearing, after which a decision is made. In this case, the planning board scheduled informal public meetings and provided notice of them to the public. After several of these meetings, the applicant voluntarily decided to comply with suggestions made by stakeholders regarding the project's modification. As modified, the project did not involve potentially adverse environmental impacts and was exempted from further environmental review. This exemption was challenged as a violation of the state-mandated environmental review process. The alternative process conducted by the local planning board was deemed an appropriate method of resolving potential environmental impacts, particularly where the applicant voluntarily agreed to modify the proposal in response to stakeholder concerns.

In Lake County Trust Co. v. Advisory Plan Commission of Lake County, 904 N.E.2d 1274 (2009), the Indiana Supreme Court held that the commission, as a governmental agency, is not exempt from sanctions under the State Alternative Dispute Rules. Such agencies are treated in the same way as any other litigant. They are subject to the court's authority to control actions, including the imposition of sanctions for noncompliance.

The trial court found that the Commission acted in bad faith by failing to approve a subdivision application after its attorneys, who had been granted full settlement authority, had agreed to its approval. Because the subdivision still was subject to the Commission's final review and approval, the court held that it did not act in bad faith. The court further held that the Commission was precluded from delegating authority to its attorneys to approve subdivision plans pursuant to a mediation agreement.

§ 4. JUDICIAL REVIEW

In land use class, the cases studied inevitably involve review by the judiciary of the decisions made by local legislatures and agencies. Those who disagree with land use decisions (the content of comprehensive plans, zoning amendments, land use regulations, the adoption of novel techniques, and decisions regarding subdivisions, site plans, special permits, and variances) may be deemed "aggrieved parties" and given the right to appeal those decisions to the judiciary, subject to certain rules of access to the courts with which they must comply. By carefully following these judicial proceedings and the standards governing judicial review, students can learn a great deal about the land use decision-making process itself, the power of government, and individual rights. The study of judicial review of land use decisions involves essential matters of our governmental system, including the separation of powers doctrine, the role of the courts, rules governing access to the courts, federal versus state jurisdiction, and the types of remedies made available in different circumstances.

Land use regulations are enacted under the police power delegated by the state to the local legislature. The police power is the authority of government to enact regulations to protect public health, safety, welfare, and morals. The United States Supreme Court has called police power regulation one of the most essential powers of government and one of the least limitable. Broad authority to regulate land uses is delegated to local governments through enabling acts that empower them to enact land use plans and regulations. This broad grant of authority, in most states, carries with it the implied authority to choose the means necessary to accomplish the purposes of conserving the value of buildings and property and encouraging the most appropriate use of the land throughout the community. Specific authority has been granted to local governments to regulate various aspects of land use, including historic districts, aesthetic impacts, building design, wetlands, and environmental impacts of land development.

Local land use regulations can be challenged in a variety of ways. They can be attacked because they violate substantive due process or equal protection guarantees, procedural due process requirements, or are beyond the legal authority of the local regulatory body. Substantive due process challenges allege that the local regulation does not advance a legitimate public purpose. Sometimes this challenge asserts that the regulation is arbitrary and capricious, such as a regulation that is adopted simply in reaction to public opposition and not on the basis of information, studies, and deliberate analysis. Equal protection claims assert that a land use classification or decision treats one parcel, or a few parcels of land, differently from similarly situated parcels with no apparent justification for the different treatment. Procedural due process challenges are brought when a land use board fails to follow a statutorily prescribed process or rushes to judgment on a land use decision, thereby violating the rights of involved parties to receive notice, to be given an opportunity to be heard, or to enjoy the benefits of a deliberate and thoughtful process on the part of the decision-maker. Ultra vires claims allege that the municipality did not have the legal authority to take the challenged action. They assert that the regulatory body acted beyond the scope of its delegated or implied authority and that its action therefore is invalid because it is an unauthorized action of government.

Since these matters are raised in most law school courses, they are briefly discussed here, mostly to reflect on the nature of the land use decision-making process and to create a context for understanding a few key cases that appear in many land use casebooks. Students should be aware that the rules on these matters vary from state to state and that any attempt to discuss them concisely involves a level of generality that may be at variance with individual practice.

A. STANDARDS

Because of the importance of police power regulations and the doctrine of separation of powers, the courts have adopted rules of self-restraint when presented with challenges to police power regulations. These rules generally presume the constitutionality of the regulation, impose a heavy burden of proof on the challenger, resolve doubts in favor of the regulator, and, in most cases, result in a low level of judicial scrutiny.

In the seminal zoning case, Village of Euclid v. Ambler Realty Co., 272 U.S. 365 (1926), the plaintiff landowners challenged the village's zoning law, which divided its property into three separate use zones. Their claim was that the law served no legitimate public purpose and was constitutionally invalid on its face. In this case, the United States Supreme Court established the standard of review to be used by the courts when a zoning law is challenged on substantive due process grounds: "[T]he reasons [must be] sufficiently cogent to preclude us from saying, as it must be said before the law can be declared unconstitutional, that such provisions are clearly arbitrary and unreasonable having no substantial relation to the public health, safety, morals, or general welfare."

Because of the importance of the police power and judicial respect for legislative and administrative decision-makers, court review of land use decisions is limited. It does not matter, in a close case, that the court might have decided the matter differently. The judicial responsibility is to review decisions made by land use boards, not to make them. In Hawaii Housing Authority v. Midkiff, 467 U.S. 229 (1984), the Supreme Court noted that "empirical debates over the wisdom of [regulatory] takings—no less than debates over the wisdom of other kinds of socioeconomic legislation—are not to be carried out in the federal courts."

Euclid involved a facial attack on a village zoning law; *Midkiff* challenged a law enacted by the Hawaii state legislature. The separation of powers doctrine dictates a posture of deference in these situations. Even when courts review the decisions of administrative bodies (planning boards and commissions or zoning boards of appeals), they defer to local decision makers whose knowledge is thought superior to that of the courts. From state to state, courts may take slightly different approaches to reviewing these decisions, requiring for example a showing of "substantial evidence" to support a decision here, or requiring "facts on the record" to sustain a decision there. These nuances are important, but they do not mask the fact that the judicial standards of review are mostly hospitable to local land use decisions.

When the courts review decisions made by planning and zoning boards, the agency is required to show the court that it has based its decision on facts that create a reasonable basis for its decision. In Citizens to Preserve Overton Park, Inc. v. Volpe, 401 U.S. 402 (1971), for example, the Supreme Court noted that a court's review should involve a "substantial inquiry" and be searching, probing, and complete. Thus, administrative decisions must be carefully decided and subject to reasonable explanation. One common basis for reversal is when a development project is severely conditioned or denied solely because of neighbor opposition. The court needs to see facts on the record that provide a reasonable or substantial basis for the decision.

One practical consequence of judicial deference to local legislative acts is that the legislature does not have to conduct detailed studies regarding the adoption of or change in land use laws, put facts supporting such matters on the record, or conduct an adjudicatory hearing on the law's adoption or change.

This is the case in all states regarding the adoption of broadly applicable land use regulations. Courts in a few states, however, regard some land use law changes as adjudicatory in nature, rather than legislative, and as a consequence place a burden of proving the need for the change on the legislature. In Fasano v. Board of County Comm'rs of Washington County, 264 Or. 574, 507 P.2d 23 (Or. 1973), the Oregon court recognized that most jurisdictions regard the adoption and amendment of the zoning ordinance to be a legislative act and entitled to presumptive validity. In *Fasano,* the court reviewed a rezoning of land to a different use to be quasi-judicial in nature—a matter requiring the collection and analysis of facts in adjudicatory hearings—rather than legislative. This less deferential approach, the court reasoned, would prevent parcel-by-parcel change affected in response to developer pressures to rezone.

The *Fasano* case reveals that legislative bodies can operate in various capacities: legislative, quasi-judicial, and, even, administrative. In Oregon, the court viewed the parcel-specific zoning amendment as a quasi-judicial matter, one applicable to a few individuals whose interests could be identified and evaluated in its proceedings. Colorado, Florida, and a few other states agree with *Fasano* and the courts will look to see whether the legislative body gathered facts that support its determination that the zoning should be changed. In these states, deference disappears and the burden of proving the reasonableness of its actions is on the legislature when it is deemed to be acting in a quasi-judicial manner.

Under some zoning ordinances, special permits and other individual parcel decisions are made by the legislative body. Here, courts are less inclined to presume the reasonableness of the body's actions and look for facts on the record supporting them. In Sunderland Family Treatment Services v. City of Pasco, 903 P.2d 986 (Wash. 1995), for example, the city council denied the plaintiff's application for a special use permit to operate a group home for troubled teenagers. The Washington state court held that the denial of such a special use permit is an adjudicatory act. The court then reviewed each of the council's findings of fact and determined that the denial was improper because it was not based on substantial evidence, but rather on general neighborhood opposition.

In other situations as well, courts will apply less deferential standards to zoning actions by legislative bodies. When, for example, a rezoning does not comply with the comprehensive plan of the community, it may be deemed invalid on its face. This may be because state law requires all zoning decisions to conform to the comprehensive plan, or because, in the circumstances of the case, the matter is regarded as "spot zoning." See, for example, Fritts v. City of Ashland, 348 S.W.2d 712 (Ky. App. 1961) and Nova Horizon, Inc. v. City Council of the City of Reno, 105 Nev. 92, 769 P.2d 721 (Nev. 1989). One way of looking at a zoning amendment that does not conform to the comprehensive plan is that the action is ultra vires, or outside the power of the legislature to act. If the state zoning enabling act requires zoning to conform to the plan, a zoning amendment that does not conform is not within the legislative prerogative delegated to municipal governments by the state legislature.

Courts adopt a number of rules to govern access to the judicial process, such as requiring subject matter jurisdiction to hear a case. In City of Trenton v. Federal Emergency Management Agency, 545 F.Supp. 13 (E.D. Mich. 1981), the City of Trenton, Michigan, appealed the Federal Insurance Administration's (FIA) determination of local floodplain boundaries. The lawsuit was dismissed by the District Court because the city did not bring its appeal within the statute of limitations established by federal law. "The City of Trenton has failed to meet the conditions established by Congress for administrative and judicial review of FIA's flood elevation determination. Where a party fails to meet the statutory prerequisites for judicial review of administrative action, the court lacks subject matter jurisdiction to hear the case."

Courts also examine whether the challenger has a sufficient interest to bring the action, if the matter is ripe for adjudication, whether available administrative remedies have been exhausted, if the choice of forum is correct, and whether the appropriate remedy is requested.

B. STANDING

Challengers are allowed to seek judicial review of parcel-specific land use decisions when they are affected by the action in some special way, different from the general public. Although land use actions are required to benefit the general public, not all local residents have "standing" to sue. However, the general judicial policy on land use issues is that it is desirable to resolve disputes on their merits rather than to deny access to the courts to challengers based on preclusive and restrictive standing rules. What courts seek, using rules of varying strictness, is to learn whether the plaintiff has a justiciable controversy, similar to the federal requirement of presenting a "case or controversy" for resolution.

Standing may be governed by statute. In the original Standard Zoning Enabling Act, adopted in many states, Section 7 limited appeals of land use actions to those "persons aggrieved." Courts may interpret this to mean that the challenger must show "special damage" or a particular "adverse impact." See, Palmer v. St. Louis County, 591 S.W.2d 39 (Mo. App. E.D. 1979). In Virginia, a person must be "severally aggrieved by any decision. . . ." The Supreme Court of Virginia formulated a two-part test to determine if a particularized harm is present. First, the party must own or occupy real property within close proximity to the property that is the subject of the land use determination to show a direct, immediate, pecuniary, and substantial interest in the decision. Second, the complainant must have alleged facts demonstrating a particular harm to some personal or property right, legal or equitable, or the imposition of a burden or obligation different from that suffered by the general public. See, Friends of the Rappahonnock v. Carolina Cty. Bd. of Supervisors, 286 Va. 38, 743 S.E.2d 132 (Va. 2013).

The owners of properties whose land use applications are conditioned or denied are clearly aggrieved and have standing to challenge the action because it directly restricts the use or enjoyment of their property. Additionally, standing is afforded to nearby property owners who challenge the approval of a land use project because they can demonstrate that they will be adversely impacted as a result of the challenged action. Proximity, by itself, is often a proxy for pleading and proving direct injury. The owner of a parcel a half-mile away from a development project approved by a local agency, however, does not have standing to challenge its approval based on proximity alone, but may have standing if she can show that hydrogeological formations and drainage patterns beneath the site indicate that her drinking water would be adversely affected by the development. Courts vary as to whether they require challengers to plead and prove their potential injury or whether it can be presumed by the location of their affected property.

Certain associations of affected individuals may also bring actions on behalf of their members. To be awarded standing to challenge land use actions, associations must be fairly representative of the community, have open membership, have the capacity and authority to maintain judicial actions, and be organized to protect the interests of those citizens allegedly affected by the land use action.

Property owners cannot challenge a land use action solely because they will suffer economic competition from a newly permitted development or business. Limiting economic competition has been held by the courts as not within the "zone of interest" of zoning and land use regulation; parties whose only injury is increased competition, therefore, are not allowed to challenge a project's approval.

In holding that the plaintiff in an Arizona case had standing, the court noted that the issue of standing in a zoning case stems from the law governing standing in a public nuisance case. A landowner must have special damages distinct from those suffered by the general public. In Buckelew v. Town of Parker, 188 Ariz. 446, 937 P.2d 368 (Ariz. App. 1996), a neighbor sued his town for its failure to abate a zoning violation on the property adjacent to his. The offending adjacent property had been used as a recreational vehicle park—a nonconforming use under the zoning ordinance—but was gradually converted to a permanent mobile home park, and the town failed to prevent this change in the nonconforming use of the site. The plaintiff's special damage claims arising from the use of the adjacent property were "noise, threats of violence, increased litter, health and fire code violations, increased danger of crime, and the destruction of his personal property . . ." The plaintiff was awarded standing to sue because these effects are distinct from those suffered by the others in the community: a matter of adjacency.

In Tenth Street Residential Association v. City of Dallas, 968 F.3d 492 (5th Cir. 2020), the Association argued that the City's demolition and historic tax credit policies made it more difficult for it to fulfill its organizational role, and therefore detrimentally impacted the ambiance of the historic neighborhood, reduced property values, threatened the neighborhood's designation as an historic district, and posed an imminent threat to each member's home.

The court noted that the Supreme Court had previously recognized that when an organization's ability to pursue its mission is "perceptibly impaired" because it has "diverted significant resources to counteract the defendant's conduct," it was deemed to have suffered an injury and thus had standing. Here, however, the time spent attending meetings and one member's efforts intervening as an interested party did not constitute "significant resources."

C. RIPENESS AND FINALITY

The question of whether an action by an aggrieved party is ripe for adjudication requires an understanding of how land use boards make decisions. Ripeness often arises as a question when a developer's proposed project has been denied by a planning board or commission. It can also arise when the local legislature rezones property and the affected property owners object. Unless and until the affected property owners have submitted proposals in good faith and been denied or limited in their development plans, how are courts to determine whether and to what extent they have been damaged? It is not sufficient to submit, for example, a grandiose development proposal, obtain a denial, and then challenge the regulations as a regulatory taking. In the ordinary context, land use agencies have a high degree of discretion to soften the strictures of the regulations they administer. It remains the law that the landowner must submit applications that give the agency the opportunity to decide and explain the reach of a challenged regulation.

In Liberty Sackets Harbor v. Sackets Harbor, 776 Fed. Appx. 1 (2d Cir. 2019), the court determined that the matter was not ripe for adjudication in federal court. Under ripeness rules in land use case, the plaintiff was required to show that there was a final decision on their subdivision application before they could seek review. The plaintiff attempted to show that it would be futile under the circumstances to pursue its application. The court was unpersuaded. Plaintiffs had not convinced the court that the defendants had "dug in their heels," or that the application would never be approved.

A ripeness issue arose in Williamson County Regional Planning Commission v. Hamilton Bank of Johnson City, 473 U.S. 172 (1985). The city rezoned the plaintiff's land, which had already been approved for development by the local planning commission. Under the rezoning, the approved, but unbuilt, project no longer complied with local law. The plaintiff claimed that this rezoning action, by itself, constituted a regulatory taking because it limited the number of homes that could be built and caused a net loss of $1 million. The Supreme Court determined that the case was not ripe and would not be until the plaintiff obtained a final decision from the zoning authority under the new law. The court held a takings claim cannot be properly decided until the aggrieved party has "obtained a final decision regarding how it will be allowed to develop its property." Because courts in takings actions look at the economic impact and the reasonable investment-backed expectations of the affected party, "[t]hose factors simply cannot be evaluated until the administrative agency has arrived at a final, definite position regarding how it will apply the regulations at issue to the particular land in question."

The *Williamson County* ripeness issue was revisited and revised by the U.S. Supreme Court in Knick v. Township of Scott Pennsylvania, 139 S.Ct. 2162 (2019). The case involved a municipal ordinance requiring that "[a]ll cemeteries . . . be kept open and accessible to the general public during daylight hours." The Township claimed that the ordinance was a codification of common law. The Plaintiff countered that, in federal court, the ordinance constituted a taking of her property. The Third Circuit had held that the federal claim was not "ripe" under *Williamson County* because no state court had denied compensation under state inverse condemnation law. The majority claimed that precluding takings claims under *Williamson County* would, as a practical matter, prevent takings claims from being brought in federal courts.

The Court in *Knick* held that *Williamson County* "was not just wrong" but that its "reasoning was exceptionally ill founded and conflicted with much of our takings jurisprudence." Further, "a property owner has a claim for a violation of the Takings Clause as soon as a government takes his property for public use without paying for it" so that the claim may be litigated at once in federal court under the Civil Rights Act, 42 U.S.C. § 1983 regardless of state "post-taking remedies that may be available" to the plaintiff because the right to just compensation rests on the Constitution and not any statute.

D. EXHAUSTION OF ADMINISTRATIVE REMEDIES

A challenge to a local land use decision may not be brought when available administrative remedies have not been sought. Where the challenger can appeal the matter to another body, such as a zoning board of appeals, or where a rehearing on the matter complained of can be had, the jurisdiction of the court cannot be invoked. Where an applicant for a building permit fails to appeal the denial to the zoning board of appeals, for example, he cannot appeal the denial to the courts. Where the only question is a legal one, or the challenge is to the constitutionality of the regulation on its face, administrative appeals need not be exhausted, because the local administrative agency does not decide such issues.

The court in Alaska rejected a property owner's due process case because it had failed to exhaust available administrative remedies. In Ben Lomond, Inc. v. Municipality of Anchorage, 761 P.2d 119 (Alaska 1988), a property owner had presented plans and secured a building permit to renovate apartment buildings, which would have created 280 dwelling units where only 234 were permitted under the zoning. When this fact was determined, the city revoked the building permit. Local law permitted the owner to appeal this determination to the zoning board of appeals or to seek a variance from that board. Alternatively, the owner could have resubmitted an application for a permit for the allowable 234 units. Instead the owner did nothing. The property was later purchased by the municipality through a tax foreclosure proceeding and demolished. A park was built in its place. The lower courts entertained the owner's due process objection, but the state's highest court reversed, denying the claim because of the owner's failure to exhaust the administrative remedies. The court noted that the municipality should have had the opportunity to hear an appeal, create a factual record, and correct any errors.

Usually, petitioners must exhaust their administrative remedies before appealing to the courts; however, a petitioner need not exhaust administrative remedies when the action raises a question that is peculiarly suited to judicial rather than administrative treatment and no other adequate remedy is available. Petitioner may bring a declaratory judgment action to challenge matter of law decisions of municipal officers and boards without exhausting all administrative remedies. See, Dembiee v. Town of Holerness, 167 N.H. 130, 105 A.3d 1051 (N.H. 2014).

E. REMEDIES

When land use decisions are challenged in state courts, a variety of remedies are available, depending on the type of action brought and the type of agency that made the decision. Remedies include writs of certiorari requiring land use bodies to certify their record for review; mandamus which require agencies to take specific actions; declaratory judgments invalidating actions because of illegality; injunctions that prevent the enforcement of illegal standards or decisions; and damages such as just compensation when a regulatory taking is deemed to have occurred.

Courts are reluctant to issue writs of mandamus ordering local legislatures to take specific actions; they are more comfortable issuing judgments that declare legislative actions valid or invalid, and simply enjoining legislatures from enforcing invalid regulations or decisions. For example, the highest state court in Georgia held in City of Statesboro v. Dickens et al., 293 Ga. 540, 748 S.E.2d 397 (Ga. 2013), that variances must be challenged as a certiorari and not a mandamus action. This reluctance to order legislatures to act is part of the important doctrine of separation of powers between the judicial and legislative branches of government. When a legislative act is challenged and found invalid, the typical approach for the court is to issue a judgment declaring the action to be invalid and enjoin its enforcement, leaving it to the legislature to decide how to correct the infirmity. Declaratory judgment actions can be brought to declare a zoning provision unconstitutional, to determine whether a rezoning conforms with the comprehensive plan or constitutes illegal spot zoning, to determine the validity of a refusal to rezone a parcel of land, to determine the constitutionality of conditions attached to a rezoning, or to determine the authority of a municipality to adopt a particular zoning provision.

The courts may require the local legislature to exercise its zoning authority in a particular fashion in the rare event that it has found that the zoning law is discriminatory or exclusionary. In Berenson v. New Castle, 67 A.D.2d 506, 415 N.Y.S.2d 669 (N.Y.A.D. 2nd Dept. 1979), a New York exclusionary zoning case, the court mandated the rezoning of the plaintiff's property to multi-family zoning, noting that "with the single exception of discriminatory zoning of similarly situated parcels . . . a judicial declaration that a zoning ordinance was invalid . . . was never accompanied by a declaration which actually rezoned that property or placed it within a particular use classification."

The judiciary is less inhibited when reviewing the actions of a planning board or a zoning board of appeals that perform administrative and quasi-judicial functions. With respect to the decisions and actions of these bodies, or the local enforcement officials who administer their decisions, courts will issue writs of mandamus requiring specific actions to be taken, such as the award or revocation of a building permit or the approval or denial of an application for land subdivision or site development. In some states, courts issue writs of certiorari to local land use bodies requiring them to certify the record of their proceedings when they act on a variance request or upon the application for development approval.

F. FEDERAL COURTS: ABSTENTION

Understanding that state courts provide a variety of remedies for land use actions that are illegal helps to explain the doctrine of abstention, which is applied by federal courts that are asked to entertain challenges before they have been presented to state courts for resolution. In Railroad Commission v. Pullman Co., 312 U.S. 496 (1941), the Supreme Court held that federal courts should abstain from entertaining matters when the resolution of a state law question would make a federal decision unnecessary. This is particularly the case where there exists an unsettled state law question that "touches a sensitive area of social policy upon which the federal courts ought not to enter unless no alternative to its adjudication is open."

In Sinclair Oil Corp. v. County of Santa Barbara, 96 F.3d 401 (9th Cir. 1996), the Ninth Circuit Court of Appeals abstained from hearing a landowner's challenge to a California county's newly adopted land use plan that it claimed was a regulatory taking. The plan designated a large portion of the plaintiff's land as environmentally sensitive and lowered the number of residential units permitted from 300 to 70. The court invoked abstention and refused to hear the case because land use planning is a sensitive area of social policy, the state court could resolve the matter by finding a taking under the state constitution, and the plaintiff presented no particularly novel legal claim or argument.

Sinclair relied on Williamson County Regional Planning Commission v. Hamilton Bank of Johnson City, 473 U.S. 172 (1985), which was overruled by Knick v. Township of Scott Pennsylvania, 139 S.Ct. 2162 (2019). The section of *Williamson* that Sinclair relied on stated, "[B]ecause the Fifth Amendment proscribes takings *without just compensation*, no constitutional violation occurs until just compensation has been denied. The nature of the constitutional right therefore requires that a property owner utilize procedures for obtaining compensation before bringing a § 1983 action." Future case law will determine the effect of *Knick* on *Sinclair*.

The *Pullman* abstention doctrine led to the denial of access to the federal courts of hotel owners who challenged the constitutionality of a city ordinance that required them to pay a substantial fee for the conversion to tourist accommodations of residential hotel rooms that provided affordable rental housing for vulnerable populations. In San Remo Hotel v. City and County of San Francisco, 545 U.S. 323 (2005), the plaintiffs were forced to litigate their legal challenges to this ordinance in state courts, where they did not prevail. In federal court, they argued that because they reserved their federal constitutional takings claim in the state litigation, the federal courts should review the matter de novo, without regard to how the issues were decided in state court. The Court refused to engage in a de novo review, holding that the full faith and credit doctrine of the federal constitution prevents federal courts from relitigating issues that have been resolved by courts of competent jurisdiction.

CHAPTER 12

MANAGING CLIMATE CHANGE

§ 1. INTRODUCTION

At the end of the last century, the literature regarding planning and planning law was saturated with discussions of smart growth. By the turn of the century, more emphasis was being placed on incorporating the concepts and principles of sustainable development. Today, we realize that effective sustainable development planning and law must also include strategies that mitigate and adapt to climate change and the effects of global warming.

The World Commission on the Environment and Development issued its report entitled *Our Common Future*, which defined sustainable development as development that meets "the needs and aspirations of the present without compromising the ability to meet those of the future." That economic development is linked to the quality of the environment is undeniable. Sustainable development comprises economic development, ecology, and intergenerational equity: a heavy load indeed. Future development must be sustainable and that the law will be a force for positive change.

Sustainable development law and practice focus on shaping land and economic development to have a lighter impact on the environment, including climate change mitigation and adaptation. Sustainable development is the currency of planners and land use attorneys; it uses less material, avoids consuming wetlands or eroding watersheds, consumes less energy, eliminates or shortens vehicle trips, emits less carbon dioxide (CO2), lessens stormwater runoff, reduces ground and surface water pollution, and creates healthier places for living, working, and recreating.

This body of law is created mainly by state and local governments, which have the principal legal authority to regulate building construction, land use, and the conservation of natural resources at the local level. More recently, it involves preserving or expanding the GHG-sequestering environment, adapting to sea-level rise, and building more resilient developments to withstand the fiercer storms associated with climate change.

The connection between sustainable land development and climate change mitigation and adaptation is particularly close. How buildings are constructed, how they are arranged on the land, and how human settlement patterns are shaped are critical to our success in curbing the causes of climate change. About 85 percent of GHG emissions in the U.S. are CO2, much of which is caused by the buildings and land use patterns that local land use plans and regulations create, regulate, and approve. Vehicle trips and miles travelled have increased dramatically in the past three decades as development patterns have spread out, consuming land at much greater rates than the rate of population growth. Today, buildings emit about one-third of CO2 in the U.S. Personal vehicles are responsible for just under one-fifth of total emissions.

Current undeveloped landscapes sequester about one-fifth of CO2 emissions.

Because local governments control land development through legally adopted land use plans and regulations, they are integral players in the process of ensuring the sustainability of buildings and communities generally. Because local governments operate at ground level, they are both aware of—and often motivated to rectify—land use crises; their citizens are there to urge them into action. In a world of finite resources overrun by sprawl, threatened by climate change, short on fuel, and long on greenhouse gas emissions, the law must keep pace.

In 2014, the world caught up with local governments in the global race against climate change. That year, the Intergovernmental Panel on Climate Change (IPCC) embraced the critical role of municipal governments in mitigating the causes of climate change. In 2015, the Paris Climate Agreement adopted by the Conference of the Parties (COP) followed suit. In 2019, the IPCC renewed its support for local mitigation as a key complement to global climate goals and initiatives. For decades, the legal and practical ability of municipal governments to shape human settlements in ways that lower CO2 emissions and enhance biological sequestration has been clear to land use practitioners.

§ 2. DISASTER MITIGATION

Following Hurricane Katrina in 2005, municipal officials and land use planners showed renewed interest in the use of planning and zoning to mitigate the devastating results of natural disasters. Building codes, land use policies, zoning and subdivision regulations, comprehensive plans, site plan review, floodplain management plans, buffers, steep slope ordinances, open space plans, stormwater management plans, transportation plans, and conservation and natural resource protection policies are some of the techniques that can be employed.

Examples of development regulations that may be employed as effective disaster mitigation techniques include: limitations on how property may be developed in flood zones; setbacks from fault lines (and shorelines and other areas prone to natural disasters), steep slopes, and coastal erosion areas; and overlay zones that introduce additional requirements over sensitive environmental areas such as wetlands, dunes, and hillsides. See, Tweedy v. Matanusak-Susitna Borough Bd. of Adj. and Appeals, 332 P.3d 12 (Alaska 2014); Parris v. City of Rapid City, 834 N.W.2d 850 (2013). The American Planning Association's 2002 Growing Smart Legislative Guidebook recommends the use of overlay districts as a natural hazard mitigation technique, and advises communities to include "procedures and criteria for the designation of. . .natural hazard area overlay districts" when drafting ordinances for areas that are prone to natural hazards. The Guidebook also encourages local governments to develop a list of uses and activities that should be prohibited in the overlay zone, therefore allowing the local government to implement its mitigation strategies in a manner that is specifically tailored to address the effects of natural hazards that pose the biggest threat. Overlay zones can be created for many different purposes. In addition to offering protection from flooding, overlay zones can be used to mitigate damage from potential disasters in watersheds, tidal basins, hillsides, and other sensitive environmental areas.

Subdivision regulations can be used to limit the intensity of development in areas located within mapped floodplains. Applications for development permits in fire-prone areas may be required to include appropriate facilities to suppress wildfires as a condition of subdivision approval. Local governments may require applicants to avoid construction that results in encroachment upon watercourses and water bodies, including avoiding the filling or excavation of, or encroachment on, wetlands, floodplains, and other lands subject to flooding. Applicants may also be directed to avoid removal of desirable vegetation. Local governments can use the site plan review process to examine proposed developments in relation to other on-site conditions, such as fault lines, steep slopes, shorelines, or other areas that are prone to natural disasters, and make decisions to grant or deny permits or add conditions to approvals based on the objectives of the local hazard mitigation plan.

Performance zoning can also be employed as part of a subdivision or site plan review to aid in disaster mitigation. For example, vegetation requirements such as tree ordinances can help to minimize flooding by preventing removal and destruction or by requiring replacement. In areas that are prone to wildfires, local governments can mitigate the impact of fires on homes by requiring buffer areas that eliminate natural fuels around residences such as requiring a clearing of small trees, fallen leaves, branches, pine needles, and the like around an appropriate perimeter of a home.

These traditional and innovative land use techniques have helped to shape the field of hazard mitigation planning. The term "hazard mitigation planning" is adopted from the Stafford Act, as amended by the Disaster Mitigation Act (DMA). Disaster Mitigation Act of 2000, Pub. L. No. 106–390, 114 Stat. 1552 (2000). The DMA provides pre-disaster and post-disaster recovery funding and technical assistance to states and local governments. Eligibility for much of this federal assistance requires that states establish hazard mitigation agencies, adopt hazard mitigation plans, and provide help to local governments to adopt hazard mitigation plans. "The purpose of hazard mitigation is to reduce potential losses from future disasters. The intent of mitigation planning, therefore, is to maintain a process that leads to hazard mitigation actions. Mitigation plans identify the natural hazards that impact communities, identify actions to reduce losses from those hazards, and establish a coordinated process to implement the plan." FEMA, LOCAL MITIGATION PLAN REVIEW GUIDE 5 (Oct. 2011); 44 C.F.R. § 201.1(b) (2019).

The FEMA Guide notes that local hazard mitigation plans are intended to, among other things, "serve as the basis for the State to provide technical assistance and to prioritize project funding." FEMA states that "[a]n open public involvement process is essential to the development of an effective plan." Local plans must be submitted to the State Hazard Mitigation Officer for "initial review and coordination." The state then forwards the plan to FEMA for "formal review and approval."

Under these federal influences, local planning has become more integrated and focused on locally specific hazards. The City of Santa Cruz Climate Adaptation Plan, for example, proposes numerous adaptation strategies that mitigate the City's vulnerability hazards. CITY OF SANTA CRUZ, CLIMATE ADAPTATION PLAN UPDATE: (2018) One of the highest priority strategies listed is the identification of areas where the City can manage retreat from the coast's rising seas. Other approaches focus on coastal erosion, flooding, wildfire, and drought. One strategy aimed at mitigating coastal erosion is the development of "setbacks adjacent to cliffs." The plan also calls for increased vegetation management efforts (such as creating and mowing fuel breaks, clearing underbrush, and protecting perimeters of parks, green belts, and open spaces) to prevent wildfires. The plan addresses drought-related hazards through strategies to "protect and preserve tree canopy and other native coastal vegetation."

"Plan Manitou" is the City's integrated comprehensive plan and hazard mitigation plan. CITY OF MANITOU SPRINGS, COLO., CITY OF MANITOU SPRINGS COMMUNITY MASTER PLAN & HAZARD

MITIGATION PLAN (2017), The Plan is the City's roadmap to guide future growth, support economic, environmental, and social sustainability, and assure that the City remains resilient in the face of future challenges. The Plan emerged from the need to create a comprehensive plan as well as address natural hazards and risks present in the community. The Plan includes strategies for addressing specific hazards and at-risk areas. For high hazard areas (including those identified as flood, wildfire, steep slope, and geologic hazard areas), one policy is to "[g]uide new development away from and discourage density increases." The use of incentives, where feasible, is suggested as a means of doing so. For flood hazard areas, policies include "[e]ncourag[ing] flood mitigation measures for existing structures," and "[d]iscourag[ing] additional development . . . in mapped floodplain areas, to the extent feasible, through the use of incentives, clustering, and other techniques." For steep slopes and geologic hazards, the policy is to "[a]void development on slopes with grades steeper than 30 percent to the maximum extent practicable."

In all of this, there is one irreducible minimum: the effect of natural disasters is local. They engage municipal officials and the professionals who advise them. They are not spectators, but the first affected and first to respond. It is at the local level that property is destroyed, lives are lost, public health is threatened, infrastructure damaged, and that the phone rings first. Local leaders must know the legal power they have and the strategies that they can design to deal effectively with this growing list of natural disasters. Local governments have the legal power to adopt comprehensive plans, zoning, subdivision and site plan regulations, and standards to protect natural resources, such as floodplains, coastal ecosystems, inland wetlands, and forests: all assets threatened by disaster events. Local governments enforce a variety of codes that affect the design and specifications of buildings themselves, including building, plumbing, fire protection, electrical, and energy codes. Municipal legislatures also adopt administrative procedures and create administrative agencies, such as planning and zoning boards, for the review and approval of development projects.

§ 3. ENERGY ISSUES

A. INTRODUCTION

L As zoning turned 100 years old in 2016, it showed its age by the failure of most communities to permit modern clean energy systems and to call for green building provisions in their zoning ordinances. In response to fears of dependence on foreign oil, high costs of energy, and interest in mitigating climate change, municipalities began reforming zoning to permit, require, and incentivize renewable and clean energy facilities and energy conserving buildings. These rapidly evolving systems include permission to use building integrated solar systems, ground- and roof-mounted solar arrays, large- and small-scale wind generation, multi-building combined heat and power facilities, micro-grids, on-site electricity generation, geothermal systems, to reduce energy use in buildings and create walkable, mixed use development near transit stations. All of these techniques mitigate climate change.

For clean energy systems to be constructed, they must be permitted by local zoning and not subject to expensive regulatory barriers that discourage their use and increase their cost. The barriers the reforms faced in 2016 were many. They ranged from the simple failure to define and permit clean energy systems, to excessive height and setback restrictions, to additional or outdated permitting requirements, which greatly increase the costs of systems or discourage their use due to the unpredictability or length and costs of the construction approval process.

Although both the federal and state levels of government have a strong interest in encouraging the deployment of renewable and clean energy systems, the power to permit these land uses has been delegated by most states to local villages, towns, counties, boroughs, and cities. Most states are not willing to preempt local control of these land use matters. As a result, it is usually state policy to defer to local discretion in these matters.

B. ENERGY CONSERVATION IN BUILDINGS

All building construction and rehabilitation projects must go through a local land use approval process. The principal method of achieving energy efficiency in new building construction and renovation is the energy conservation code. This code is one of several promulgated by the International Codes Council. These codes are adopted in most states and are enforced by local governments. The energy conservation code contains minimum standards for the design, construction, and installation of the building shell or envelope, mechanical systems, and lighting. By vigorously enforcing this code, dramatic progress can be made in energy conservation and climate change mitigation, particularly in buildings whose energy source is fossil fuel.

Land use law in some states allows local governments to enhance the energy code by adopting additional standards aimed at achieving greater energy efficiency. A creative example is found in Marin County, California. The county requires large homes under 4,000 square feet to exceed the energy conservation code requirements by 15%. County of Marin, Cal., Ordinance § 19.04.100 (2011). If the home is over 4,000 sq. ft., but less than 5,500 sq. ft., it must exceed the state code in efficiency by 20 percent. For homes between 5,500 and 6,500 sq. ft., the requirement is 30 percent. Homes over 7,000 sq. ft. must be "net zero energy" users; a goal that green builders can actually achieve.

In New York, the town of Greenburgh amended its local code to require that "all new one- or two-family dwelling or multiple dwelling (townhouse) of three stories or less [b]e built to achieve a HERS [Home Energy Rating System] Index of 70 or less on the Residential Services Network (RESNET) Home Energy Rating System (HERS) . . . ." Town of Greenburgh, N.Y., Code § 100–20 (2011). The town of Blooming Grove, New York, uses a zoning density bonus to encourage home developers to adopt Energy Star. Energy Star can achieve energy savings in excess of 30 percent greater than the base energy code. It governs appliances, heating and cooling systems, the thermal envelope, electrical, ventilation, and equipment efficiency. Blooming Grove, N.Y., Town Code § 235–14.1(A)(3) (2011). The town awards a 10 percent increase in the number of homes that can be constructed under local zoning in exchange for making them fully Energy Star compliant.

Local subdivision and site plan regulations can be amended to govern building orientation, layout, or landscaping on sites, which can be used to reduce energy consumption in new buildings. Land use laws can require homes in subdivisions to be clustered and designed to conserve energy or equipped with solar panels (or at least to be wired and built to accommodate them). Land use boards can require developers and their design consultants to follow an integrated design process, where they collaborate during the early stages of the project review process to achieve the greatest possible energy conservation and cost reduction. It is at this stage that decisions can be made about building orientation, form, shading, energy-efficient exterior lighting, window size and location, rooflines and extensions, reflective roofing, height-to-floor ratios, and building features that relate to passive ventilation and cooling.

Land use laws can achieve extraordinary energy efficiency by permitting and encouraging the use of combined heat and power (CHP) systems in individual buildings and interconnected energy systems in certain mixed-use districts. By employing CHP—a mechanical system that can be used to produce electricity, heating and cooling in higher density, mixed-use neighborhoods—the potential for energy efficiency, and therefore energy conservation, is remarkably greater than if used on an individual parcel of land. To increase the use of district energy systems (DES), the local land use regulatory system can be adjusted to allow or incentivize them. DES must be made an allowable use under local zoning and site plan regulations, as well as local building and energy codes. They, too, may be encouraged through bonus zoning provisions that provide additional development densities for developers who adopt DES technologies.

Microgrids usually operate at the scale of multiple buildings, a city block, or a larger neighborhood and are, therefore, ideally subject to local planning and regulation. They can be prevented or furthered by land use standards. Pittsburgh used its delegated land use power to adopt zoning and land use regulations to enable microgrids to develop. Pittsburgh Zoning Code, Article VI, § 915.07.B. The City Council amended its municipal code to add a Performance Point System that incentivizes sustainable development. It awards developers density bonuses for points that they accumulate by developing sustainably, including the development of distributed energy systems such as microgrids.

C. ZONING FOR SOLAR ENERGY

Local officials who want to encourage solar energy systems are adjusting the local land use system first by adding a solar energy component to the comprehensive plan or adopting a special solar energy policy or plan to guide the reform of land use regulations. These local governments are then amending zoning regulations to permit and encourage these systems.

The primary, and most common, barrier to solar energy system implementation occurs when solar energy systems are neither defined nor permitted in one or more zoning districts. Without explicit definitions of solar facilities, they cannot be permitted by reference in the district use provisions of local zoning. In addition, the lack of clear clean energy- or solar-related definitions misses the opportunity for municipalities to send a signal to developers, property owners, and installers that they are open for clean energy business. Municipalities are beginning to fix this problem by amending their zoning code to include definitions of the different solar energy systems available based on type, size, and/or energy capacity. Since solar energy systems vary significantly by type, location, size, and energy capacity, zoning definitions generally are based on these factors. Where these characteristics align with the intensity of use or impact of a solar energy system, they justify different land use regulations for each type and guide local planners as to where to allow each type of system to be constructed. Municipalities can choose to permit solar energy systems by designating them as principal, accessory, secondary, or specially permitted uses. They can subject them to modified and expedited site plan review, waiving design standards enforced by local Architectural Review Boards, and providing exemptions from historic district review standards for conforming designs and proper locations.

Solar easements, not recognized by common law in most states, can be created by local government regulation to ensure access to sunlight over the life of the solar system. Typically, these regulations require written and recorded solar easements that define easement dimensions, how the easement will terminate, and compensation for easement maintenance or interference, among other provisions. Some localities require developers to install solar energy systems or, short of that, make buildings solar-ready. Other communities incentivize, rather that require, these solar facilities, typically by providing density bonuses for solar panels, solar readiness, and solar access easements.

D. LOCAL REGULATION OF WIND ENERGY

A group of wind turbines is known as a wind farm, and the positioning of even a single turbine can be a highly controversial issue. While wind farms offer a clean alternative to fossil fuel combustion, siting these utilities often inspires the "anywhere but here" argument commonly associated with locally unwanted land uses. There are two typical types of wind turbines; each carries with it a unique set of land use challenges.

While wind turbine design has changed throughout history, the most prevalent design is known as a horizontal access turbine. Under this design the generator is located on top of a support structure (usually a pole) with three blades that spin in the wind. The generator and the blades have to be located in areas that receive sufficient wind and that are high enough to remove it from any obstacles that would block wind access. The difference between the wind turbine designs is the size of the unit and the amount of power it can generate.

The personal use turbine is the smallest variety of wind turbine. With support poles ranging between 80–110 feet, these turbines can supply enough energy to power a home. In residential zones, it is the close proximity to other houses that can cause trouble with neighbors. Two cases involving personal wind turbines are Rose v. Chaikin, 187 N.J. Super. 210 (N.J. Super. Ch. 1982) and Rassier v. Houim, 488 N.W.2d 635 (N.D. 1992). Both cases dealt with the noise generated from the turbines. In *Rose* the court found that the defendant's placement of a turbine (that was operating above the town's noise ordinance level) ten feet from his neighbor's property line was an actionable private nuisance. The *Rassier* case involved a similar situation; however, in this case, the defendant was operating its wind turbine for two years before the plaintiff positioned its mobile home 40 feet from the turbine. With several neighbors testifying for the defendant, the judge ruled that the plaintiff "came to the nuisance" and allowed the turbine to continue.

The second design type is the commercial wind turbine. These are much larger units with support structures up to and over 200 feet tall and blades measuring 80 feet or more in length. These larger structures require a great deal more land use planning than their smaller counterparts. Noise and safety concerns are more prevalent and necessitate the use of setback requirements. Aesthetic issues abound with the larger turbines, prompting some communities to ban wind turbines or wind farms altogether, while others require certain paint schemes and prohibit support roads from being placed on ridge lines. Significant planning is also required to avoid disrupting bird habitat and migration patterns.

When identifying where wind energy projects may be sited, municipalities with zoning can decide to limit the use in one or more zoning districts "as of right," or they may prefer to allow the use subject to special permit review, providing an opportunity to ensure that the proposed development meets additional review criteria to ensure compatibility with the surrounding area. In addition to being listed as a specifically permitted use, smaller wind energy facilities may be considered as an accessory use, particularly in an agricultural area. The clearest way to ensure this is to list wind energy/farms/turbines as an appropriate accessory use to other agri-business activities.

Opponents of wind projects have raised concerns regarding the noise generated by wind turbines. Establishing a buffer zone will allow the sound to diminish before it can reach a receiver. The suggested distance for a commercial turbine is between 1,000 feet and half a mile. Set-back requirements have other benefits as well, as they may be used to protect nearby property from the effects of potential thawing of ice build ups that may occur at turbines sited in colder climates.

The visual impacts of wind turbines may be also the focus of community concern. For a wind turbine to be effective, it must be placed above trees, buildings, and other obstacles that will disturb the wind flow. These requirements often restrict wind development to rural or remote areas. Several factors go into a wind farm's aesthetic impact: lighting, coloring, and signage are obvious ones, but spacing can also be a factor. The size of the turbines must also be considered, as smaller turbines can be placed closer together and have blades that spin faster, while large turbines have slower rotors and must be placed further apart, but are visible from a longer distance. The distance between turbines is determined based upon the distance needed for the wind to replenish. While turbines may need to be constructed at certain heights, zoning ordinances can provide maximum allowable height limitations to ensure that the turbines are not any higher than necessary. Through a local site plan review law, municipalities can effectively examine the proposed layout of a wind project including spacing, how the wind turbine array is set against the landscape, buffering, and other visual impacts.

Unlike traditional energy generating facilities, wind power is virtually emission free, yet concerns still exist over the effect wind power facilities will have on the environment. These concerns can arise in a number of different contexts, such as bird and bat collisions with the turbine's rotors, disrupting native habitats during building, or soil erosion or the invasion of non-native plants in the soils disturbed during after construction. These environmental harms can be mitigated with careful attention to appropriate design measures, including following natural terrain contours to the maximum extent possible and quickly restoring land disturbed by construction activities.

§ 4. TRANSIT ORIENTED DEVELOPMENT

Transit Oriented Development (TOD) is a modern zoning strategy with exceptional potential to reduce GHG emissions. According to the Presidential Climate Action Project, "[t]he greatest potential for reducing greenhouse gas emissions . . . is to reduce vehicle miles traveled (VMT)—the miles Americans drive each year." PRESIDENTIAL CLIMATE ACTION PROJECT PLAN § 7:6 (2007). TOD land use plans and zoning encourage mixed-use, compact development in transit neighborhoods. They locate housing and jobs near transit stops and significantly reduce the number and distance of vehicle trips.

Encouraging land use patterns that house and employ more people in urban, transit-connected areas will cause a significant reduction in VMT, while placing households in smaller, more energy-efficient homes and offices will further reduce fossil fuel consumption and CO2 emissions. When neighborhood density is increased for both residential and commercial uses, the distance between origin and destination is shorter, and walking, bicycling, and mass transit services are more feasible. In order for increased densities to be tolerated, standards requiring attractive building, landscape, and streetscape design must be employed.

The successful development of transit stations and rail and bus lines is dependent upon land use densities and mixed uses. There must be a large enough number of commuters in a relevant area to provide a base level of ridership. In addition, ridership must be sufficiently diverse to ensure that people are traveling to work, to shop, to seek entertainment, and to go home at various times during the day, thereby increasing the cost-efficiency of the transit system.

Local land use plans and zoning, which determine population density and building uses, control how much the population will increase over time in a certain area, and what transportation needs new people will have. This, in turn, dictates the demand for various types of transportation services. Locally, this planning is done at the neighborhood level and should be guided by objectives contained in the city's comprehensive plan. To make transit systems feasible, land use planning among localities in a transportation region must be coordinated with transportation planning and development, which occurs under federal programs in urban areas at the metropolitan-area scale.

Many state enabling statutes require or encourage local governments to include a transportation element in their comprehensive plans. Increasingly, these transportation elements have incorporated planning strategies intended to encourage people to drive less and to walk, bicycle, and use mass transportation more frequently. Arizona's planning enabling statute, for example, requires cities with more than 50,000 people to prepare a bike transportation element as part of their comprehensive plan. Ariz. Rev. Stat. Ann. § 94611.05(E)(9) (2011). Nevada's enabling legislation supports planning for mass transit, bicycle, and pedestrian infrastructure. This statute encourages local planning to include a transit element that "[s]how[s] a proposed multimodal system of transit lines, including mass transit, streetcar, motor coach and trolley coach lines, paths for bicycles and pedestrians, satellite parking and related facilities." Nev. Rev. Stat. Ann. § 278.160(1)(R) (2011).

Even where communities are not currently served by transit systems, they can create compact, mixed-use neighborhoods that reduce car trips and miles traveled. Zoning controls in "transportation efficient districts" can limit the size of housing units and combine retail, office, and residential land uses, putting services, shops, and jobs in closer proximity to homes. Communities not yet served by transit can design one or more priority growth districts and create overlay zones for them that allow greater densities and more land uses than permitted in the underlying zoning districts. By clustering development strategically, these growing localities position themselves for future service by commuter rail or bus rapid transit, thereby becoming "transit ready."

Suburban areas that adopt higher density, mixed-use zoning will find it easier politically to adopt strong environmental protection ordinances applicable to the land outside high-density zones. Where state law permits, density bonuses may be provided in transportation efficient districts and cash contributions made by developers in exchange. This money can be used to purchase development rights from landowners in sensitive environmental areas outside the higher density zone, areas that mitigate climate change through sequestration. This balance between development and conservation can be accomplished within TOD areas as well—highlighting again the ability of zoning to create sustainable settlement patterns and mitigate climate change.

APPENDIX

AN INTERNET GUIDE TO LAND USE RESEARCH

§ 1. INTRODUCTION

Students of land use law cannot conduct comprehensive research in the field today without surfing the 'Net. The Internet has become a virtual library providing access to resources beyond what the traditional legal online databases have to offer. For example, while the proprietary law related sites offer comprehensive access to federal and state statutes, regulations, and caselaw, there is sparse access to information about municipal laws and ordinances pertaining to planning and zoning. In addition, proprietary sites provide online access to law review articles, but they do not capture non-commercial publications that contain legal analysis of various planning and zoning related issues. Today, many non-profit and advocacy organizations post position papers, scholarly articles and reports, and other law-related information (such as amicus curiae briefs) to their websites. And of course, planning and law professors often provide course websites with a host of interesting information not readily available from other sources.

Local governments are increasingly offering a web-based presence to post otherwise difficult-to-access public information including zoning ordinances and land use laws. The availability of these ordinances online can assist land use law students in a number of ways. They provide an opportunity actually to see how various provisions are drafted and how they work in practice. It is one thing to read a case about nonconforming uses, but it is another thing to actually read a working provision in a current zoning ordinance, and to be able to compare and contrast different approaches to nonconforming uses in different zoning laws.

For land use practitioners, the availability of online zoning codes can serve as models (although attorneys should always draw their own conclusions as to appropriate enabling authority and constitutionality). Second, they can provide quick access to local ordinances that are not otherwise published in a compilation and available commercially or in a law library. In addition, the posting of minutes of meetings online by municipalities can prove to be important information for attorneys challenging decisions of planning and zoning boards and local legislative bodies. In the past, this information was only available via request to the municipal clerk's office and often required a formal Freedom of Information Law request.

An important caveat, however, is just because the information is electronically published and posted to the Internet does not ensure its veracity or the accuracy of the legal analysis (if any), and it does not guarantee, for example, in the case of a local zoning ordinance, that it is the most up-do-date version of the law. Furthermore, various studies, reports, and articles that are posted on websites may not always be dated, and it is possible to review documents that have been superseded by new statutes, regulations, or caselaw. Due diligence is required to make certain that any information gleaned from the Internet is accurate and based on current legal information. Whether or not the data sought are individual documents, it is a good idea to ascertain when the website was last updated. However, even where websites are regularly updated, the reader must keep in mind that while this may mean that new information has been added, it does not mean that outdated information has been removed from the site. Many studies, reports, and articles, easily posted on websites, lack peer review and do not undergo the same rigorous cite-checking exercise as would a law review article.

With all of the above disclaimers, the Internet remains a valuable legal research tool for land use practitioners, and it provides a wealth of information for course papers. This chapter is intended to interest the reader in exploring some of the sites dedicated to land use. It is by no means a comprehensive review of what is out there (after all, that changes daily). The sites suggested are well established sites that are currently operational and routinely updated by the hosts. The sites reviewed are organized into several major categories: 1) Comprehensive Sites—or sites that focus on land use law with links to other major land use law resources online; 2) Government Sponsored Sites—these are websites hosted by government agencies that contain a significant amount of land use law information; 3) sites where a significant number of land use codes can be accessed; 4) sites sponsored by non-profit organizations involved in various aspects of land use law; and 5) miscellaneous sites of interest.

Cyburbia is a portal for all kinds of land use planning and regulation information. A special section of the site offers a variety of information on planning and zoning law. See, http://www.cyburbia.org/directory/index.php?t=sub_pages&cat=1. Information available includes links about architectural design, development guides, subdivision, land use law, property rights, signs and billboards, wireless facility siting, and zoning and land use regulations. In addition to indexed resource information, this site offers forums to facilitate the exchange of ideas and "top rated" links to sites that include planning sites for, among other things, leading municipalities. http://www.cyburbia.org/.

§ 2. GOVERNMENT SPONSORED SITES

The websites included in this section are federal government sites of interest. Land use researchers should remember to review the websites of state agencies in the jurisdictions where they practice (or are researching laws and policies) to obtain very helpful information. For example, community development agencies and environmental agencies in each state typically make available online relevant statutes and regulations, opinion letters, guidebooks and publications, and other forms of technical assistance. While many federal government agencies may have information relevant to land use law issues, the three sites selected below offer the most comprehensive information. All of the federal agency websites may be accessed by visiting the U.S. Government's Official Web Portal at http://www.firstgov.gov/. In addition to accessing all federal agencies off of the site, links are provided for each of the official state and territorial government websites.

U.S. Department of Justice, Office of Civil Rights, Housing and Civil Enforcement Section, offers information on their website about the federal Fair Housing Act and the Religious Land Use and Institutionalized Persons Act. They produce a newsletter on religious freedom that includes information about enforcement activities related to RLUIPA, https://www.justice.gov/crt/combating-religious-discrimination-and-protecting-religious-freedom-12, and the website provides information about cases and matters within which the Section is involved. See, https://www.justice.gov/crt/housing-and-civil-enforcement-section.

U.S. Department of Housing and Urban Development offers the Regulatory Barriers Clearinghouse to support state and local organizations seeking information about laws, regulations, and policies affecting the development, maintenance, availability, and cost of affordable housing. This site, as called for in the "American Housing and Economic Opportunity Act of 2000," contains a huge database searchable by keyword, author, topic, geographic location, and publication type. The site also offers a biweekly newsletter and an extensive bibliography of sources. Additionally, by registering as a "HUD user" individuals can receive research assistance at no charge from the Customer

Service System. http://www.huduser.org/rbc/. In addition, HUD's client information and policy system, HUD CLIPS, https://www.hud.gov/guidance, offers searchable databases linking to, among other things, the Federal Register, Codes, Congressional Record, Guidebooks, Handbooks and Notices, Inspector General, Letters, Office of General Counsel Documents and Legal Opinions. http://www.hud.gov/. HUD also provides case studies on zoning and affordable housing, https://www.huduser.gov/portal/casestudies/Zon_AfforHousing.html.

U.S. Environmental Protection Agency offers a variety of land use law-related information throughout its substantial web presence. Information regarding creating sustainable, healthy and equitable communities can be accessed at: https://www.epa.gov/environmentaljustice/resources-creating-healthy-sustainable-and-equitable-communities.

The environmental justice homepage is located at http://www.epa.gov/compliance/environmental justice/index.html and offers, among other things, links to environmental justice laws and statutes, cases and settlements, policy and guidance, and data and reports. Links to the homepages of the Federal Interagency Work Group on EJ as well as the National Environmental Justice Advisory Council are also available. Environmental laws and regulations are available at https://www.epa.gov/environmentaljustice and include existing laws, legislation pending before Congress, regulations and proposed rules, and EPA Dockets. In addition, land use practitioners can access legal, policy, and program information about all of the programs under EPA's jurisdiction. http://www.epa.gov/.

Partnership for Sustainable Communities—A Joint Initiative of US HUD, DOT and EPA— On June 16, 2009, the U.S. Department of Housing and Urban Development (HUD), U.S. Department of Transportation (DOT), and the U.S. Environmental Protection Agency (EPA) joined together to help communities nationwide improve access to affordable housing, increase transportation options, and lower transportation costs while protecting the environment.

The Partnership for Sustainable Communities (PSC) works to coordinate federal housing, transportation, water, and other infrastructure investments to make neighborhoods more prosperous, allow people to live closer to jobs, save households time and money, and reduce pollution. The partnership agencies incorporate six principles of livability into federal funding programs, policies, and future legislative proposals. Among the items the site offers is a federal resource guide for sustainable rural communities, see: https://www.sustainable.org/governance/community-regional-state-and-federal-relations/146-interagency-partnership-for-sustainable-communities-.

§ 3. LAND USE CODES

As mentioned in the introduction, the availability of land use codes online provides good starting places for the drafting of new zoning ordinances and land use laws. There are very few commercial services or non-profit or government sponsored websites that provide comprehensive lists of links to individual municipal land use codes. The two commercial sites reviewed in this section offer searchable access only to those codes adopted by municipalities who happen to be clients of the code publishing company.

There are several ways to attempt to find an online version of a particular code or code provision of interest. The easiest way is to find state-based websites that may exist with links to these codes for all municipalities within the state, such as the California Land Use Planning Information Network reviewed below. Where these lists do not exist, use the search engine to determine whether the particular municipality has an online presence and if so, whether they post their laws and regulations. If you are looking for model language for particular land use laws or code provisions, enter key words, such as "adult business use" or "nonconforming use" into the search engine, and dozens of zoning ordinances from across the country will be ready for you to "click" and review.

E-Codes, or municipal codes online, is offered by General Code Publishers. Organized alphabetically by state, the site provides municipal codes from hundreds of municipalities in 21 states and Canada. Once the user follows the links to a municipal code of interest, the code can be searched by key words. Obtaining local codes can also be a challenge as they are often not easily accessible. This site provides the beginning of a clearinghouse type function for this purpose https://www.generalcode.com/library/.

Municipal Code is a commercial publisher of municipal codes including zoning ordinances and other land use laws. The company offers free online access to more than 1,500 municipal codes from across the country. The site also has pamphlets detailing how state laws affect local codes in Georgia, Minnesota, Florida, Texas, Michigan and Virginia. Member attorneys can also register for the attorney list service which may include sending an ordinance of the month, fielding requests for sample ordinances or serving as a platform for debate among municipal attorneys on topics of current interest. http://www.municode.com/.

New York State Local Law Search is an electronic database of local laws and county codes in New York filed with the Department of State on or after January 1, 1998. This is a publicly searchable database and offers researchers sample local laws for all kinds of land use regulations. https://locallaws.dos.ny.gov/.

§ 4. NON-PROFIT ORGANIZATIONS

There are literally dozens of websites offered by non-profit educational and advocacy organizations that relate to one or more aspects of planning and zoning law and policy. The sites selected below are representative of the breadth of land use law websites in cyberspace. When using search engines to find information on controversial topics, it is important that users attempt to find out about the host or sponsoring organization. So, for example, when exploring the topic of eminent domain, a search using the key words of "eminent domain" will take the researcher to articles, reports, and publications of organizations whose mission it is to challenge the constitutionality of these government actions, as well as to government and non-governmental organization sites that support the appropriate use of this power. The legal analysis offered on the various sites must be considered and weighed based upon the political and philosophical leaning of the host organization.

The **American Planning Association** offers a comprehensive and searchable website with information, analysis and links on planning, environmental, and land use law. In addition to containing a large and comprehensive searchable archive, the site also has an entire section dedicated to legislative and policy initiatives. This portion of the site provides a daily update on legislative activity at both the state and federal level and provides a bi-weekly electronic newsletter. The site also contains *amicus curie* briefs filed by the APA since 1997. Attorneys can also use the site to find articles and publications of interest on particular topics. http://www.planning.org.

National Association of Home Builders (NAHB) offers a searchable site that provides access to Association reports on a wide variety of land use and development issues. The site provides links to current state and federal legislative initiatives, economic forecasts and current housing data, federal and state regulatory programs, business management tools, and links to NAHB positions on virtually every aspect of housing policy. Additionally, this site links to state and local chapters across the country and provides information on upcoming educational events and opportunities. The site also links to the NAHB library and serves as a clearinghouse for NAHB publications. The clearinghouse is searchable by keyword, topic, intended audience and publication year. Users can also register for NAHB's weekly newsletter reporting on the economic, industry and legislative developments. http://www.nahb.org.

The **Smart Growth Network** (SGA) offers **Smart Growth OnLine**, which provides access to publications and guidebooks on incorporating smart growth principles into state and local planning and zoning codes. The site offers a large variety of studies, reports, and links organized topically around community quality of life, design, economics, environment, health, housing, and transportation. http://www.smartgrowth.org.

Smart Growth America offers a variety of online publications regarding smart growth policies and initiatives from across the country. While primarily policy oriented, land use and legal themes run throughout the various studies supported by SGA in conjunction with numerous federal agencies, not-for-profits, and state and local governments. SGA also offers a bi-weekly email newsletter that can be requested from the website. http://www.smartgrowth america.org/.

The **Community Rights Counsel** is a non-profit public interest law firm that provides legal assistance to local communities. The site offers the "Taking Litigation Handbook," which is the self-proclaimed "first soup-to-nuts guide to avoiding, litigating and defeating takings challenges to land use laws." The site also tracks pending and recent Supreme Court decisions and certiorari petitions. Additionally, the site provides *amicus curiae* briefs submitted by the Counsel dating back to 1999. All monthly newsletters issued by the Counsel are archived to November 2004. http://www.community rights.org/.

The **Pacific Legal Foundation** (PLF) is a non-profit organization dedicated to the protection of private property rights. Its website offers a listing with information and status of the lawsuits with which PLF is involved. Its quarterly newsletter is online and the site offers links to the websites of other similar-minded organizations. http://www. pacificlegal.org/.

The **Lincoln Institute of Land Policy** provides access to a wealth of policy and legal research topics on domestic and international land use and tax policy. While policy and legal research articles are intermingled, the site is searchable by keyword and topic. This site offers a database of research papers funded by the Institute through fellowships with graduate students, faculty, and professional fellows. The site also offers updates on ongoing research initiatives and provides information on upcoming educational seminars. Additionally, the site provides access to the Institute's online database of publications. http://www.lincolninst.edu.

The Urban Land Institute offers a forum for land use professionals and policy-makers to come together. The site offers access to recently issued reports from the Institute on an array of topics from housing, to infill development, urban revitalization, smart growth, and finance. The site also has a topical and keyword searchable archive containing the Urban Land Institute magazine, electronic newsletters, and annual forecasts. http://www.uli.org.

The **National Association of Realtors** offers links to a number of studies and smart growth initiatives of interest to realtors. In addition to providing policy research, the site offers a quarterly update on federal and state legislation on growth and development. There are also links to selected state resources and legislative initiatives as well as the invaluable National Association of Realtor's "Growth Management Fact Book." In addition, the site offers a Field Guide to Zoning at https://www.nar.realtor/field-guides/field-guide-to-zoning-laws-ordinances, and articles about zoning basics, the impact of zoning, zoning boards, legal information and zoning reform. A field guide to inclusionary zoning is also available. https://www.nar.realtor/zoning.

§ 5. ACADEMIC SPONSORED SITES

Many research centers based at law schools and planning schools offer good websites with publications by faculty, staff, and students on various land use and zoning topics. In addition, these sites typically offer links to other state specific sites as well as to national sites of interest. These sites may also contain links to cases and offer interesting briefs and model ordinance language. Below are some of the leading academic sites that have law-related planning information.

Land Use Law is hosted by Professor Daniel Mandelker at Washington University School of Law. While the site is designed to assist law students, it offers good leads to practitioners who are looking for information on plans and ordinances, as a number of models are posted to the site. Recent cases of national significance are available, as are articles on a variety of topics of current interest. Photos relating to some of the significant land use cases are also offered on the site. The site also provides numerous links to other websites of interest hosted by non-profit organizations. http://law.wustl.edu/landuselaw/.

Land Use Law Center at Pace University's Elizabeth Haub School of Law offers among other things the "Gaining Ground Information Database," (GGID) a free and ever-expanding online database featuring best practice models used by government to control the use of land in the public interest. It includes a collection of federal, state, and local ordinances; commentaries; research papers; research aids; and much more. To access the GGID, visit www.landuse.law.pace.edu and click on "Gaining Ground Database" in the navigation menu. For other resources on the scholarship of land use law, click on the Center's Publications & Resources page, also available in the navigation menu.

Florida State University College of Law offers the Journal of Land Use and Environmental Law available on its website. The Journal is archived from 1994 to the present. https://law.fsu.edu/journals-and-advocacy-teams/jluel.

Georgetown Climate Center is part of Georgetown Law School and it seeks to advance effective climate and energy policies in the United States and serves as a resource to state and local communities that are working to cut carbon pollution and prepare for climate change. Their website offers reports, presentations and documents on topics including: clean energy, adaptation, and transportation. http://www.georgetownclimate.org/.

National Center for Smart Growth Research and Education is a non-partisan center for research and leadership training on Smart Growth and related land use issues nationally and internationally, located at the University of Maryland. The website boasts that faculty and staff associated with the Center have produced a large body of research focusing on the diverse dimensions of Smart Growth, including its relationships to the environment, to transportation and public health, and to issues of housing and community development. Dozens of these papers and reports related to land use, housing, and transportation are available on the site. http://www.smartgrowth.umd.edu/.

Sabin Center for Climate Change Law at Columbia Law School offers a comprehensive website on climate change and sustainable development issues. The site offers, among other things, a searchable database of publications, https://climate.law.columbia.edu, links to resources including model local laws at: https://climate.law.columbia.edu/content/resources, and a blog on climate law: http://blogs.law.columbia.edu/climatechange/. The comprehensive website address is: http://columbiaclimatelaw.com/.

Institute on Land Use and Sustainable Development Law at Touro Law Center provides training, technical assistance, and research on a wide variety of land use topics. It also offers a blog at: https://tourolawlanduse.wordpress.com/. See, http://www.tourolaw.edu/LandUseInstitute/institute-land-use-sustainable-development-law.

§ 6. MISCELLANEOUS TOPICS OF INTEREST

In conducting land use law research on the Internet, one effective strategy is to simply enter a search term to see to what sites the search engine directs the user. For example, if your community wants to fight the siting of a big box development, simply search for "big box retail" and hundreds of articles, publications, and organizational websites will appear with valuable information from case studies to speakers to model zoning language. The following sites offer examples of online information in the area of sign and billboard regulation, the leading land use and property discussion forum via list serv, zoning and religious land uses, fair housing, and historic preservation. There are hundreds of sites on these and other land use planning and zoning topics.

The **Becket Fund for Religious Liberty** is a non-partisan non-profit organization dedicated to preserving religious freedom. One of its main endeavors is the "Sacred Spaces" project dedicated to protecting the rights of religious institutions in land use law through RLUIPA. The site provides narrative history of recent RLUIPA cases, various court decisions from around the country, press releases, and *amicus curie* briefs submitted by the Fund. http://www.becketfund.org/.

Information about Fair Housing Act laws is maintained by **Civilrights.org network**, a project of the Leadership Conference on Civil Rights. Links to the Federal Fair Housing Act and other related federal laws are provided, as well as links to state laws. http://www.fairhousinglaw.org/fair_housing_laws_fh_act.html.

The **National Trust for Historic Preservation** is a private, non-profit membership organization dedicated to saving historic places and revitalizing America's communities. The Trust is currently featuring information on five issues of interest: chain drugstores, historic schools, housing, smart growth, and transportation. The Trust's Legal Defense Fund participates in amicus briefs to courts across the country, and publishes a regular newsletter, available online, highlighting its litigation efforts and summarizing cases of interest. The legal advocacy section of its website provides links to the U.S. Supreme Court, federal district courts, the code of federal regulations, federal agencies with jurisdiction over some aspect of preservation, and professional organizations. https://savingplaces.org/.

Planetizen is a professional practice and an academic study focused on the future of built environments and connected natural environments—from the smallest towns to the largest cities and everything in between. The website provides news, a blog, and information about planning schools, as well as training including preparation for the AICP exam. http://www.planetizen.com/.

U.S. Green Building Council has a mission to promote sustainability-focused practices in the building and construction industry. It developed LEED—Leadership in Energy, Environment and Design—which is a certification program for buildings and communities that guides their design, construction, operations, and maintenance toward sustainability. It's based on prerequisites and credits that a project meets to achieve a certification level: Certified, Silver, Gold and Platinum. http://www.usgbc.org/.

Summaries of current case law and new legislation and regulations of interest can be found on **Law of the Land**, a blog maintained by Touro Law Center professor and former dean, Patricia Salkin. The blog offers more than seventy categories for readers to learn about and watch trends. https://lawoftheland.wordpress.com. For a focus on eminent domain and regulatory takings, Professor Robert Thomas of William and Mary Law School authors the **Inverse Condemnation** blog—https://www.inversecondemnation.com/inversecondemnation/.

A number of law firms offer clients and members of the public newsletters, blogs, and memorandum on developments in land use. For example:

Sheppard Mullin hosts the **Real Estate, Land Use and Environmental Law Blog**—https://www.realestatelanduseandenvironmentallaw.com, and California-based Perkin Coie publishes the **California Land Use & Development Law Report**—https://www.californialandusedevelopmentlaw.com/about/.

Dalton Tomich based in Michigan has a land use blog with a special focus on the Religious Land Use and Institutionalized Person Act—https://www.attorneysforlanduse.com/blog/. The Connecticut-based law firm of Robison & Cole hosts the **RLUIPA Defense Blog** at https://www.rluipa-defense.com/.

Farrell Fritz hosts a land use blog that focuses on New York issues, and Long Island in particular—https://www.lilanduseandzoning.com Silverberg Zalantis also hosts the **New York Zoning and Municipal Law Blog**—https://blog.szlawfirm.net/ and **The Climate Change Attorney Blog** - https://www.climatechangeattorney.com/.

The **Municipal Minute** is the blog of Chicago-based Acel Glinck—http://municipalminute.ancelglink.com/.

The **Rocky Mountain Sign Law Blog** is hosted by Colorado-based Otten Johnson Robinson Neff + Ragonetti—https://www.rockymountainsignlaw.com/.

§ 7. SEARCH ENGINES ON THE WEB

There are a number of different search engines on the Internet. These search engines help researchers to navigate through the Internet. More popular search engines are Google at http://www.google.com; Yahoo! at http://www.yahoo.com; Lycos at http://www.lycos.com; MSN at http://www.msn.com; Ask Jeeves at http://www.ask.com; Alta Vista at http://altavista.com; and Excite at http://www.excite.com. To make sure your research is thorough and comprehensive, in addition to trying a variety of search terms, it is a good idea to try the terms in an assortment of engines because they may have different results.

§ 8. CONCLUSION

Finding land use law information on the Internet is easy. The challenge is sorting through all of the information to ascertain what is actually useful. Bookmark interesting sites in the favorites section of your browser so you can easily revisit them for updates and new searches. Remember legal research skills on the web demand the same level of attention and detail as more traditional legal research. Verifying accuracy of content from a substance perspective requires review and exercise of independent judgment on the part of the reader. Just because information is published in cyberspace does not make it automatically true. One can get "lost in cyberspace" for hours on end uncovering free, interesting, useful, and relevant land use planning and zoning information. Don't forget to check out the dozens of comprehensive blogs that also provide access to current information and thought on land use law.

Send us your favorite land use website for the next edition of this Nutshell. We can be reached at patricia.salkin@touro.edu Happy surfing!

INDEX

References are to Pages